Murray Leinster

Murray Leinster
The Life and Works

BILLEE J. STALLINGS *and*
JO-AN J. EVANS

Foreword by James Gunn

McFarland & Company, Inc., Publishers
Jefferson, North Carolina, and London

"A Logic Named Joe," copyright © 1946, 1974 by the Heirs of the Literary Estate of Will F. Jenkins a/k/a Murray Leinster; first appeared in *Astounding*, March 1946; reprinted by permission of the Estate and the Estate's agents, the Virginia Kidd Agency, Inc.

"To Build a Robot Brain," copyright © 1954, 1982 by the Heirs of the Literary Estate of Will F. Jenkins a/k/a Murray Leinster; first appeared in *Astounding*, April, 1954; reprinted by permission of the Estate and the Estate's agents, the Virginia Kidd Agency, Inc.

Excerpts from "What's in a Pro?" copyright © 1953, 1981 by the Heirs of the Literary Estate of Will F. Jenkins a/k/a Murray Leinster; first appeared in *The Writer*, July, 1953; reprinted by permission of the Estate and the Estate's agents, the Virginia Kidd Agency, Inc.

"Writing Science Fiction Today," copyright © 1968, 1996 by the Heirs of the Literary Estate of Will F. Jenkins a/k/a Murray Leinster; first appeared in *The Writer*, May, 1968; reprinted by permission of the Estate and the Estate's agents, the Virginia Kidd Agency, Inc.

The Murray Leinster/Will F. Jenkins letter from John W. Campbell is used by permission of A.C. Projects, Inc., writers/owners of "The Campbell Letters."

LIBRARY OF CONGRESS CATALOGUING-IN-PUBLICATION DATA

Stallings, Billee J., 1928–
   Murray Leinster : the life and works / Billee J. Stallings and Jo-an J. Evans ; foreword by James Gunn.
      p.   cm.
   Includes bibliographical references and index.

   ISBN 978-0-7864-6504-0
   softcover : 50# alkaline paper ∞

   1. Leinster, Murray, 1896–1975. 2. Authors, American—20th century—Biography. 3. Science fiction, American—History and criticism. I. Evans, Jo-an J., 1938– II. Title.
   PS3519.E648Z88   2011   813.'52—dc23   [B]   2011025614

BRITISH LIBRARY CATALOGUING DATA ARE AVAILABLE

© 2011 Wenllian J. Stallings and Jo-an J. Evans. All rights reserved

No part of this book may be reproduced or transmitted in any form or by any means, electronic or mechanical, including photocopying or recording, or by any information storage and retrieval system, without permission in writing from the publisher.

On the cover: Will F. Jenkins, also known as Murray Leinster, in the mid–1940s; background © 2011 Wood River Gallery

Manufactured in the United States of America

McFarland & Company, Inc., Publishers
   Box 611, Jefferson, North Carolina 28640
   www.mcfarlandpub.com

Acknowledgments

Jim Gunn — whose encouragement from the start is responsible for this biography.

Fred Pohl — who cheered us on and supported our efforts.

Michael Swanwick — whose editorial comments and generous gift of time were invaluable.

Bob Silverberg — an outstanding example of the true professional who is both helpful and kind in his advice to newcomers.

Lee and Diane Weinstein — multitalented supporters and promoters of science fiction who have been of extraordinary help in this venture.

Steven H. Silver — for maintaining the Murray Leinster website, a treasure for fans.

Bob Harned — dear friend, cheering section, and tireless researcher and proofreader.

And all those contributors who remember our father and were kind enough to share their own memories of him.

Table of Contents

Acknowledgments — v
Foreword: The Dean Revisited by James Gunn — 1
Preface — 3

- ONE • The Beginning: 1909 — 5
- TWO • A Southern Family — 13
- THREE • The Early Days: 1910–1919 — 22
- FOUR • Entering Science Fiction: 1919–1921 — 33
- FIVE • Marriage: The 1920s — 38
- SIX • The 1930s — 61
- SEVEN • The New York Years: The 1940s — 86
- EIGHT • The 1950s — 117
- NINE • The 1960s — 132
- TEN • After Mary's Death — 152
- ELEVEN • On Writing — 164

Appendix A. "A Logic Named Joe" — 175
Appendix B. "To Build a Robot Brain" — 187
Bibliography — 195
Index — 215

No two people who've been through the identical experiences would write them in just the same way.
Letter from Will to his daughter Jo-an, November 4, 1963

Foreword:
The Dean Revisited
by James Gunn

Murray Leinster became part of my life as soon as I picked up a science-fiction magazine, which was in 1934, when I was eleven. By that time he had been publishing science fiction for 15 years, starting even before there were science-fiction magazines. His real name was William Fitzgerald Jenkins, but he wrote SF mostly under the name of Leinster. The name became synonymous with science fiction for me, for his stories not only were everywhere, they were there first. He originated more SF concepts that any writer since H. G. Wells. And, as I learned later, he was a rarity of the times, a writer who actually made a living at it.

His career began so early and lasted so long that he became known as "the Dean of Science Fiction." His first story, "The Runaway Skyscraper," was published in 1919, and his last one in 1967, a period covering almost 50 years and six decades. (It would not be surpassed until Jack Williamson, who lived to be 99 and wrote until the end, published work in ten decades.) Jenkins died at the age of 79. During his life he published 1,500 short stories and almost 100 books. He also was an inventor who patented a number of devices, including a front-projection system used to create special effects for motion pictures.

It was only looking back upon his birth year, 1896, that I realized he was only a year younger than my father and a year older than my mother. He was of their generation, but he seemed contemporary until his typewriter stopped. In 1962, at the age of 66, he was voted one of the six favorite *modern* writers of science fiction, and his novelette "Exploration Team" won a Hugo award the same year. He was one of the most anthologized writers of SF until his death, and his name comes up regularly when some new development in technology is traced to a story he wrote decades before, like "A Logic Named Joe," published in *Astounding Science-Fiction* in 1946, which anticipated the internet.

Earlier than that, though, he had written "Sidewise in Time" (1934, *Astounding Stories*), which provided a framework for the alternate history story that has burgeoned into a separate genre in recent years — so iconic that the award for the best alternate history story is called the "Sidewise." Even earlier was his ecology story, "The Mad Planet" (1920), which described a world in which plants and insects have grown huge, leaving humanity dwarfed and hunted. His novel *Murder of the USA* may have been the first of the atomic-attack treatments and was written, surely, before the first atomic bomb was dropped on Hiroshima.

Then there was "First Contact," which was the first story to consider the consequences of a meeting of alien cultures at the same technological level and suggest that there is a way to get around the natural distrust of the other (which offers a lesson for our own quarrels). He manages this by bringing together two spaceships in a place in the galaxy remote from both. Neither has any reason to trust the other and every reason to distrust any suggestion short of mutual destruction to prevent the other from following it home and endangering the entire species. Leinster, however, finds an ingenious solution: make tolerance more profitable to both.

My favorite early Leinster story (it seems strange to pick a favorite from among so many) is his 1934 "Proxima Centauri," which not only anticipated the generation starship concept that Robert Heinlein explored further in "Universe" and many more since, but imagined the kind of spaceships creatures who evolved from flesh-eating plants would build, and, even more important, how they would behave, and how that kind of knowledge could not only save a couple of crew members but also the human species.

Leinster very early understood that science fiction was the literature of the human species.

Science fiction is what it is today because of writers like Murray Leinster — and there were few like him. Now two of his daughters give us the rare opportunity to see the great writer from the perspective of his own children and let us understand what it was like to grow up with an icon as father.

James Gunn, writer, anthologist and a professor emeritus, is director of the Center for the Study of Science Fiction at the University of Kansas.

Preface

Two sisters, both long past their youth and living on opposite sides of the Atlantic Ocean, chat almost daily by email, occasionally switching to internet telephoning via their laptops for more detailed discussion. There is nothing exceptional about this staple of 21st century life, except that the internet and computers were described more than sixty years earlier by their father in a story, "A Logic Named Joe," published in the March 1946 issue of *Astounding Science-Fiction* magazine. The story described personal computers called logics, easy enough for a child to operate and linked to other logics, so that one can call logic to logic (internet telephoning) and obtain a vast range of information. The story, in effect, represents the connected or wired world we now know more than half a century later.

Born on June 16, 1896, Will F. Jenkins, often writing as Murray Leinster, was among the most prominent writers of science fiction for nearly fifty years. He began with "The Runaway Skyscraper," which appeared in 1919 when he was in his early twenties. He published more than 1,500 short stories, novellas, and novels, writing variously as Will F. Jenkins, Murray Leinster, William F. Jenkins, William Fitzgerald, and even Louisa Carter Lee and Florinda Martel. His output was not only huge, but varied. As well as science fiction, he wrote love stories, murder mysteries, adventure stories, westerns, fantasy, television and film scripts, and mainstream fiction.

Some of his earliest efforts were published in H. L. Mencken and George J. Nathan's *The Smart Set* magazine. His first short story, "My Neighbor," was printed in the February 1916 issue under the name "William F. Jenkins." He appeared regularly in the most popular magazines of his time, adapting his writing to new markets as they developed. His stories are in textbooks, in endless anthologies, and in translations all over the world.

Will often said, "I think of something impossible, and then write a story about it." In this way, he initiated new fictional concepts: "Sidewise in Time," the first parallel universe story (*Astounding Stories*, June 1934); "First Contact," confronting the implications of the first contact between human and alien spaceships (*Astounding Science-Fiction*, May 1945); and "Symbiosis," presenting a novel but effective weapon against biological warfare (*Collier's*, June 1947).

He was a frustrated scientist. His father's job loss when he was 13 ended the possibility of college and the career in chemistry he wanted. He tinkered throughout his life, endlessly inventing and leaving bits of experiments all over the house, to his wife's frequent dismay. The most successful result of his tinkering was a filming method, Front Projection, patented in 1955.

Throughout his life, however, Will remained sensitive to the fact that his formal education ended in the 8th grade. Articulate and intelligent though he was, he never gave himself full credit for his extensive knowledge of an enormous variety of subjects acquired over the years from voracious reading and conversations with people in all walks of life.

Most importantly, he dreamed. He once said to his youngest daughter, "I couldn't live without my fantasies." His imagination — and constant study of philosophy, theology, history and science — fueled his writing for all of his life.

• ONE •

The Beginning: 1909

Will told stories. More precisely, he loved to tell stories. He loved to be at the center of a captivated audience. Whatever tale he told might not always be the complete story or even the true story, but, if it entertained you or made you laugh, that was good enough for him.

He told saucy stories (to men only, after ushering them into the kitchen), kids' stories (to entrance children who flocked to him as to a magician), funny stories (rejoicing in the roars of laughter that followed), and stories about oddities and curiosities (always to amuse). But, fed by a lifetime of omnivorous reading, he also turned out a steady stream of short stories, novelettes, novels and scripts in a writing career that began in his teens with epigrams in *The Smart Set* and ended more than fifty years later.

The tapping of his trusty old Remington ran as a counterpoint to our childhoods. Will worked far into the night as we slept, while he perched on a plain wooden chair tilted onto its back legs, squinting slightly against the curls of smoke floating gently up from the small, curved, brown Wellington pipe clenched firmly between his teeth.

How should we begin his story?

Will would tell us. "This makes a good story," he would say, his eyes sparkling, puffing on his pipe enthusiastically.

It might be the one about how he happened to be in the *Today's Woman's* office just after the atomic bombs ended World War II. He entertained the editor, Eleanor Stierhem, with the tale of the much earlier visit to his home by the FBI. Agents asked him whether a story, published in *Astounding Science-Fiction* that described the atomic bomb in detail, was a leak. (It wasn't, and Will explained why.)

Or, it might be how he wrote his first science fiction story, the often-told tale of looking out of his window to see the hands of the clock on New York's Metropolitan Tower running backwards as it was reset, giving him the idea for "The Runaway Skyscraper," first published in *The Argosy* in 1919.

But, "Hell's bells," as Will would say, this is *his* story after all, so we will start with one of his favorites, the one about how it all began, when he was twelve years old, at school in Norfolk, Virginia, where he was born.

"General Robert E. Lee is directly responsible for my being a writer and for whatever of my writing you've read," he told the audience at the 1970 Disclave (Washington, D.C., Science Fiction Association convention).

On January 8, 1909, the powers that be of the Charlotte Street School had done the unthinkable for Norfolk, Virginia, in that time. They had forgotten it was Robert E. Lee's birthday. At 10 o'clock, somebody noticed. The principal rushed around to alert the teachers and to ask them to read to their students about General Lee, and then to ask them to write compositions about him, after which everyone could go home and breathe a sigh of relief that the sky had not fallen.

Will, a member of Mrs. Clay's sixth grade class, picked up his pencil and began to indulge his inclination for "nice long words," he later reported. He finished his work and happily left for the day. A few days later, Superintendent of Schools R. A. Dobie came around and was so impressed with the composition that he sent it off to the Norfolk afternoon paper, the *Ledger-Dispatch*, as an example of the outstanding quality of the Norfolk schools under his supervision. They printed it on January 28, 1909.

Robert E. Lee

Of all men, if I were asked, I should say Robert E. Lee comes the nearest to being ideal of any man the world has ever known.

Born in 1807, his whole life of sixty-three years shows a character of marvelous beauty. Gentle, yet firm, strong, resourceful and above all, faithful to what he believed his duty, no man could make a better example to follow.

At eighteen years of age he entered West Point, the appointment being secured by General Andrew Jackson, who had taken a fancy to him. Many people marveled at the fact that during the whole of his four years at the academy he never got a demerit.

At West Point his marvelous military talents began to show so strongly that he graduated second in his class of forty-three.

His mother died shortly after this and he was left alone but far from friendless, for his dignified, yet genial manners made friends of all who came in contact with him.

Having served as lieutenant of engineers for part of the Mexican war, he was highly complimented and promoted for bravery at the storming of Chapultec [sic].

His talents were versatile in the extreme. At one moment he was a philosopher, at another a capable engineer, at another a brilliant soldier.

He could have been as great a man as Alexander in a military way, as great a historian as Pliny, as great an engineer as De Lesseps, but he was faithful to his duty,

and when it called another way he answered its call and he remains today as great a man as ever lived, not in power but in mind, morals, and faithfulness to duty.
                                                                WILL F. JENKINS

Captain Manly, a Confederate veteran, of whom there were quite a few around in 1909, read the article and was so impressed that he sent Will $5, an enormous sum for the time.

Will had a use for the money. As later correspondence shows, he was a reader of *Fly: The National Aeronautic Magazine*, which billed itself as *A Popular Aeronautic Magazine for Men, Women and Children*. It was published in Philadelphia by the Aero Publishing Company. The detailed plans for a glider that were printed in the March 1909 issue must have caught his eye.

Later in 1909, *Fly* organized the National Junior Aero Club, open to boys between 12 and 21. The object as stated in the magazine was, "The advancement of the public interest in and the development of the science of aviation." The article goes on to say, "Had Bishop Wright, when a more or less obscure clergyman, frowned upon the interest displayed by his boys, Wilbur and Orville, in the various toy flying machines they made, it is possible that flight would not now be in its present stage of development."

Membership in the club was $1. It included a subscription to the magazine, a button, and the opportunity to compete in a number of contests. One offered a prize of $5 for the best photograph and description of a glider made by a member that was submitted that month.

The $5 sent by Captain Manley was enough to buy the materials needed for his glider project, and the $5 prize money provided an additional incentive. Will's interest is demonstrated in an exchange that appeared in the February 1910 issue of *Fly*. In it, the editor of the National Junior Club News page wrote:

One of the most interesting and most faithful correspondents of the Junior Editor began writing really before he became a member of the Junior Club. His name is W. Jenkins (and I am sorry he has never told me just what the W. stands for), and he lives at "The Tazewell," Norfolk, Va. Here is his first letter:

Dear Sir,
Enclosed find jingle to be sung to tune of "My Irish Rose." I have on file every number of *Fly* magazine since its first issue. Was so struck with it that I have hopes of a yearly subscription as a Christmas gift from my elder brother.
Have an order being filled for materials for a half-size glider, ten feet wide. I have been an "aero-maniac" almost since I can remember, and have constructed several models of the Langley type. One of them, five feet by two, is at my elbow now.

Fly magazine cover — 1909 (contained plans for glider).

I have designed a launching machine that works perfectly. It consists of a band traveling over two large rollers after the manner of a belt conveyer. Lay the model on it and start the rollers and the model is shot into the air with considerable momentum.

I think that a sort of turbine engine to be run by compressed air will be invented in the near future. The compressed air might be taken up in the form of liquid air and reduced to its normal state by alcohol burners under an airtight tank.

My newsdealer sold out all copies of FLY in town before I got there so he simply had to order me one (at least) more. He ordered three and they will be gone this evening.

This is my first letter to you, but I feel like an "old 'un" compared to many of the new experimenters. Though I am but thirteen years old I have been experimenting about four years.

Yours, W. Jenkins

For the benefit of those of the Juniors who may be wondering, I will tell you that the expected Christmas present materialized, for George, the "elder brother," gave the subscription. A letter since received from this member states that he is about to put a small glider, boy-carrying, as he calls it, into commission, and he will send photographs of it when he gets it into working order. But he isn't satisfied to conduct his experiment alone, and so is trying to form a local club among the boys he knows in Norfolk. Don't you wish him success?

Here is his "jingle," entitled "Aero-Plano-Jane:"

> With gauntlets on her fingers
> And goggles on her nose,
> Aeroplanes to carry her
> Wherever she goes;
> The motors all are chugging,
> And the guy-wires whistle, too,
> Aero, aero, Aero-Plano-Jane.

Will's photograph and description of his glider were printed in the March 1910 issue of *Fly* resulting in another $5. He wrote as follows:

I finished my glider on January 15, and, of course, I tried it the same day. Although the trial took place on level ground and without a breath of wind, I rose nearly two feet several times. Since then, on the twenty-sixth, I took it to Cape Henry, nearly seventeen miles from Norfolk, but easily reached by trolley, and tried it out again. Cape Henry has fine sand-hills for gliding, one of which slants one in ten for nearly a mile.

My first glide was only eight feet, as I wanted to get the "feel" of my glider, but my last flight, in which I broke one of my uprights, covered over forty feet.

The name of my glider is "Condor." It is ten feet wide. The distance between the planes is two feet and the planes are three feet wide. It is made in four sections to permit being carried on the trolley car. The sections are each five feet long and three feet wide and fasten together in a flat bundle. They are spliced by bolts two inches long and one-eighth inch in diameter. Following are other dimensions of the glider:

Main strips, ⅜" × ¾" × 5'.
Ribs, ⅜" × ⅛" × 3'.
Uprights, ⅜" × ⅜" × 3'.
Tail strip, ⅜" × ⅜" × 4'.

Bracing was done with small iron wire covered with unbleached cotton. The ribs are nailed to the main strips with the smallest nails obtainable and the cover is sewed to the ribs with No. 10 thread.

As I could get no spruce [*spruce was specified in the 1909 plan*] in Norfolk, I used oak throughout, the largest being the arm-sticks, ½" × ½" × 2'. I weigh seventy-two and one-half pounds and the glider weighs about fifteen pounds and has about sixty square feet.

Will and his glider "Condor."

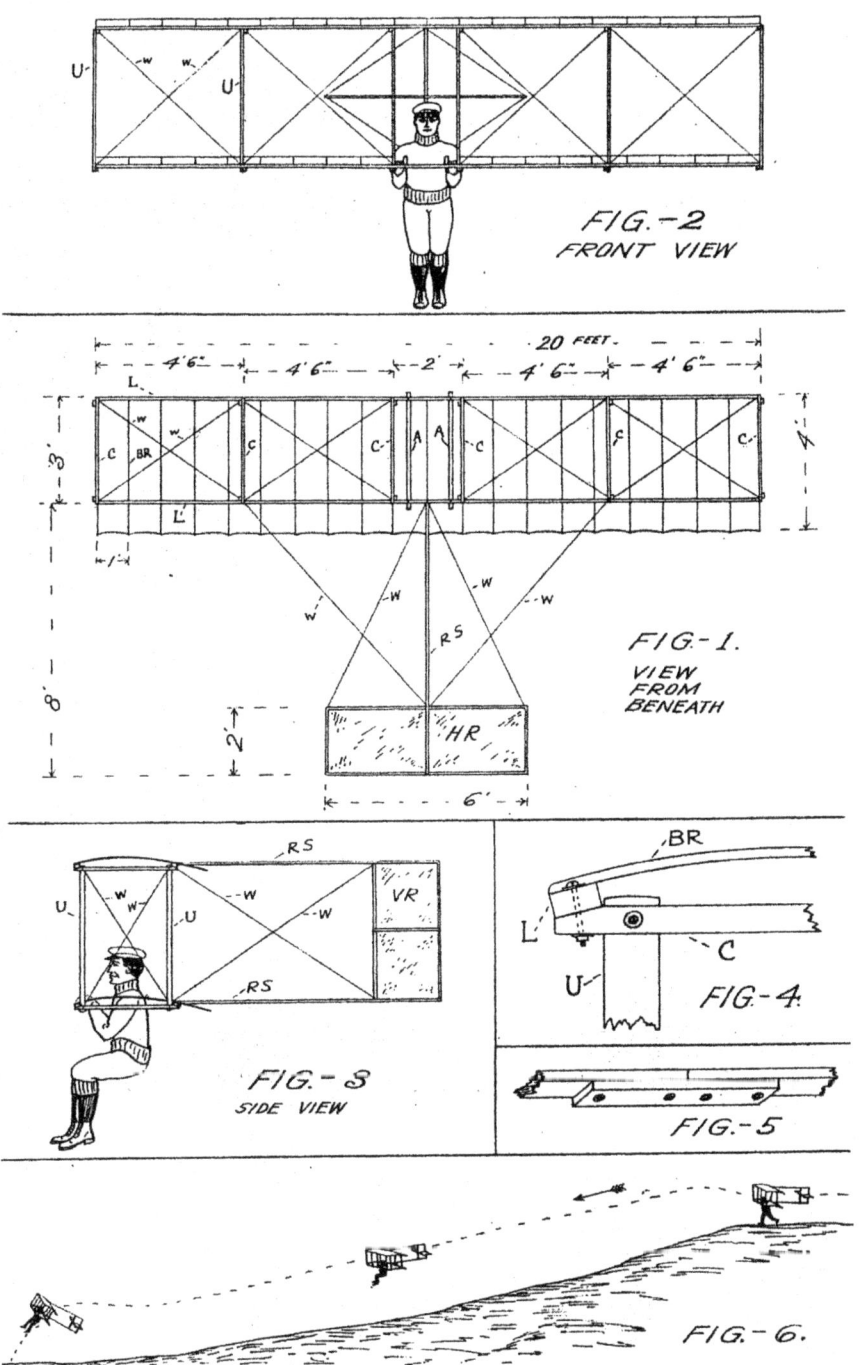

Plans for "Condor" from *Fly* magazine, March 1909.

The wood was sawed to order, but I put in every bolt and nailed the ribs myself. A friend helped sew the ribs. I put it together in an apartment and monopolized the sitting room for three weeks. If it isn't the first in Virginia, it is the first ever made in an apartment.

"And this," Will would say triumphantly, waving his pipe as he finished retelling the story of receiving $5 from Captain Manly, and another $5 for his contribution to *Fly* magazine, "is how I got the idea that I could make money from writing."

After that, Will never looked back. He elaborated on the theme in his guest of honor speech, "Recollections from My Past," that he delivered to the audience at Disclave 1970, which was sponsored by the Washington, D.C., Science Fiction Association, "From the time I was thirteen 'til I was seventeen, I worked on the belief that if people would pay me for writing about General Lee and gliders, sooner or later they would pay me for writing about other things. When I was seventeen I sold some epigrams to *Smart Set* for five dollars. During the first year I was selling stuff, I made seventy-two dollars by writing. In my eighteenth year I did better. When I was twenty-one...."

• Two •

A Southern Family

Will was deeply proud of his southern heritage, showing each of his daughters a typewritten copy of their paternal family tree practically from the time they could read. He often referred to his great-grandfather eight generations back, the first of his family to arrive in the newly settled colonies, Governor John Jenkins.

John Jenkins was first recorded in *Cavaliers and Pioneers*, in March 1655, living on a 400-acre land grant on the Eastern Shore in Virginia. Later, on September 5, 1663, Sir William Berkeley, governor of Virginia and a lord proprietor of Carolina, gave him a 700-acre grant south of the Perquimans River at Harveys Neck. This was an area that is now part of North Carolina, and it is noted that he was already living there. The lords proprietors later appointed him colonial governor of Albemarle County, which included the area where he lived, and he died in office in 1681.

Will was born on June 16, 1896, and named William Fitzgerald Jenkins. He was the fifth son, but only the second one living, of George Briggs Jenkins and Mary Louisa "Mamie" Murry. The Fitzgerald name came from his great-grandmother on his father's side, Elizabeth Fitzgerald Jenkins. Her tombstone in Cedar Hill Cemetery, Suffolk, Virginia, proudly records that her parents, Matthew and Elizabeth Fitzgerald Madden, were from Dublin, Ireland.

Will used to say that he came from a long line of lawyers. Elizabeth's son, Will's grandfather James Edward Jenkins, was a lawyer as was James Edward's first cousin John Summerfield Jenkins. James Edward graduated in 1846 from the College of William & Mary and practiced law in Suffolk, Virginia.

Will's uncle John Baugh Jenkins, who was his father's brother, was also a lawyer.

Will's paternal grandmother, Mary Virginia Briggs (James Edward's wife), was the daughter of Merit Briggs, a prosperous merchant. Mary Virginia's brother (Will's great uncle) George Washington Briggs was a doctor, graduating from the University of Virginia in 1849. Before the War Between the States, he practiced in the Church Hill section of Richmond in a house that is still standing. The Historic Richmond Foundation lists it in its publication as the Merritt Briggs House (one of the variations of the spelling of Merit) after his father, who owned the house.

During the war, Dr. Briggs was a surgeon, a field and staff officer with the rank of major. Later he practiced medicine in Suffolk (formerly Nansemond County) and for a time edited a weekly agricultural newspaper, *The Rural Messenger* in Petersburg, Virginia. At the time of his early death, Dr. Briggs was a professor of horticulture at the Agricultural College of Maryland, later the University of Maryland.

Robert Crawley Jenkins, the only brother of Will's paternal grandfather (James Edward Jenkins), was also a doctor, practicing in Perquimans County, North Carolina.

James Edward Jenkins and Mary Virginia Briggs married in 1848, and George Briggs Jenkins (Will's father) was born a year later. By 1854, when they purchased a home and office on Main Street in Suffolk, Virginia, there were two more children, Mary Lucretia and Ann Elizabeth.

In 1857, attracted by the promise of the new frontier in St. Louis, Missouri, they sold the Suffolk property and by 1860 were ensconced in St. Louis with the youngest children, James Webb, Robert Crawley and Henry. James opened a law office in a location that is now under the arch in St. Louis. George and the two eldest girls were left behind with their grandparents, Merit and Lucretia Briggs, at The Exchange plantation near Lake Cohoon in Suffolk. George learned his skills in bookkeeping and accounting while working in their store there.

Missouri was deeply divided early in 1861 at the beginning of

Mary Virginia Briggs.

the Civil War. When Lincoln looked for troops in this border state, Confederate sympathizer Governor Claiborne F. Jackson sent a telegram to the secretary of war saying, "Not one man will the State of Missouri furnish to carry on any unholy crusade." There arose two state governments, and citizens were forced to choose between the Union and Governor Jackson's Missouri state government. The Union won out, and Jackson and his government were forced into exile.

Clearly, it was time to leave and return home to Virginia, but Will's grandfather James and his family faced a difficult journey, and the exact timing is unknown. Another baby, John Baugh, had arrived in November 1860, and they would be returning to Suffolk, a city that had been occupied by Union soldiers since May of 1862. Sometime during this ordeal, little Henry died.

The family got back to Suffolk in time for the birth of their eighth child, Charles Winborne, on June 14, 1863. They were stunned by the death two weeks later on July 3 of James' first cousin and fellow Suffolk lawyer John Summerfield Jenkins during Pickett's Charge at Gettysburg. Nineteen days after that, on July 22, James, 39 years old with a month old baby and six other living children, enlisted in the Confederate Army.

He was soon transferred to the 14th Virginia Cavalry where he served as clerk to a well-known Confederate brigadier general, James Dearing, notable as the last general to die of wounds sustained in the war. It is thought that James probably accompanied General Dearing on the retreat from Petersburg. General Lee planned to move west and south in an attempt to join General Joseph Johnston's forces in North Carolina. They marched toward Lynchburg, Virginia, where badly needed supplies were waiting. Lee hoped to stop General Grant by destroying the bridges over the Appomattox River. In the attempt at High Bridge on April 6, General Dearing was fatally wounded. Union soldiers were able to save the wagon bridge over the river, and their troops were able to cut off Lee's options. Lee was forced to surrender to General Grant at Appomattox on April 9, 1865. James' parole was signed on April 25, and he was able to go home to Suffolk.

Will's father, George, was 12 years old in 1861 at the start of the war. He wanted to help and volunteered as a messenger. The family did not want him to travel alone, so they assigned a young slave boy to accompany him. Because slaves were not allowed to cross county lines unless with their owners, Little Billy was given to George. George taught Billy to read and write, although it was against the law to teach that to slaves at the time, and he later told his children of lying on the books to hide them when the officers came to their tent. The two remained in touch, and Will remembered Uncle Billy coming around as an older man still visiting the family.

The war and reconstruction period left Virginia devastated and in ruins.

Will's grandfather James, having lost his citizenship because of his service in the Confederate Army, probably could not practice his profession. Another baby, Mathew, was born in 1867, but James' health was broken, and soon he was dying of tuberculosis. Their personal property — horse, wagon, hogs, hay and the lot — was sold off piece by piece. After his death in 1868, Mary Virginia, left with seven minor children at home, moved to a farm in Isle of Wight County that had belonged to her father. In 1873, having contracted tuberculosis herself, she died.

Will's father, George, became 21 in 1870 and was making his own life. He was the oldest grandchild, and his grandfather Merit Briggs remembered him in his will. At Merit's death in 1867, George inherited three parcels of land in Isle of Wight County, which he soon sold. He took a job as bookkeeper in Enoch Gale's shoe store in Norfolk, Virginia, living with the family. There he became enamored with their daughter Emma Dryden Gale. They married around 1873, and Louisa Dryden Jenkins, Will's much-loved half-sister Lula, was born in 1874. A son, Tommy, was born on February 18, 1878, but died 5 months later. Emma's health was poor and, after she died on November 15, 1881, her mother, Louisa, continued to take care of little Lula.

George met the woman who would become his second wife and Will's mother Mary Louisa "Mamie" Murry, in Portsmouth, Virginia, where she was known as a belle. Her red-haired niece, Grace Davis, recalled the story of when Mamie gave herself a party for her 18th birthday and invited 18 guests — all male! She lived with her family on Court Street in Portsmouth and scribbled the address, along with a boyfriend's name, in her Episcopal prayer book.

Her maternal grandfather, James Cannon, was a captain on the Old Bay Line, serving on several ships that sailed from Baltimore to Portsmouth including the side-wheeler *Adelaide*. He was well known and popular in both cities. In those days, steamboat travel was quite formal, and the captains wore frock coats and high silk hats and often served tea from a silver service. A photograph shows him in formal dress, clean-shaven with longish hair curling around his ears and the searching eyes of a sailor. Captain Cannon's daughter Mary Elizabeth Cannon married Oliver Perry Murry in Baltimore, Maryland, on October 27, 1861. Maryland did not join the southern states in seceding, but it was definitely pro–Confederacy. In spite of the war, the young couple moved to Portsmouth, Virginia, where they opened a grocery store. Mamie (Will's mother) was born in Portsmouth on January 13, 1863, and was soon joined by two younger brothers, Oliver "Ollie" and Charles.

Tragically, on a Sunday afternoon in May 1868, Mamie's father, Oliver Perry Murry, was drowned in the Elizabeth River on a recreational sail from Portsmouth to Norfolk. On the return trip, the small boat capsized in the middle of the river, and he and his companion climbed on the upended bottom. Then, according to a newspaper account of the time, Oliver said, "I'll swim to that schooner, get a boat and take you off." Family legend said that he didn't want to take off his new boots, and they weighed him down. He sank and didn't make it to the schooner. His companion, however, stayed with the boat and was rescued. Oliver's body was not found for several days, and, in true tabloid tradition, the newspaper article detailed what parts had been nibbled by crabs.

Oliver was an Episcopalian, and had a Masonic funeral. Although his obituary said he was a local grocer, records of the time show that he also had a wholesale license to sell liquor.

Early publicity photograph of Will circa 1920.

Mary Elizabeth was pregnant at the time and bore a fourth child who died. She later remarried and had four more children with her second husband, George W. H. Watts. Mamie's brother Oliver "Ollie" Murry, half-sisters Grace Watts Syer and Virginia "Jenny" Watts Davis, Ollie's daughter Margaret Murry Holland and Jenny's children Grace and George Davis were the family members most known to Will's children.

Mr. Watts must have been a Methodist because the second set of children was brought up in the Methodist church and all were strict teetotalers.

Will's father, George Briggs Jenkins, was apparently a dashing suitor. A neighbor later told Mamie's niece Grace Davis that, when he was a small boy, he used to follow George and Mamie, running after the carriage as they drove around town because he thought they were so elegant and glamorous. George and Mamie married on May 25, 1885. She was 22 years old, and he was 36 with a twelve-year-old daughter Lula and a resident mother-in-law.

Will's story of his parents' marriage includes a ghost. As his mother told the tale, right after she was married, she was resting in a room off the entrance hall of what would now be her home. While waiting for her new husband to finish overseeing the delivery of their luggage, she heard someone coming

Left: Mary Louisa "Mamie" Jenkins. *Right:* George Briggs Jenkins at 21.

down the stairs. She rose to see who it was and saw a young woman cross the hall and go out the front door. When George came in, she asked who the woman was. George asked for a description and when Mamie gave it, he turned pale. Mamie had unwittingly described Emma, his first wife and Lula's mother, now long dead.

Those first years must have been difficult for Mamie. Three little boys, Oliver, a second Oliver, and the first George, came quickly and died shortly after their births. George Sr. must have grieved deeply as well, having lost his first son, born to his first marriage, also in infancy. Mamie and George's fourth son, George Jr., was born in 1890 and soon became his mother's darling. Six years later, with this intricate family history, Will came along. Apparently he was a cranky baby, did not eat well, and was prone to temper tantrums. His traditional southern mammy doted on him, however, so it was a happy time for him. She often sang an old, rather gruesome lullaby, which Will remembered and sang to his own children when they were babies:

> Lammo, lammo, where's the little sheep
> Down by the haystack fast asleep.
> The buzzards and the flies keep peckin' at his eyes
> 'Till the poor little sheep cried, "Mammy."

His half-sister Lula, whom he always called S'Lula for Sister Lula in the southern tradition, also spoiled him. She was a schoolteacher, still single and living at home. She passed down a treasured memory of Will, sitting in his high chair with his soft brown hair curling around his ears and a delighted smile on his face. He had turned his cereal bowl upside down on his head and was enjoying his spot in the center of attention as the gooey mess made its way down to his shoulders.

Will remembered a happy boyhood. One of his close childhood friends was Cornelius "Neely" Bull. They were bright and curious boys, and Will told stories of their playing with a pet raccoon and dropping a cat from a second story window to see if it would land on its feet, an early experiment. He was pleased when he and Neely reconnected many years later during World War II, and Will had a chance to share another invention with him.

Life was happy and secure for the family of four. Lula, Will's half-sister, married, and George Sr., Mamie and their sons, George Jr., and Will, were comfortable and surrounded by family and friends in Norfolk, Virginia. But the good times ended in 1910, and life changed dramatically for Will. The Norfolk and Southern Railroad, where his father, George, had been paymaster for 25 years, went into receivership, and George, 61 years old, lost his job. With the job went the life Will had known since birth.

The next two years are hazy. We know from Will's correspondence with *Fly* magazine that he was living in The Tazewell in late 1909 and early 1910. The Tazewell, located at the corner of Tazewell and Granby Streets in downtown Norfolk, was new at the time, and revered as the first hotel in the area with automatic elevators and air-conditioning. It was built in 1906 on the site of the home of Littleton Walter Tazewell, a former governor of Virginia, in anticipation of the tri-centennial of the founding of Jamestown to be celebrated the next year. It exists today as a boutique hotel and is listed as one of the Historic Hotels of America, a program of the National Trust for Historic Preservation.

In April 1910, the census found the

George Briggs Jenkins in his 50s.

Mamie, Will, and George Jr. circa 1910.

family living in New York City on West 139th Street. George Sr., was working as an accountant, and George Jr., as a bookkeeper, both in an accountant's office. Mamie, Will's mother, was at home, and Will, aged 14, is listed as "having attended school any time since September 1, 1909." This was probably the three months of eighth grade he talks of attending before his formal education ended.

There is evidence that Mamie and George Jr., and possibly Will, returned to Norfolk that year. The 1910 Norfolk city directory shows George Jr., living in The Tazewell and working as a clerk at the Norfolk and Southern Railroad, which had reorganized. In 1911, both George Jr., and Mamie are recorded as living at The York Apartments in Norfolk.

Will talked of going to Cleveland with his father sometime during this period and reading and studying in the library there. He may have done so at this time, however, there are no records of either of them living in Cleveland.

By 1912, according to the Newark, New Jersey, city directory, George Jr., was working for the Prudential Insurance Company there. Only George Jr.'s name is listed, probably as head of household. According to family members, all three of them lived together in Newark. George Jr., and Mamie were enumerated at the same address in the 1920 census. George Jr. was listed again in 1920, along with Will, in Norfolk at the home of their half-sister Lula.

Where George Sr. was between 1910 and 1920 is unknown. He next appears in the 1920 census in New York City, living alone and working as an accountant. Later he went to live with his daughter Lula in Culpeper, Virginia, where she had moved, and he died in 1926.

During this unsettled period, Will was unable to go to school regularly. Not surprisingly, as he often said, he failed English. He gave up, did not go back to school, and joined his brother at the Prudential Insurance Company in Newark as an office boy. He hated it, and, determined to find another way to earn a living, he decided to become a writer.

• THREE •

The Early Days: 1910–1919

Will said he read every book on writing in the Newark Public Library, where the now impoverished family of three — Mamie, George Jr., and Will — often spent time to keep warm. He undoubtedly devoured *The Smart Set* magazine as well.

Its first issue was published March 10, 1900, with the subtitle "A Magazine of Cleverness." It was the ultimate in sophistication and chic and certainly attracted this impressionable young man with literary aspirations.

The Smart Set was launched by Colonel William D'Alton Mann, a wealthy and colorful speculator, who gambled that he could make money in publishing. His weekly tabloid, *Town Topics*, was very successful, and he reasoned he could appeal to the same audience with an entertaining magazine focused on the peccadilloes of New York's high society, true or fictionalized. It would also include stories and verse. Its first editor, Arthur Grissom, was a hard working journalist with a literary flair. Although he died less than two years after its first issue, the magazine bore his imprint for a long time. It went through many changes in leadership over the next few years, perhaps facing its greatest challenge with Mann's involvement in a libel suit he brought against Norman Hapgood, editor of *Collier's Weekly,* and the Colliers (father and son) themselves. They had accused him and *Town Topics* of blackmail. The court found him "not guilty" but *The Smart Set*, even though not directly involved, suffered.

In 1908 in order to economize, Mann took over the editorship himself. He decided to add a literary editor and a regular book review column and contacted 28-year-old Henry Louis Mencken, a Baltimore newspaperman, about the position. (Mencken later shortened his byline to the more familiar H. L. Mencken.) Mencken accepted with the caveat that he could do most

Will may well have read this September 1911 issue of *The Smart Set* when he was 15 years old. His first epigram was printed two years later when he was 17.

of his work in Baltimore. The following year he was introduced to a new staff member, George Jean Nathan, who was to join the magazine as drama critic. Nathan had two years of experience in reviewing for newspapers and weeklies in Manhattan. Despite the difference in their backgrounds (Mencken, the stereotypical tough newsman, and Nathan, age 27, elegant and a bit snobbish, with Ivy League Cornell University and two years' study in Italy under his belt), they bonded immediately. During their fifteen-year relationship, they transformed the magazine by recruiting new talent as well as soliciting work from well-known writers. Their policies made a significant impact on American literature.

Some of the best-known writers of the time were published in the magazine. *The Smart Set* is credited with discovering F. Scott Fitzgerald, O. Henry and Eugene O'Neill. Edna St. Vincent Millay was a 22-year-old recent Vassar graduate when she submitted a short story, "Barbara on the Beach." It was published in November 1914, her first appearance in an adult magazine, and she soon became part of the literary and Bohemian Greenwich Village crowd.

Nathan used his contacts in Britain and France to solicit new material, and the poet Ezra Pound sent over a couple of new author James Joyce's "Dubliner" stories which they printed. Joyce was a Pound protégé, so the proof pages of *A Portrait of the Artist as a Young Man* soon followed. It was rejected as "too long." Mencken regretfully informed Joyce that they did not print serials, and it should not be cut.

James Branch Cabell also appeared first in its pages. He was a Virginian who became notorious with the 1919 publication of his novel entitled *Jurgen, a Comedy of Justice*. Although it was labelled obscene by the New York Society for the Suppression of Vice, this did not seem to bother the usually straight-laced Will, who was so impressed by the description of a fantasy empire that he had a framed map of Jurgen hanging on the wall of his home for many years.

When Mann had sold the magazine in 1911 to John Adams Thayer for $100,000, Thayer offered the editor's job first to Mencken and then to Nathan. Both refused, fearing correctly that Thayer really wanted to be his own editor. By 1913, when Will was beginning to be published in *The Smart Set*, Thayer realized he needed help and brought in Willard Huntington Wright, a model of precocity. Wright had studied in three colleges between the ages of fifteen and eighteen when he left Harvard because "they had nothing more to teach me." At nineteen, he was literary editor of the *Los Angeles Times*.

He was a handsome man with a cleft chin and a magnificent upswept moustache. Mencken had encouraged him to apply for the editor's position, and Wright got along well with both Mencken and Nathan, and their idea to make their work fun. Will remembered their escapades with fond amusement.

As *The Smart Set* editor, Wright was brilliant but flawed. His controversial editorial policies (some called them pornographic) and reckless spending left *The Smart Set* with financial and image problems. Thayer fired him, and the magazine struggled until it was taken on by Colonel Eugene R. Crowe (one of its chief creditors), and Eltinge Warner, who was then beginning to build a publishing empire. After many personal struggles, Wright became a very popular mystery writer under the name S. S. Van Dine, creating the hero Philo Vance.

By chance, Eltinge Warner and his wife were passengers on the S. S. *Imperator* where Warner met Nathan while strolling on the promenade deck. The elegant Nathan (they used the same London tailor) impressed him. When *The Smart Set* deal came up, Warner immediately thought of Nathan, remembered he worked for *The Smart Set*, and offered him the editorship. Nathan, believing in Warner's financial acumen and feeling that he would not interfere in editorial decisions, agreed, on the condition that Mencken would be coeditor. Mencken accepted but again reserved the right to work from Baltimore. He would be the first reader of manuscripts, and he and Nathan would meet twice a month to confer.

Despite the demands of his growing stable of authors, Mencken found time to encourage an aspiring young writer, who had been successfully submitting epigrams, sending Will a letter: "You seem to know precisely the sort of epigrams *The Smart Set* needs, and we shall be very glad to have you submit them regularly." He did so. Each sale brought him $5, and Will was on his way. There were no bylines on epigrams, so it is impossible to identify his.

Will loved to tell of his first visit to *The Smart Set* offices (around 1913). He said George Jean Nathan almost fell off his chair when he saw the author of such pithy and sardonic sayings. "I'd been providing it with dabs of such writing, and had been asked for more. It was perfectly normal for me to be consulting with its editors, but I happened to be seventeen years old. I was a freak."

Each issue of *The Smart Set* included one novella, several short stories, poems and sketches, in addition to epigrams. Will began to submit other material, and his first longer piece, "My Neighbor," appeared in the February 1916 issue under "William F. Jenkins" when he was 19 years old. This was followed by seven more contributions that year, including the short stories "The Anti-Climax" in July and "We Were in the Smoking Room" in December.

At times, Mencken had trouble filling *The Smart Set* magazine and solved his problem by encouraging both his well-known authors and the new young writers he was fostering to adopt a variety of pen names. Thus Murray Leinster was born.

Soon, Will began appearing in *The Smart Set* as both William F. Jenkins and Murray Leinster (pronounced Len-ster).

The name was derived from Will's mother's maiden name, Murry, and indirectly from his middle name, Fitzgerald. Wyndham Martyn, an English writer and friend later known for the Anthony Trent novels, told him that the Fitzgeralds in Ireland were descended from the Dukes of Leinster, so he adopted the name.

In their sometimes-desperate solicitations of new manuscripts, even Nathan and Mencken felt some of the submissions were pretty bad. They decided to start new magazines to publish some of their rejects and nicknamed them louse magazines. One of these was *The Parisienne,* later edited by Wyndham Martyn. Story locales were changed to France to reflect the current infatuation with all things French, and the first issue came out in July 1915.

Although Will's epigrams had been appearing regularly in *The Smart Set,* what may have been Will's first bylined piece, "Love" by Will F. Jenkins, was published in *The Parisienne* in August 1915 six months before the short story "My Neighbor" appeared in *The Smart Set.*

> "Love," said the scholar, "is the product of the creative imagination, the process being the creation of a distorted and thereby improved image of the beloved object which is therefore substituted for the object itself."
>
> "Love," cried the jester, "is a nimble flea that bites me, and whose bites I cannot scratch."
>
> "Love," said the young merchant, "is the wakening voice in a nightmare of pettiness."
>
> "Love," said his father, examining his son's accounts, "is the genius of bankruptcy and the Nemesis of bank accounts."
>
> "Love," said the theologian, "is excellent evidence of the divine origin of man."
>
> "Aye," answered the benedict, "and the absolute proof of his invincible sapheadedness."
>
> * * * * * * *
>
> "Love," quoth Zeus, "is my only rival." So to crush his rival, he instituted marriage.

A playlet, also bylined Will F. Jenkins, "On the Country Club Verandah," appeared in the February 1916 issue. *The Parisienne* was very popular and financially successful, so Nathan and Mencken sold it at a profit and started another louse magazine, *Saucy Stories,* to compete with *Snappy Stories*, which was still published by Colonel Mann.

Writers might submit a story to *The Smart Set* and find it later in *The Parisienne* or *Saucy Stories,* but no one objected because the latter were able to pay higher rates.

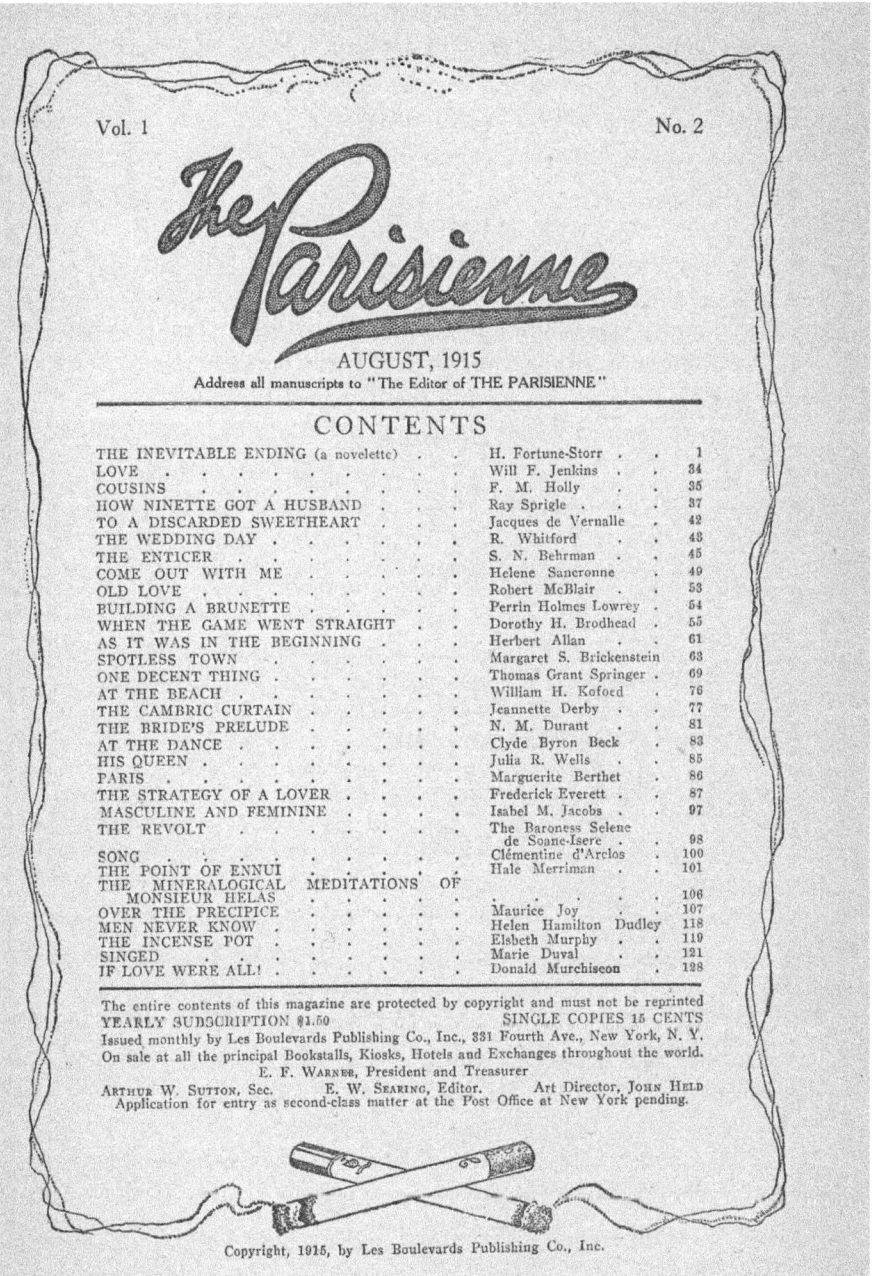

The August 1915 issue of Parisienne — probably Will's first published byline, for "Love," a poem.

Will had already sold to *Snappy Stories* beginning with "You Woman!" under the Murray Leinster byline in April 1917. When Mencken found out that his protégé was appearing in other magazines, he flattered the young writer by asking him to save "Will F. Jenkins" for his "better" work, such as that published in *The Smart Set* implying that he had a future in the better magazines.

Will's first story in *Saucy Stories*, "The Third Love of Aileen Duzant," was published as by Murray Leinster in March 1917. Will's brother George had watched the first checks come in and had become interested in writing, too. Many years later, Will complained in a letter to his daughter Jo-an: "My brother saw me getting money for such stuff, met the literary group I got into and proceeded to write. He sold his first five stories; I didn't."

George had joined Will in writing epigrams, poems and sketches for *The Smart Set* and *The Parisienne*. One of George's earliest pieces, "My Wife," appeared in the November 1916 issue of *The Parisienne*. Interestingly, George was never married.

"My Wife" by George Briggs

She is as fragrant
As the aroma of a good cigar to the nostrils of a man
Who has just sworn off smoking.
She satisfies my desire for the useless and expensive
And is as necessary as a cocktail before dinner.
I wish I had discovered her desirability
Before we were divorced!

George also used more than one name for *The Smart Set*, usually "George Briggs Jenkins, Jr.," and "George Briggs." Sometimes he and Will collaborated, as on a play called "The Beautiful Thing" in the August 1919 issue bylined "Murray Leinster and George B. Jenkins, Jr." George also began appearing in *Snappy Stories, Saucy Stories* and *Breezy Stories*.

Carl R. Dolmetsch, in his book *The Smart Set, A History and Anthology* (New York: Dial Press, 1966) quotes George J. Nathan as saying in 1955, "There never was anything quite like it ... but there ought to be. Where can beginning writers of today get that kind of exposure?"

Will cherished that early relationship with *The Smart Set*. Years later he wrote this to his daughter Jo-an, "Query: would you like a Xerox of Mencken's letter to me acknowledging that he'd put some of my stuff in a book of his and offering to settle for a large beer?"

When Will's boss at Prudential got word of his budding writing career, however, he called him in to inform him that the company frowned on outside work, but would overlook it if Will would report on any misbehavior of other employees. Will, indignant, promptly quit and, except for a spell in the army in World War I and his stint with the Office of War Information during World War II, he never took a job again.

With over a year of writing and selling stories behind him, Will registered for the draft on June 5, 1918. George had registered in Newark, the year before listing his mother as next of kin. Will registered in Washington, D.C., using the St. James Hotel as his address and also listing his mother as next of kin. Why he was in Washington is unknown. The record showed George of medium height and build with light brown hair and gray eyes. Will was described as tall (although he was actually 5'7") and slender with brown hair and dark brown eyes. George entered his occupation as "Clerk, Prudential Insurance Company," while 21-year-old Will confidently wrote "Author." George was called up quickly and, according to Will, served overseas. Will said he had the devil of a time getting in because he was underweight and used the well known "stuffing himself with bananas" trick to add more pounds.

He was disappointed that he did not go overseas but was sent instead to the Office of Public Information in the 19th Division, a training unit. (Still in action during the Iraq war, the 19th or Iroquois Division was the subject of a flurry of internet exchanges complaining that a National Guard unit was being sent to Iraq without any weapons. It was explained by the army that regulations authorized all equipment "from typewriters to weapons" and that training units such as the Iroquois did not need weapons but would have them issued to them by another unit if they were needed. To those who knew him, the picture of Will Jenkins going to war with his trusted Remington upright typewriter is somehow appropriate.)

Mamie in Newark.

In spite of the demands of their military service until the war's end in November 1918, stories by both young men kept appearing in print.

In February 1918, Will first appeared in *Breezy Stories* with "Sacrifice," but he soon branched out beyond the light, trendy, humorous pieces he had been selling to *The Smart Set* and *Snappy, Saucy* and *Breezy Stories*. He added ones with an adventure, western or mystery flavor using his pen name, Murray Leinster. He found a new market adding the Munsey magazines *All-Story Weekly* and *The Argosy* to his publishers and was averaging two stories a month among these publications.

Coincidently, in 1896 the year Will was born, Frank Munsey decided to take advantage of the development of pulp paper, a cheap alternative to what was previously available. Munsey had entered the publishing business in 1882 with a boy's adventure magazine, *The Golden Argosy*. He converted *The Golden Argosy* to a monthly, dropping the *Golden*, targeting adults and printing all fiction. Using the new paper and untrimmed pages, he was able to price the magazine at ten cents a copy and sales took off. Because of pulp paper's giant advantage — it was cheap, so magazines printed on it could be cheap — there was tremendous growth of the genre. Street & Smith entered the field in 1903 with *The Popular Magazine* and Munsey added *All-Story Weekly* to his group in 1905. *The Argosy* started to publish weekly in 1917 still selling for 10 cents a copy. It printed all fiction, soon including science fiction; therefore *The Argosy* and *All-Story Weekly* became important new markets for Murray Leinster.

His first Munsey story was "Atmosphere" in *The Argosy*, January 26, 1918. This was followed by adventure stories in *All-Story Weekly*: "You Can't Get Away with It," February 2, 1918; "A Cabin in the Wilderness," April 6, 1918; "Grooves," October 12, 1918; "Footprints in the Snow," June 7, 1919; "W.S.S.," August 2, 1919; and "Oh Aladdin" on November 1, 1919. "Evidence," published July 12, 1919, was a western murder mystery.

Five more Murray Leinster stories appeared in *The Argosy* in 1918: "In Cold Blood," May 4; "The Hour After Supper," July 13; "Jiggy Jazz," September 21; "Honesty," September 28; and "Izzy," November 16.

Will's relationship with *Argosy* continued through its various name and editorial changes. The skills he learned in these early years prepared him well, and, when *Argosy* switched to slick format and a varied editorial content in 1942, Will switched also and continued to sell to them, changing to the Will F. Jenkins byline. In April 1963, it printed "Night to Survive," which had originally been published in *The Saturday Evening Post*.

While Will was experimenting with new genres and finding new markets, George, other than one appearance in *Detective Tales* in February 1923, never emerged from his early style. The bulk of his work appeared in *The Smart Set* and *The Parisienne*.

In 1968, in a letter to his daughter Jo-an, Will reflected on this time:

> oh, yes. I found a Pleiades Club annual volume for 1918–1919. It contains the first item of my writing to be included in a hardcover book. And it's terrible! But it was amazing to see the names of so many people I used to know who for a time were more or less famous. Richard le Gallienne (Eva le Gallienne's father) to you *may* be the name of a famous actress. But he was highly literary and much admired.
>
> If you were to find somebody of my generation they would prick up their ears (providing they were intellectuals fifty years ago) if somebody said Berton Braley, Lillian Bennet-Thompson, Dorothy Dix, Thomas Edgelow, Archie Gunn, Bernard Hamblin, Joseph Hergesheimer, Fanny Hurst, George B. Jenkins, Jr., Reginald Kauffman, Harry Kemp, Murray Leinster, Elias Lieberman, Wyndham Martyn, Cleveland Moffett, Channing Pollack, H. Thompson Rich, Walter Adolph Roberts, Francis Rolt-Wheeler, Herb Roth, Margaret Sangster, Clinton Scollard, Elizabeth Sharp, Thomas Grant Springer, Robert W. Sneddon, Archie Sullivan, Margaret Widdemer, Clement Wood... It is most singular to come upon the names of all these people I knew more or less well, of whom I have all sorts of irrelevant memories, who at one time were recognizable entities with known achievements and with status ... the fact that reputation even in one's field is just what Bill Shakespeare said. It's a bubble. It bursts.

The Pleiades Club was a literary society that was founded in Greenwich Village in 1896 and published yearbooks through 1936. It started when a group from the artistic community, who were regulars at an Italian restaurant (Maria de Prato's on MacDougal Street), decided to formalize their gatherings. Mark Twain is perhaps the best known now of the first members. They met weekly for dinner and entertainment, music, poetry readings and the like, and, as the membership grew, moved to larger quarters. They saw their mission as promoting the arts of "Music, Drama, Art and Literature," providing an appreciative audience and helping needy artists with free scholarships. It is possible that he met the poet Strickland Gillian there. He certainly brought up his children reciting Gillian's so-called world's shortest poem, "On the Antiquity of Microbes." In its entirety it reads, "Adam had 'em."

The Pleiades Yearbook 1918–1919 included "The Ass," a short story by Murray Leinster, and "In the Subway," a humorous poem by George B. Jenkins, Jr.

Will always said that if he had been able to continue in school, he would have become a chemist. However, his scientific interests extended beyond chemistry into physics and the biological sciences. The thought of combining his interests in science and writing by producing science fiction was not yet in his mind, even though science fiction had begun to attract major attention as long ago as 1864 with Jules Verne's *Journey to the Center of the Earth* and

From Earth to Mars in 1865. H. G. Wells wrote *The Time Machine* in 1895, *The Invisible Man* in 1897, and *War of the Worlds* in 1898. Mark Twain wrote his story of time travel, *A Connecticut Yankee in King Arthur's Court*, in 1889. Edgar Rice Burroughs' *Under the Moons of Mars* (later published in book form as *The Princess of Mars*) was printed as a series in six issues of *All-Story Magazine* beginning in February 1912. Notable in the story was that the hero, John Carter, rescued and married Princess Dejah Thoris and the fruit of their union was an egg. Burroughs' more enduring *Tarzan* was printed in its entirety in one issue of *All-Story* in October 1912. Even Arthur Conan Doyle wrote a number of science fiction stories beginning with *The Lost World* in 1912. This series about the exploits of rich, eccentric Professor Challenger was concluded in 1929.

For now, Will was spurred by the reality of actually making a living by writing, so he continued to seek out all possible markets and tried to write a minimum of a thousand words a night. Of those early years, one of his favorite lines was, "I only starved to death twice."

In 1919, in the mix of adventures, westerns, mysteries and other stories published as by Will F. Jenkins or Murray Leinster, there appeared also the first of his attempts at science fiction.

FOUR

Entering Science Fiction: 1919–1921

> *The whole thing started when the clock on the Metropolitan Tower began to run backward. It was not a graceful proceeding. The hands had been moving onward in their customary deliberate fashion, slowly and thoughtfully, but suddenly the people in the office near the clock's face heard an ominous creaking and groaning. There was a slight, hardly discernible shiver through the tower, and then something gave with a crash. The big hands on the clock began moving backward.*
> "The Runaway Skyscraper," published in
> *The Argosy* magazine, February 22, 1919

"The Runaway Skyscraper" was Will's first science fiction story. Sam Moskowitz, science fiction writer and editor, well known as a historian of science fiction, tells the story of how it all happened in his profile of Will, "The Strange Case of Murray Leinster," in the December 1961 issue of *Amazing Stories*.

Although Will had achieved his goal of supporting himself by writing, he told Moskowitz he had gotten fed up with the kinds of stories he had been writing and selling to *Argosy* since 1917. So he told *Argosy*'s editor, Matthew White, Jr., he was finished with that stuff for a while. He casually mentioned he was working on a story beginning with the line, "The whole thing started when the clock on the Metropolitan Tower began to run backward." White immediately sent back a letter saying he wanted to see it.

"I had to write it or admit I was lying," Will said.

Matthew White was an interesting man. He was personable, a prolific writer, and also a drama critic. Will's memory of him included his snow-white whiskers and a slight lisp. His editorship, some said his genius, in the early 1900s greatly contributed to the growth and success of the magazine.

Cut from "The Runaway Skyscraper."

An article in the January 1908 issue of *The Writer* laid out White's editorial rule that was the secret of *The Argosy's* success: "Pique the reader's curiosity, then gratify it." The article quoting White continued as follows.

> "*The Argosy*," he says, "never has a story written backward — that is to say, the editor never hits on some frenzied position for the hero, and calls on an author to write a story around it. The editor considers what phase of life is likely to be most interesting to the big majority of readers. This being settled upon, the author is told to carry his hero along in a series of experiences that would be liable to happen to anyone under such conditions. *The Argosy*," says Mr. White, "...does not print stories which wander off at the end into hazy nothingness, which some writers are pleased to call 'artistic finish,' but which, as a matter of cold, hard fact, is neither finish nor art. Neither do readers of *The Argosy* have to waste time in wading through a tame introduction to get at the kernel of the narrative. Stories must capture interest at the outset."

Will's first line certainly piqued curiosity, including his own. The idea for "The Runaway Skyscraper" came when he looked out the window and noticed the clock on the Metropolitan Life Tower, one of the tallest buildings in New York at the time, was running backwards. It was being reset. What if time was really running backwards? How could he gratify his curiosity? He began the process of developing literary plots he followed all his life.

"The Runaway Skyscraper" captured the interest of Harold Hershey, one of the editors of *Thrill Book*, a new publication planned by Street and Smith in 1919. He and fellow editor Eugene Clancy had been having difficulty finding stories for the new magazine. They had planned for it to be an all-fantasy magazine but could not find enough material and decided to add science fiction, straight adventure and mystery stories. He knew of Will's work from *The Smart Set* in addition to *Argosy* and approached Will, asking him for something for *Thrill Book*. Will came up with three stories. "A Thousand Degrees Below Zero" was published July 15, 1919. Its plot involved an evil inventor whose machine could draw heat from all objects it was directed onto, killing all living creatures and destroying the rest. This plot with changes in the inventions was a basis for many further Leinster stories.

The story was a success and was quickly followed by "The Silver Menace" in two installments on September 1 and September 15. Here, the seas are turned into gelatin by a swiftly multiplying life form.

"JuJu," an adventure story set in Africa, appeared in the October 15 issue, and Murray Leinster had achieved enough interest that his name was on the cover. Unfortunately, this, the sixteenth, was the final issue of *Thrill Book*.

Will continued to read everything he could get his hands on and on every subject. This took him to French entomologist Jean Henri Fabré who wrote *The Life of the Spider, The Life of the Fly, Social Life in the Insect World,* and many others.

Will, in the Author's Note of *The Forbidden Planet* (Gnome Press, 1954) said about them, "These books, while absolutely factual, are much more interesting than most fiction and can be read as if they were make-believe instead of the sound and honest work they are."

He also commended the work of Ralph Beebe on the army ant in *Edge of the Jungle* and Maurice Maeterlinck for *Life of the Bee*. Will introduced all of these books to his children at an early age, and they devoured them as well.

"The Mad Planet," which came out in *Argosy* on June 12, 1920, was a result of this interest. In what could be a prescient warning of global warming, changing climate conditions had resulted in a world where plants and insects had grown to enormous size and were dominant, and man was reduced to a primitive, hunted state. The hero, Burl, an early genius, begins to lead mankind out of this predicament. The popularity of the story resulted in "The Red Dust," printed in the April 2, 1921, *Argosy*, bringing Burl back with even more exciting adventures. A spaceship crash strands its crew on a planet where a dangerous experiment had been tried, then abandoned and forgotten. A cloud of dust containing primitive bacterial plant and insect life had contaminated the planet, and the crew must fight to survive.

It is interesting that these stories were basically narrative and included little dialogue. Will loved to break rules and, in this case, was defying the critics who said a reader's interest could not be maintained with pure narrative.

Third in the series, "Nightmare Planet," didn't come out until June 12, 1952, also in *Argosy*, and Moskowitz said, "It was an older, more philosophical, more thoughtful Jenkins writing this story, but the magic of the first two carried through." When the three stories were put together in a book, *The Forgotten Planet* (Gnome Press, 1954), he moved the locale to another planet for scientific reasons. Moskowitz called it "a book of such magnetic appeal it is unlikely to become a forgotten classic."

Now confident that he could make it with his writing, Will turned to settling his personal life. Although his brother George was living comfortably with his mother, in Newark, New Jersey, Will, now in his twenties, was eager to be on his own. He complained that Mamie looked through his mail, and that she boasted to the neighbors about the number and size of the checks he was receiving. It is doubtful that he stayed very long with his mother and brother after leaving the army when the war ended in 1918. He often referred to time spent in Greenwich Village, but the easy, freewheeling Bohemian atmosphere, though stimulating in some ways, probably did not appeal to Will for long (he spoke disparagingly about it in later life). What he was seeking was a secure family life.

Will made long visits to his half-sister Lula and her family in Norfolk, Virginia. Lula had married the Rev. George William Cox, a Baptist minister, in 1910, and they had a daughter, Francis [*sic*], and a son, George Jr. Lula's marriage was particularly fortunate for Will, as it was through his brother-in-law that Will was introduced to Gloucester County, Virginia, the place which soon became the home of his heart, no matter where else he lived.

Gloucester is in the southeastern part of the Commonwealth of Virginia in what is referred to as the Tidewater region. Technically, it includes all areas where water level is affected by tides, and Gloucester, Portsmouth, Norfolk, Suffolk, Hampton, Newport News, Yorktown, Williamsburg and Richmond are all in Tidewater.

There is a great deal of local pride in being from Tidewater Virginia perhaps because of its rich colonial history — the first English settlement at Jamestown in 1607, and the first continuous English-speaking settlement at Hampton in 1610. Norfolk, where Will was born, continues to be Virginia's primary port as it has been since the 1700s. At the time of the Revolution, it was the largest community in Virginia.

There may be no place other than Tidewater Virginia that more closely represents the quote from William Faulkner's *Requiem for a Nun*, "The past is never dead; it is not even past."

There is pride of family and heritage, and these Virginians know who their ancestors were, even distant cousins, for generations back, and their lives are remembered and celebrated. Many of these early settlers were educated and cultured and traveled to England and France. There were wharfs on almost every Tidewater farm that had access to water. The network of rivers and creeks made them useful not only for local travel, but many were also accessible to ocean-going vessels. This allowed these early residents to go abroad for business or to send and receive products, keeping up with the latest trends and fashions.

The Rev. George W. Cox, "Uncle Will" to Will's children, was from Gloucester County. His brother and sisters, Ned Cox and Miss Ada and Miss Emmie Cox, owned and managed the Botetourt Hotel in Gloucester Court House, and Will became a frequent visitor, falling in love with the area in the process. As early as 1917, he rented a writing room at the hotel. Gussie and Hylda Lawson and Edith Lawson Hatch, nieces of the Coxes all lived there. They were shirt-tail relatives, the southern term for people related by marriage, and they formed a friendship that lasted the rest of their lives.

The rural, small town life where everyone has known you forever, and everyone knows everything about you — and there are few surprises — suited Will perfectly. He liked familiarity; he liked to go to the same places, to be with the same people with whom he felt comfortable and unchallenged. This gave him the stability and security he longed for after his unsettled teen years. Although at this time he was living primarily in Newark, New Jersey, and New York City and visited his half-sister Lula in Norfolk frequently, for the rest of his days, Gloucester was the only place he ever really wanted to be.

• FIVE •

Marriage: The 1920s

During one of his stays in New York, Will met Mary Mandola, the Greenwich Village–born daughter of Attilio and Marianna Mandola. Attilio had arrived in New York in 1891 from Sarno, a town in the region of Campania in the province of Salerno, Italy. Marianna came two years later with their two-year-old son, John. Four daughters (Rose, Mary, Julia, Adeline) and a second son (Rudolph) were born in Manhattan.

Will and Mary met on the beach at Coney Island, and Will said later: "I thought she was the prettiest kid I'd ever seen." She had beautiful brown eyes and very white skin that never tanned in the years in the hot Virginia sun. Although she was 22 and Will just a year older, he thought she was a teenager.

Born on March 14, 1897, Mary had grown up on Thompson Street in Greenwich Village and had fond memories of roller-skating in nearby Washington Square. Intellectually, she was a good match for Will. She graduated from Washington Irving High School, and the breadth of Mary's education there made her more than just a pretty girl; she had a literary and artistic education that made her especially appealing to the young writer.

Washington Irving was the newest high school in New York City. Its brand-new building opened at 40 Irving Place in Greenwich Village in February 1913. The school itself, however, started earlier, coming from the 1906 joining of the prestigious Wadleigh High School for Girls and Girls Technical High School. In organizing the new school, the principal, Patrick McCowan, believed in integrating the curricula, combining academic instruction in the liberal arts with the technical skills of typewriting, stenography, commercial art, dressmaking and home economics. He developed a creative atmosphere that made the school a model for education in that time.

A repertoire course, which included literature and the arts, was required. Students studied the poets, including Whitman, Thomas Gray, Lord Byron, Wordsworth and Shelley. However, the policy was that poetry must be not only be studied, but also recited on a regular schedule in performances that encouraged and trained future actresses. School plays included Shakespeare productions and performances of operas such as Bizet's *Carmen*. Metropolitan Opera stars visited. Washington Irving was the first school to have an art gallery and, in art classes, each student had her own worktable. The integration of art and dressmaking inspired an interest in fashion design. Girls learned to tailor on living customers and sold their own creations from a room next to the library.

Mary had been interested in studying law and had taken a few classes, but the death of her mother when she was 18 and her training at Washington Irving led her to focus on fashion design. A few years later, the actress Claudette Colbert also developed this interest while at Washington Irving. Colbert's major interests were art and acting, and she had been encouraged in those studies at school. However, her early eclectic training served her well, and when she went on to study at the Art Student's League, she helped pay the tuition and support herself by dressmaking. After she achieved great success as an actress, she continued to remember what she had been taught and took great interest in the style and fit of her costumes. She always remembered her high school and sent an autographed picture that is still on view in the library.

Mary worked for a French custom dressmaker — always called Madame — in the Village after she graduated, and she designed and made her own stylish clothes for her petite 5'2" frame. Her portrait, showing a sweet-faced, dark-

Mary Mandola circa 1920.

Mary's wedding picture, 1921.

haired young woman in a romantic black and white dress she designed, was displayed in the photographer's window as a sample of his work for several months.

Mary's father, whose youngest child, Rudy, was only six when his wife died, soon remarried. He moved their home and his established real estate brokerage business to Brooklyn.

Mary was very close to her older brother John, who limped badly from an accident in his teens. John provided a limousine service for the early motion picture studios then located in Fort Lee, New Jersey, and Astoria, in Queens, New York City. He also started the first commuter airplane service to Atlantic City, New Jersey, the Bluebird Airline and Limousine Service. Although Mary never drove after she was married, she had a license and was proud to have learned in her brother's Cadillac.

Will was very much in love, and it is obvious that he was thinking about her in the fall of 1919 when staying with Lula and her family in Fentress (a section in Norfolk), Virginia. The evidence of this poem suggests that their meeting on the beach may have taken place that previous summer. The poem, dated October 25, 1919, and signed Murray Leinster, survives:

> I gaze, unseeing, from my small high window
> And lean outside to seize my little share
> Of faint, infrequent, vagrant breezes,
> While longing for a country fair

> Where cities do not make the very night winds
> Hot-breathed and dust-filled torments, where
> I might recline upon broad moonlit beaches
> And watch your face, framed in your dark, dark hair.
>
> I sigh, and know sighing foolish,
> For was there ever such a lovely place,
> Where I might find you shyly waiting
> Until I saw you, shadow veiled in lace?
> For all I know, tonight you may be sitting
> In this same city's drab, dull covered space
> In some small room, by some high attic window
> A wistful look like mine upon your face.

Will had been selling regularly and, during their courtship in New York City, Will and Mary's usual hangout was Keens Steakhouse near Herald Square on West 36th Street. Keens was originally the meeting place of the Lambs Club, the well-known artists and writers club. It opened to the public in 1885 and continued to be frequented by the literary and theater crowd, including publishers, producers, newspapermen and playwrights. Originally gentlemen-only, the gender barrier was broken in 1905 when Lily Langtry, actress and paramour of King Edward VII of England, sued for admittance and won.

Keens is still known for its huge collection of churchwarden pipes, some of which hang from the ceiling in the dining room. Keens' Pipe Club continued a tradition from 17th Century England when the long stemmed clay pipes were kept at the owner's favorite inn, because they were too fragile to transport. Members of the club included Teddy Roosevelt, Babe Ruth, Will Rogers, Albert Einstein, General Douglas MacArthur and even opera singer Grace Moore.

Will's first venture into the movies was "The Purple Hieroglyph," a short story that was published in *Snappy Stories* March 1, 1920. It was a mystery melodrama, and one of the last of his stories to appear there. It was filmed by Vitagraph Studios in their Brooklyn location and released in October 1920. Vitagraph was founded in 1897 by Albert E. Smith and J. Stuart Blackton, and by 1907 was producing most of the films made in America. Warner Brothers bought the company in 1925.

The Purple Hieroglyph was the working title of the movie, changed later to *The Purple Cipher*. *The Purple Hieroglyph* would be filmed twice more, first as *Murder Will Out* in 1930, featuring Lila Lee, Noah Beery and Hedda Hopper, and then as *Torchy Blane in Chinatown* in 1939.

Torchy is a newspaper reporter who is involved with a police detective in solving crimes. This familiar plot was used in a series of Torchy Blane films starring Glenda Farrell. A five-cassette collection is currently available. The

Chinatown story involves a rich young man engaged to a U.S. senator's daughter, three murders, blackmail, an Oriental gang, a speedboat kidnapping, and a rescue by a U.S. submarine. Some shots were made in the shipyards of San Francisco and at the San Diego Naval Base.

In 1921, Will added Mencken and Nathan's new magazine *Black Mask* to his list of markets. However, in spite of these successes and continuing short story sales, he wanted more to offer his bride and decided to write a play. His agent, Bob Hardy, submitted it to the Shuberts, then the leading Broadway theater producers. He was again visiting Lula in Virginia when he heard they had accepted it and fired off a letter to Mary with a proposal. When wooing her, he had told her, "Just think, our children can say their father is a writer." He said he was "walking on air" when she accepted, but then he got another letter from Hardy saying, although the play was accepted, the date of production was indefinite, and no money would be forthcoming until then. (The play was never produced, and Will never made any money from it.) He was "tearing his hair out," he said later. Mary, in the meantime, had other concerns.

The slightly built, ambitious young writer with the soft Virginia accent was undoubtedly unlike anyone else she had met, and Mary was understandably worried about marrying a man whom she really didn't know very much about. Although sheltered and naïve, she gathered strength and took the train to Portsmouth, Virginia, to meet more of Will's family, including his half-sister Lula, Lula's husband and children, and the uncles and aunts on his mother's side who lived nearby. She was delighted to meet another engaged young woman on the trip, and that made her feel better. More importantly, getting to know Lula and more of the family gave Mary the confidence to go ahead, and the wedding took place in New York on August 9, 1921.

Knowing Will, he had probably drawn an idyllic picture of life in the area of Tidewater Virginia that he had come to love and so was able to convince the city-bred Mary to give living in rural Gloucester a year's trial. As he later told the story, "Thank goodness, she liked it."

For her, that first long drive down to Virginia was novel and exciting. She saw her first cow, and Will had to stop the car so she could get out and examine it. Later she enjoyed discovering that horses were for riding as well as pulling wagons. A house was found to rent in Ark, a settlement in Gloucester County, where their first daughter, Little Mary, was born on May 6, 1922.

They searched and soon found what became Will's dream home, a deteriorating story-and-a-half colonial built in the late 1600s. It sat on several acres high over the north bank of the York River at Clay Bank in Gloucester County across from Williamsburg. Long abandoned, it had recently been the residence of a flock of chickens. It was quite small, as were those early colonial houses, but full of charm with low ceilings, beautiful wide board floors, the original HL hinges and box front door lock with a foot-long key. There were three working fireplaces. Best of all, there was a view to die for. As you looked west, the sun scattered diamonds on the water every morning, and set off an explosion of color over that same river at night.

Will and "Little Mary" at Ardudwy in 1922.

Mary and Will faced a daunting task but went ahead and bought it, signing the papers on August 26, 1922, just over a year after the date of their marriage. In homage to his Welsh ancestry, Will named it Ardudwy.

The original Ardudwy is in northwest Wales and is prominent in Welsh mythology. Historically, Collwyn or Colwyn, depending upon your source, was lord of Ardudwy and progenitor of one of the Fifteen Noble Tribes of Gwynedd. He is credited with restoring Harlech Castle in the tenth century.

A 1909 article in *The Washington Post* that was circulated widely among the various Jenkins families of the time traced their lineage to Sir Leoline Jenkins and Judge David Jenkins calling them father and son. There is no verifiable family link to either man, they were not father and son, and there is no indication that they were related to each other. However, ancestral records of some English Jenkins families lead back to Colwyn of Ardudwy.

Like Harlech Castle, Clay Bank's Ardudwy needed restoring and Will and Mary were equal to the task. First came the scrubbing. Mary's younger sister Adeline came down to help, and Will remembered her crying hysterically when her fingernails became soft from the lye soap, and how he comforted her, telling her they would harden again. They did.

The house was in Clay Bank, a farming settlement that was little more than a post office and a county store. It was just up the hill from Clay Bank wharf where the steamboat from Baltimore landed. The landmark clay banks, visible from the river, are in front of Ardudwy.

Clay Bank, rural and remote as it was, was also a community center of sorts. Before reliable automobiles and trucks and widespread railroad service, all transport, commercial and pleasure, was by boat. A series of wharfs extended to the channel up and down the river and the bay, and Clay Bank wharf was a focus of activity at least twice a day when the steamer that went from Baltimore to West Point, Virginia, and back docked there. It was not until World War II that trucks completely replaced the freight service it provided. In the early days, when there was not much in the way of entertainment, people would stroll out to see the boat come in. A walk to the wharf shed at the end was a favorite activity for courting couples, even more popular later in the evening. There was a smell of saltwater, mud flats and old rope, but it was not unpleasant if you were used to it.

At the foot of the wharf, there was an area with the shipping office, a store and post office, and the home of the merchant and postmaster, Louis Groh. Will had bought the Clay Bank property from Groh, and his wife, Frieda, became a close friend of Mary's, with their babies coming along close to the same time. The York River is four miles wide at Clay Bank, and there was a rail line from the shore to the wharf shed and loading dock at the channel. A double-ended cart was designed to be pulled by a mule and ride the rail. In the 1930s, Barneymule was in charge of pulling the truck for the mile-long rail trip along the wharf stem.

After his freight had been loaded onto the steamboat and another load had filled his truck, he was led around to the other end of the cart and hitched up for the trip back. Some of the more unusual shipments were daffodils that were grown as a crop for the northern market and watermelons. Will and Mary reported that they once scratched a name and address on the rind of a watermelon, added stamps, and the melon safely reached Mary's family in New York.

From the first, Clay Bank was a popular gathering place for family and their extended circle of friends. Mamie and brother George came, Lula with her family, and Will's father, George, after he moved in with Lula. Mary's brothers and sisters and their families often arrived for vacations and holidays. The several acres of lawn, a sandy beach for oyster roasts, crabbing off the wharf, and the wide York River for swimming were big attractions.

Adeline and unknown friend (in overalls) hitch a ride with Barneymule on his load of watermelons.

Five • *Marriage: The 1920s*

Mary in her brother John's car during a visit on his way to Florida.

Visitors to Ardudwy, coming within sight and the salty smell of the river, would watch for a narrow dirt lane on the right just before the Clay Bank store. They would make a sharp right turn onto it and drive uphill past a field on the left where in the spring there were daffodils, and, later in the season, a crop of corn. By 1930, the old, white-painted, story-and-a-half colonial house was half-hidden by a high privet hedge. For a time, there was a sign at the entrance saying "Ardudwy."

It was likely that Will would be at the open door, for it was rare for anyone to be coming up the lane unless they were coming to see the Jenkins family. Engine noise, headlights at night, or a cloud of fine dust during the hot, dry summers announced your impending arrival. His first words in his soft Tidewater accent would be, "Come on in. Let's have a memorial for my seventh great grandfather." He was referring to a saying, popular at the time. The governor of North Carolina was supposed to have said to the governor of South Carolina, "It's been a damn long time between drinks." Will would be quick to explain that when his first ancestor in America, John Jenkins, was a governor in the 1600s there was no North and South Carolina, it was all Olde Albemarle County. "So," he would say, "we consider that he was talking to himself."

Friends were always welcome, and they were encouraged to bring guests, so there was an interesting mix. Like other young couples, Will and Mary had many parties continuing the socializing and camaraderie they had enjoyed in New York. The Lawson sisters, Gussie and Hylda Lawson and Edith Hatch would bring down guests from the Botetourt Hotel. They were often the traveling men, salesmen who made regular stops in Gloucester. The Jenkins girls particularly looked forward to a visit from one of the tobacco salesmen recalled as a Mr. Berkabile. He was a very talented amateur magician and entertained them by pulling quarters out of their ears and other tricks.

Gussie was a charmer, always beautifully dressed with finger-waved hair, a fresh manicure and smelling sweetly of cologne. Hylda was more reserved. She wore trousers when no one but Katherine Hepburn did and had a thriving business growing and selling jonquil bulbs and making wreaths. Edith was married but also lived at the hotel where Mr. Hatch, who worked in Richmond, visited from time to time. She was also beautifully dressed and "went to business" as was the term at the time.

Meanwhile Will had to worry about supporting his growing family. He was polishing his craft and had learned that, even at the going rate of half a cent to a cent a word, he could make a living if he was versatile enough and wrote enough stories that sold.

Fortunately he had been doing well since his marriage. William Clayton's *Telling Tales* and *Clues* printed several stories in the twenties. A long relationship with Street and Smith began with appearances in *Top Notch Magazine*, *Detective Story Magazine*, and *Cowboy Stories*. In September 1923, he began a long run in *Short Stories* under Doubleday-Page and later Doubleday-Duran with "In Account with Destiny." It continued with 29 more stories through 1948 and ended in 1958 in Leo Margulies' revival of the magazine under the new American Short Stories Corporation. His first story in Doubleday's *West*, "Howdy," appeared in January 1926.

The Munsey Company, publishers of *Argosy*, started a new magazine, *Love Story*, in 1921. They had been publishing Will's adventure stories in *Argosy* and were familiar with his versatility, so they wrote to him about a series they planned to initiate based on some British six-penny novels they had purchased. Would he be interested in taking on writing romances for *Love Story Magazine*? Resourceful as usual, Will was able to respond positively. They were paying half a cent a word, so he was happy to give it a try. He created Louisa Carter Lee out of his half-sister's first name, Louisa, and two venerable Virginia surnames, Carter and Lee. Writers often took women's names for romance stories and triple names were considered elite and were very popular.

"A Chivalrous Silence" was published in two parts in August 1921. Louisa

Five • Marriage: The 1920s 47

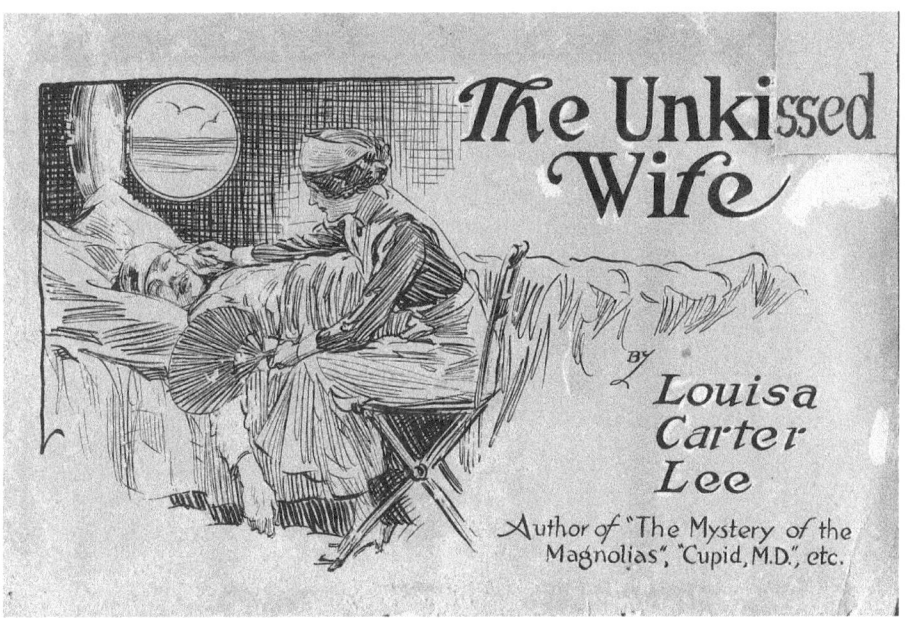

"The Unkissed Wife" appeared in *Love Story Magazine*, March 25, 1922.

was very popular and, in 1926 alone, 12 of Louisa's stories were printed in *Love Story Magazine*. Chelsea House published two Louisa Carter Lee novels, *Her Desert Lover* in 1925, and *Love and Better: A Love Story* in 1931. Later he estimated Louisa was earning about $200 a week at this time, good money in those days when two thousand dollars a year was a living wage for many of the middle class. Louisa was popular, and there were plans to expand. Will invented a male love novelist, Dana Furnam, and proposed a serial with Louisa and Dana writing alternating chapters. But all of a sudden he couldn't do it.

He said in his Disclave 70 speech, "I was living a real romance and couldn't write the phoney stuff any more." The Munsey Company tried to encourage him: "They offered a cent a word, then two cents and finally three cents a word if I would just go back to being my old Louisa. It would have meant five, six hundred dollars a week — in the early Twenties! And I just couldn't do it."

But a check was a check, and he managed to write "the phoney stuff" occasionally as late as 1937 when *Thrilling Love* published a story by him. The Louisa Carter Lee name surfaced again in May 1949, when "Red Canyon" was reprinted in *Movie Magazine*. But he wasn't happy about it. In the end, he fell so out of love with what had been a solid income earner that, later, when his daughter Billee was in her early teens and was caught reading *Love*

Story Magazine, he stood the copies up on the mantelpiece, thinking to embarrass her by allowing people to see what trash she was reading.

Much later, Will wrote to his daughter Jo-an about this period:

> Man I've been reading stories sold as far back as 1921, and I writhe at how bad, and how immature and how simply sickly those yarns are. I must have sold more utterly lousy stories than anybody else in the world. — I suspect that if I ever got famous enough for somebody to propose a "Complete Works" that I'd rise up from my grave to strangle him. But the necessity isn't likely to arise.

Meanwhile his family was growing. A second daughter, Betty (Elizabeth Madden Jenkins), was born on April 2, 1925. Louisa's retirement, and the notoriously slow pay of the pulp magazines made things difficult for a time, but Will continually checked on new and unusual markets for opportunities to sell the same story more than once. A western story, "Ample Water," bylined Murray Leinster, was published in *Sunset* in January 1925, and in the *Brooklyn Standard Union* newspaper on Sunday, May 3, 1925. It contained the Leinster trademarks, an engaging animal, in this case a rabbit, and an evil antagonist, defined by his actions and not by words.

Will once commented disparagingly of his brother, "When George doesn't sell a story for a couple of months, he gives up and gets a job editing." Will never gave up.

Hugo Gernsback launched *Amazing Stories* in April 1926. He is credited with being the father of science fiction and developing some of the most successful writers in that genre. Gernsback wanted Will, and writing for Gernsback with his idea of a magazine devoted to scientifiction as he called it should have been a natural for Will. It was an idea whose time had come. However, there was a crucial issue, payment, and by now Will was already firmly established as a name writer because of his regular appearances in *Argosy, Short Stories, Clues, Telling Tales* and others. Gernsback was notorious for being slow pay or no pay.

Gernsback had been publishing a number of science-oriented magazines like *Radio News, The Electrical Experimenter,* and *Science and Invention,* and had identified a market for this genre. Munsey's *The Argosy* and *All-Story* had started to print some science adventure and he might have brought out a new magazine, but he died in 1926 without trying the new format. *Blue Book Company* was printing some science fiction. Street and Smith's *The Thrill Book* had failed, so they were not ready for another attempt. It was only Gernsback who dared take the plunge and try an all science fiction magazine.

Will did appear in the June 1926 issue of *Amazing Stories* with a reprint

Opposite: "My wife merely feels faint," he says in "The Unkissed Wife."

of "The Runaway Skyscraper" from *Argosy*. This issue of *Amazing Stories*, like the first two, was made up primarily of reprints, including "The Star" by H. G. Wells and *Journey to the Center of the Earth* by Jules Verne. Because he paid his authors very little if at all, Gernsback was having trouble attracting new stories, including from Will, and he soon had the reputation of using only reprints. He undoubtedly would have been more successful in getting new material if he had not been so parsimonious.

Gernsback had tried out set rates on H. G. Wells: $100 for a novel and $50 for short stories. This was not so bad in those days for the short stories, but, for a 60,000-word novel like *War of the Worlds*, it came out to ⅙ of a cent a word. This was further complicated by a possible confusion that the rate agreed upon was in pounds rather than dollars. The pound being worth $5 at the time, this was serious confusion, and Gernsback soon stopped printing Wells' stories, probably because he didn't want to meet Wells' price.

Amazing Stories went on to reprint Will's "The Mad Planet" in November 1926 and "The Red Dust" in January 1927, both originally in *Argosy*.

Gernsback paid $45 for the reprint of "The Red Dust" but, more importantly, Robert T. Hardy, Will's agent at the time, negotiated a payment upon contract rather than publication. "The Red Dust" was 23,000 words, so the $45 represented about ⅕ of a cent a word. Gernsback liked to plead poverty and asked writers for special consideration while he was launching his new magazine. As the magazine went into its second year, authors got tired of that excuse, especially in light of his lavish personal life-style.

Hardy had been with Will since *The Smart Set* days when he had represented several of their authors. Striking at well over six feet tall, Hardy had a reputation for a good rapport with his authors, and his advice to Will seems to have been good as well. He surely must have helped this youthful beginner negotiate a then uncommon relationship with Munsey. At that time, the potential for reprint sales for science fiction was not anticipated, and publishers regularly retained all publishing rights. Will's contracts retained the rights for him, a practice he continued. This was a particular bonus for his wife, Mary, in later years, as foreign rights became a reliable source of income. From the first sale, Will told Mary that all money from foreign rights would be hers personally, to spend as she chose. Even if he had to borrow from her occasionally, he respected that gift and always paid her back.

Because of Will's reputation from *Argosy*, Gernsback was eager to obtain new stories from him. He heard Will had written a new novel called *The Strange People* and asked to see it. He also requested a sequel to "The Red Dust" and up to six new stories a year, but Hardy's advice was that he wouldn't pay enough to make it worthwhile.

Hardy wrote to Will saying:

> I don't know whether it would pay you to undertake to write this for two cents a word, if payment was on acceptance. I am not sure it would, as he probably wouldn't order them in advance, and if you didn't sell them to him you might have some difficulty in disposing of the stories elsewhere. Don't you think you could put your time better elsewhere?

Hardy was not convinced of the viability of this new genre and thought of science fiction as freak stories and not particularly marketable. *The Strange People* sold later to *Weird Tales* and was published in March, April and May 1928. Their usual rate was at least a cent a word.

Gernsback lost *Amazing Stories* in 1929, when he was sued into bankruptcy. He further developed the reputation of "paying upon lawsuit," when science fiction writer Donald A. Wollheim sued him in 1935 for not paying for two of his stories in *Wonder Stories*.

However, Gernsback's encouragement of fandom was a major contribution to the future of science fiction and of benefit to Will. Gernsback started a "Discussions" letter column in the January 1927 issue of *Amazing Stories*, providing an opportunity for communication among the widespread science fiction fans who were beginning to form into clubs. These fans were a nucleus for a generation of writers and editors and a market for the additional science fiction magazines to come that would give Will an outlet where he could combine his passion for science with writing moneymaking fiction. He called his science fiction writing "a hobby," as he tells in his editor's introduction to *Great Stories of Science Fiction*, published by Random House in 1953.

> The sort of mental exercise these writers have done for their own satisfaction may not appeal to everybody, but to me it's fun. Anybody's hobby has some attraction and science fiction has been a hobbyist's hobby up to now. I think it is an intelligent hobby without being in the least "intellectual" in the repulsive meaning of the word.
> The sort of people who practice it may have something to do with that. A good many of the writers are simply addicts, like myself, who have been writing it for fun because there is no money in it. I view with some alarm that presently there may be profit in it.

Will was moving toward his interest in science fiction, and the field was beginning to open up. Although writing was still a precarious way of making a living, he was able to do so because of the steady markets he had developed in adventures, mysteries and westerns. If one magazine closed, he found other outlets. The film *Good as Gold*, which starred popular cowboy star Buck Jones, came out in 1927. It was based on "The Owner of the Aztec," printed in *Western Magazine*, May 5, 1926. A few beginning stories in 1924 in *Triple X Weekly*, a Fawcett publication, led to a series of four serials in 1928 through 1931.

Alfred H. King published one, *The Kid Deputy*, in hardcover in 1935. Four of Murray Leinster's most enduring stories were published in *Argosy* in late 1929 and 1930, "Darkness on Fifth Avenue," "The City of the Blind," "The Man Who Put Out the Sun" and "The Storm That Had to be Stopped."

Sam Moskowitz in *Seekers of Tomorrow* (Cleveland: World Publishing Company, 1961) specifically refers to these stories in identifying what he considers the basic theme of most Leinster stories, man battling against nature. Moskowitz says, "A majority of Leinster's stories emphasize that it is the battle, not the ultimate victory, that is important. Man courageously, sometimes magnificently, fights a mindless, implacable creature, phenomenon, or condition. Even if some man has caused the situation, he is rarely the antagonist."

He says Will, writing as Leinster, "recognizes man against nature and he will permit the *appearance* of man battling against man but disallows the Freudian concept of man against himself."

He mentions "Ribbon in the Sky" (*Astounding Science-Fiction*, June 1957) as an example where Will tells of people who believe they will become ill if they come in contact with people in other communities, and do, because they believe they will. Will indicates that he believes the cure "is physical action, not psychiatric treatment."

Moskowitz attributes this attitude to Will's Catholic faith. However, he says Will, a convert, did not push his faith on others, did no proselytizing, and embraced his new faith because "it represented his attitudes even as a youth." Moskowitz felt that Will's stories represent how he himself felt about things rather than pushing religious beliefs saying: "Things happen and man responds to events. In science fiction, where what happens is frequently more important than why it happens or to whom it happens, this tendency has easily been overlooked."

Joe Rico, a Fellow of the New England Science Fiction Association (NESFA) and editor of *First Contacts: The Essential Murray Leinster* (The NESFA Press, 1998), was particularly interested in how Will's Catholic faith affected his stories. He wondered if it was a convenience or had a spiritual basis. Rica says, "Villains redeeming themselves, or at least being implored to repent, are a common theme in his SF stories ... as well as people realizing they may be in the wrong. It struck me as a Catholic attitude."

Will loved storytelling in every form, and he particularly enjoyed those that came out of everyday life. His Catholic faith contributed to one of his favorites that emerged during the 1928 election when Al Smith, a Catholic, was running against Herbert Hoover (who won). Although Will had been brought up as an Episcopalian, and Mary had been raised as a Catholic, it had not been an impediment to their marriage. Later, as Will read and studied, he embraced the Catholic faith as his own. There were few other Catholic families in Gloucester at that time, and those were viewed with suspicion.

In the summer before the election, Will gave a lift to a man walking by the side of the road on his way to the Court House. Many people still walked everywhere in those days, and drivers were expected to pick them up. Since Will drove into the village twice a day for the mail, he did a lot of transporting of neighbors and always enjoyed the opportunity for conversation. Since the suitability of a Catholic for president was a major concern at the time, the subject often came up. On this particular day, his passenger expressed his worries, and Will discussed, in his usual thorough manner, Catholicism in general, why there was no chance of the pope running the country from Rome, and some of his own beliefs. His passenger scratched his head, thought a bit, and finally said, "Mr. Jenkins, I don't understand how you can believe something that just ain't so."

The whole country was suspicious of Catholics at that time. Although the activities of the Ku Klux Klan had diminished in the 1870s, there was a second Klan started around 1915. Members opposed minorities, including blacks and Jews, labor unions and Roman Catholics. This time it was a national organization, not restricted to the South and very strong in other areas of the country, but there is no doubt that there were members and sympathizers in Gloucester.

When Alanson Crosby, a good friend of Will's, was editor of the weekly *Gloucester Gazette*, he printed something that offended the Klan, and they threatened him. Will and Mary invited him and his wife to stay at Ardudwy in Clay Bank where outside floodlights could be turned on offering some protection. They did stay, but, fortunately, the Klan did not turn up.

Lewis E. Allen, editor of the *Gazette* when Alanson Crosby was on leave writing a book (and later Will's brother-in law), came to Gloucester from Ohio State University's School of Journalism. He kept in touch with Charles E. Yost, his former editor at the *Fayette Review* in Ohio, writing about Gloucester and what was going on there. He received the following letter from Yost dated November 16, 1928, which said in part:

> I do not think you need to fear [those] people. If they are at all like the Ku Klux here, all you need to do is keep a sharp lookout behind after dark. And yet, a mob like that has about as much sense as an angleworm. It may be well for you to go armed. I would hate to have you get into trouble and possibly shot by such people. It wouldn't be so bad to get shot by an intelligent civilized man, but such a bunch, no.

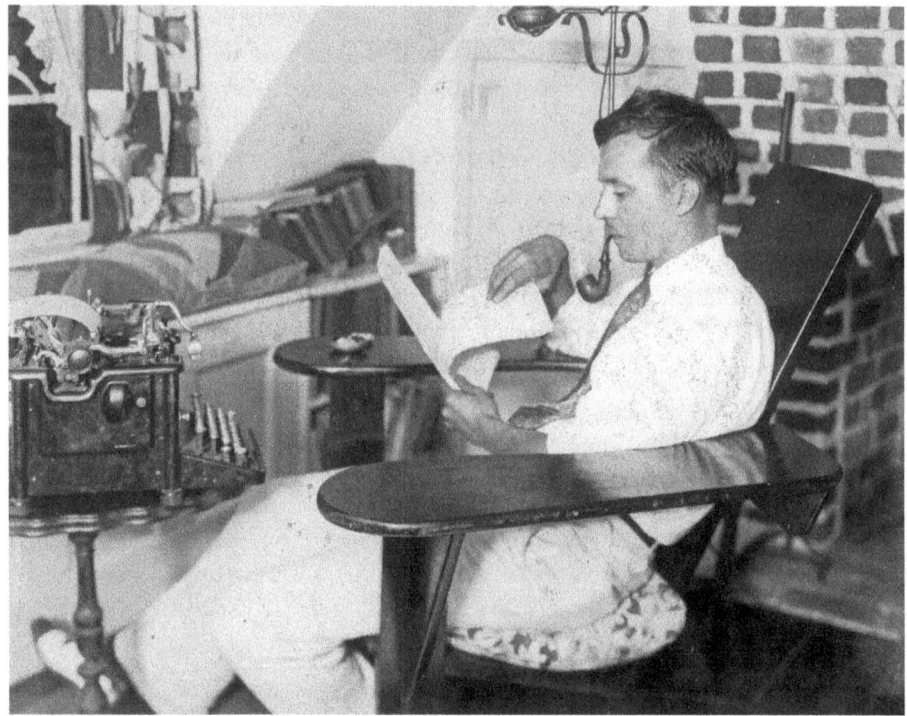

Will took his typewriter anywhere. Here he is in the master bedroom circa 1930.

Perhaps because of the isolation of the house, Will did keep a gun. It was an automatic pistol, and he slept with it under his pillow and carried it in the glove compartment of the car when he traveled. It seemed very out of character for a man who, though he loved living in the country, in some ways never really adapted to it. He did not hunt or fish. When he got up every morning, he put on a white shirt and tie, and, except in hottest weather, a jacket, and sat down at his typewriter as if he were in an office in the city.

Will's own children were well aware that the gun was a "do not touch," but one time when relatives were visiting, a young cousin found it and shot it through the bathroom door, fortunately missing everyone. After that, Will was more careful about putting it away.

A third daughter, Wenllian Louise Jenkins, was born in 1928. Will said Mary had promised him twin boys for his birthday, June 16, and, instead, he got another girl two days early on June 14. He said her name was the Welsh feminine for William (it isn't), and she was nicknamed "Billy." Will called her "Bill." Later, in her teens, she changed the spelling of "Billy" to a more feminine "Billee," but Will continued all his life to spell her nickname "Billy."

Five • Marriage: The 1920s

Will told Billee that she was named after her 14th great-grandmother and that the Welsh name started with a "G." However, he used the spelling without the "G" for the supposed ancestor when he typed the version of the family tree that went beyond Governor John Jenkins back to Colwyn of Ardudwy. He probably preferred the spelling without the "G" as it was closer to William.

Later research on the name Gwenllian shows that it was the name of the daughter of the last real prince of Wales, Prince Llywelyn, who was killed by order of King Edward I of England, December 11, 1282. The infant princess was a threat to the crown, but her life was spared, and she was banished to a priory in Lincolnshire where she died in 1377. The king took the title prince of Wales for his eldest son, where it remains.

Work continued on Ardudwy, the Clay Bank house, but sometimes things did not progress fast enough to suit Mary. When she wanted to open up the living room by removing a wall, and, it didn't happen quickly enough, she got impatient. One morning, Will woke up to loud noise and found her attacking the wall with a hammer.

Clay Bank house around the late 1930s.

Dining room fireplace at Ardudwy.

Reliable electricity had been added when a Delco plant was installed in one of the ancient outbuildings on the property. It was a type of generator that used batteries to supply the house with electricity. From then on, the building was referred to as the power house. (The Rural Electrification Act bringing electric power to unserved areas was signed in 1936 during Franklin

Roosevelt's presidency.) The outhouse or outdoor toilet that Will called the escusado was retired, and indoor plumbing was installed in a small room they had playfully labeled the Neckers' Nook. The new bathroom was papered with silver building paper and called the can.

Eventually, there were installed a new roof, new dormers and bay windows, and the screened porch was glassed in. To entertain the children, Will and Mary painted murals in the kitchen showing dinosaurs picnicking. Later they stripped the paint from the doors and woodwork, as well as from the 1820 mantels, and added knotty pine panels to the end walls of the living and dining room. They were interested in making a comfortable home, not restoring a museum, and like many other homeowners in the 1920s and 1930s, they embraced the charm of spinning wheels, cobbler's benches, braided rugs and ladder back chairs. They took a colonial house and made it Colonial Revival in the fashion made famous by Wallace Nutting. They made it comfortable and livable.

Will used his inventiveness in household projects. He converted doors to the kitchen and bathroom into extra storage by adding shelves to the full thickness of the doorjamb with slats to keep things from falling out.

Will knew a little Spanish (therefore the escusado), and a smattering of other languages including Latin. Will's brain was like a sponge. He was a quick study and loved to learn new things. Mary's brother John had married Carmen DuBlan, daughter of a proud Mexican family reputed to be descended from Emperor Maximilian's finance minister, Ignacio DuBlan. He probably picked up his knowledge of Spanish from those in-laws, and he loved to drop in words or phrases like escusado for toilet and the admonition to the children "en boca cerrada, no entran moscas" ("flies do not fly in a closed mouth").

The family tradition was that the DuBlan family was angry when their son married a gringo and sent the mother and three children back to New York when he died. Carmen was a translator at the League of Nations. Her brother "Natcho" was a wannabe writer who mixed with the same literary crowd that Will had belonged to in New York. Will and Natcho carried on a correspondence by letter over many years while Natcho traveled back and forth to Mexico and Venezuela on various jobs, planning stories, novels and plays that never quite came to completion. This relationship was probably the origin of Will's stories of being involved in the early 20th century Mexican revolution.

Will's family having grown to five, he retired the old Packard and bought a seven passenger Pierce Arrow. He was so proud of this car that he kept a floor mat as a souvenir after it was sold, showing it to his daughter Jo-an many years later. Around the same time, he bought Mary a gray squirrel coat and the older girls muskrat coats with raccoon collars. Life was good.

Betty, Mary and Billee in the Pierce Arrow at left, Mary and Will standing center, Rudy Mandola, far right, with unidentified friends circa 1930.

Then a tragedy occurred. On October 1, 1929, when Will's brother George Jr., was 39 years old, he died of appendicitis in Newark, New Jersey, where he was living with his mother, Mamie. As is common in such times, Will needed to find someone to blame and turned on his mother. He accused her of not getting a doctor to treat George, but instead, sitting around with her Christian Scientist friends and praying over him.

Mamie had always been an Episcopalian, but, lonely in Newark and away from family and friends in Portsmouth where she had lived all her life, she had found friends and companionship in the local Christian Science Reading Room. Although Will was in Gloucester in southern Virginia and nowhere near Newark at the time of George's illness, he decided that, because of these friendships, George had not had proper medical treatment. Sadly, death from appendicitis was not uncommon in those days before antibiotics. One of Mary's young nieces died of appendicitis at around the same time, but Will did not consider this, and his grief at his brother George's death made him irrational. For years, Will would tell people: "My mother killed my brother."

There was a second issue. Will insisted that George was married to a friend of theirs named Helen Hysell. George had been helping to support Mamie, but Will wanted the money George left to her at his death given to Helen and was outraged when she refused.

There is no documentation of any kind that there was ever a wedding between Helen and George. Will's wife, Mary, always said firmly that they were never married. Supporting that belief is that the 1930 census records (a year after George died) show Helen Hysell (not Jenkins) living with her mother in Essex County, New Jersey. Mamie said to a granddaughter years later, "George told me he didn't have to marry that woman."

Perhaps it was Will's strong puritanical streak that made him believe that what must have been a close, possibly intimate, relationship between George and Helen needed to have included marriage. He had an old fashioned, almost Victorian view of women and once told his granddaughter Gail, "When I grew up, it was immoral to kiss a woman above her wrist." One of his editors, unsuccessfully trying to get him to spice up his stories said, "Will Jenkins doesn't believe in sex." That probably stood him in good stead in later years with *Astounding Science-Fiction*. Kay Tarrant, assistant editor in John Campbell's day, was notoriously straight laced and blue-penciled anything the slightest bit questionable. Although Will's speech was colorful and his kitchen stories legend, his published stories were strictly family rated, and he never gave her a problem.

Helen Hysell appears as one of the authors of "The Day of the Dead" (Chapter 6) along with Will, Leslie Burton Blades, Rosalind Blades, George B. Jenkins, Jr., and Cynthia Wooloford, which was printed in *Black Mask Magazine* in July 1921. In the 1920 census, she listed her occupation as "magazine writer," however, only one other published piece can be traced to this name, a sketch, "Conquest," that appeared in *The Smart Set* in April 1921. Leslie Burton Blades published several stories between 1919 and 1928 in magazines such as *All-Story, Telling Tales, Munsey's, Breezy Stories, The Danger Trail* and *Argosy-All-Story Weekly*. There is no trace of publications by Rosalind Blades. Cynthia Woolford [sic] had a 10-line sketch in the March 1922 issue of *Snappy Stories*. Her name rang a bell with Will's daughter Billee, who remembered her mother tearfully telling her that Will had been madly in love with someone else before they were married and her name was Cynthia. Coincidence?

Against all evidence, Will would not let go of his conviction that George and Helen had been husband and wife. He called her "Helen Jenkins" when he listed her as co-author of a story, "Lethion," that was printed in *Complete Detective Novel Magazine* in April 1933. Sadly, as a result of this dispute, Will did not speak to his mother for over twenty years, although for much of that time they lived barely forty miles apart. So traumatic was this event that, fifty years after George died, people who knew the family were still asking, "Do you think they were married?"

Mamie was, of course, devastated by George's death. Although she never referred to the estrangement with Will when her granddaughter Billee later reconnected with her, Mamie may have remembered George's words to her when Will married. "We must be kind to Mary. She has to live with Will." After 17 years in Newark, Mamie returned to Portsmouth when George died. She lived to be 96, dying in 1959. She was buried in Elmwood Cemetery in Norfolk next to him. On her tombstone is inscribed "George's mother."

• SIX •

The 1930s

The birth of *Astounding Stories* in January 1930, with Murray Leinster's "Tanks" in the first issue, launched a 36-year relationship that continued until 1966 when *Analog* (the latest of its various names) published "Quarantine World."

William Clayton started the magazine under the name *Astounding Stories of Super Science* with Harry Bates as the first editor. Bates had been working for Clayton editing his adventure magazines. He is best remembered as the author of *Farewell to the Master*, which was made into the movie *The Day the Earth Stood Still* in 1951. Many consider it the best science fiction movie of all time. It was inducted into the Science Fiction Hall of Fame in 1983 and remade in 2008.

Clayton's other publications included *Snappy Stories*, where Will had been appearing regularly. *Astounding Stories* was a breakthrough in science fiction publishing in that it regularly paid two cents a word on acceptance. Murray Leinster rated four cents a word. The usual going rate for "the pulps" had continued to be half-a-cent a word paid on publication, and the date of publication was indefinite. This increase was important because Will and his family lived from check to check, and the Jenkins girls grew up hearing, "We'll do that next check."

"Tanks," published in January

Will and a favorite pipe circa 1935.

1930, is set in 1932 during a war between the United States and "The Yellow Empire." Fogs of gas and vast armadas of tanks, supported by air cover including helicopters, are used by both sides. The infantry has little role. Two bitter infantrymen with disdain for tanks tell the story and have a large part in the victory. The story was very popular with readers and often considered to be one of the best published in the early *Astounding Stories*.

After "Tanks" came "Murder Madness," Will's only serial in Clayton's *Astounding Stories of Super Science*. It was published in four parts beginning in May 1930 and later in hardcover as a straight mystery (Brewer and Warren, 1931). It was about an attempted South American takeover involving a drug that would turn its victims into homicidal maniacs.

Later stories were "The Fifth Dimension Catapult," January 1931, and its sequel "The Fifth Dimension Tube," January 1933, which warranted the cover picture and author's name. Isaac Asimov named "The Fifth Dimension Tube" as one of his favorite Leinster stories. Rarely reprinted, the novel combines a brilliant professor-inventor, his beautiful daughter and a handsome potential suitor with racketeers, general greed, treachery, a desperate small town police chief, and a giant lizard wearing a golden collar. It is classic vintage Leinster.

"Morale," published in December 1931, predicted a conflict in 1942 when a super tank called The Wabbly invades New Jersey, and the enemy seeks to win by breaking the civilians' morale. Spookily ahead of its time, it predicts the significant role of propaganda and the sustaining of morale in a future war. Will could not have predicted the possibility of his own involvement in this role. It came in 1942 when he joined the Office of War Information, a newly formed government agency that had this responsibility.

Clayton went bankrupt in 1933, and his last issue of *Astounding Stories of Super Science* was dated March 1933. It contained "Invasion," a story that depicted a struggle between Russia and the United States. Murray Leinster's name was on the cover, and Jack Williamson's "Salvage in Space" was the featured story.

Street and Smith purchased *Astounding*. They immediately installed F. Orlin Tremaine as the editor, moving him over from Clayton's publishing house. There was scarcely a hiccup between the publishing of "Invasion" in March 1933 and "Beyond the Sphinxes' Cave" in November 1933 when Tremaine took over.

"Beyond the Sphinxes' Cave" assumes that the ancient gods of Greece are real and living here on earth. It merited a splendid cover, complete with a warrior in ancient Greek fighting garb who holds a gorgon's head shooting rays from its eyes toward a figure wearing hazardous materials protective

Sphinx cover on *Astounding Stories* (copyright © 1933 by Street & Smith Publications, Inc., reprinted by permission of Dell Magazines, a division of Penny Publications).

garments that include a gas mask. He was standing close to a golden-thong-clad beauty. Murray Leinster's name was prominently displayed.

Tremaine had no science fiction experience when he got the job but was generally liked and respected. Fred Pohl says in his book *The Way the Future Was* (Ballantine Books, 1978), "Tremaine was no scientist and he was likely to come up with some galumphing horrors, but the virtue of that defect was that he was able to publish some pretty fascinating stuff that any scientifically trained person would never touch."

Astounding printed an additional four stories and a five-part serial of Will's before 1938 when Tremaine was moved up in the hierarchy, and 27-year-old John Campbell took over as editor. These included some of the most important of his career. "Sidewise in Time" appeared in June 1934 and is generally accepted to be the first story in science fiction presenting the concept of a parallel universe.

Will used the title for a collection he edited in 1950 (Shasta Publishers, 1950) and dedicated the book to "F. Orlin Tremaine who presided at the birth of the title story." Will says in the introduction to the book, "I think I can honestly say that I wrote these yarns for fun. It happens that I like to fool around with ideas like some people do with drill-presses or vegetable gardens or blondes. It's a hobby."

He goes on to tell the story of its origin.

> Being the sort of person I am, an explanation of the cosmos which ignores pattern in events — ignoring purpose — simply doesn't hold water long enough for swallowing. I also believe in free will. To reconcile the two, one day, I set to work to design a maze for a rat, in which he would have absolutely free choice, over and over again, of two paths, and yet would have to come out of a pre-posed exit. It's easiest when you use two levels, by the way. It worked out amusingly enough. But when I started to give him more that two choices, I began to need extra dimensions to design the thing in and that gave me a charming background of practical data when one day Orlin Tremaine — then the editor of *Astounding Stories*— mourned over the fact that all the changes had been rung on the time travel theme. Travel forward in time had been done to death. Ditto backward in time.
>
> "Ah," I said nonchalantly, "but how about traveling sidewise in time?"
>
> I sketched for him a multi-dimensional universe in which everything that possibly could happen, somewhere did, and everything that could have happened, had.

What happened was chaos in which Roman soldiers marched into Joplin, Missouri, dinosaurs roamed the streets of Atlanta, Georgia, and flocks of passenger pigeons, extinct since the early 1900s, filled the skies. Pickett's charge succeeded at Gettysburg, and the Confederacy was alive and well.

Will made the protagonist a professor at a "jerkwater" college in Fredericksburg, Virginia, who anticipated the cataclysm and proceeded to take advantage of it.

Will has been accused of racism because of his descriptions of scenes of Roman slavery used in the story, and of pandering to his Southern roots, using the story to perpetuate an unrequited Southern desire for the actual winning of the war by the South. For Will, making this change in history was undoubtedly what he called a twist, what he always looked for as a basis for a good story. Professor Minott was an anti-hero, typical of the evil geniuses Will used in his plots from his first stories. Saving the world was up to the scientists and mathematicians left with the job of replicating Minott's work for the common good.

Joe Rico, who edited the collection *First Contacts: The Essential Murray Leinster* which includes "Sidewise in Time," says he discussed Will and race relations with Hannibal King. King is African American and painted the cover art for *First Contacts*. King agreed that for a Southerner of this period, Will was ahead of his time.

"Sidewise in Time" has been reprinted in at least eight anthologies. The Sidewise Awards for Alternate History, created in 1995 by Steven H. Silver, Evelyn C. Leeper and Robert B. Schmunk, take the name from this Murray Leinster story. The awards recognize the best alternate history story and alternate story novel of the year. The awards are given at Worldcon, one for the long form and one for the short form.

"Proxima Centauri" appeared in *Astounding*, March 1, 1935. In this story, a spaceship takes generations to travel to the stars, requiring it to be completely self-sustaining. Will explains the birth of the story in this same introduction to the book *Sidewise in Time*.

> "Proxima Centauri" came out of two separate speculations. (I read science fiction for the same reason I write it. I like the stuff.) I'd read a yarn that didn't convince me and I began to debate what non-mammalian creature I could believe might develop a culture. Insects are out, for me. They are complicated machines with built-in reflexes. (You dig up a mining-wasp grub some day — I have — and watch the food-mother wasp trample all over the grub, hysterically looking for but can't recognize because she can't find the tunnel that ought to lead to him.) Reptiles and fishes don't click with me. I can't imagine emotions in gentlemen fish who haven't even a fin-waving acquaintance with their wives. No ... the creatures I did devise are possibly just as unlikely, but I think they are pleasantly gruesome. And the *Adastra* was designed for interstellar travel at less than the speed of light. Other people have written about self-sustaining spacecraft since. Perhaps before. I don't know. Anyhow, there's the yarn.

Isaac Asimov included both stories in his anthology *Before the Golden Age*. He commented in his introduction to the story "Sidewise in Time" in that book that its alternate-history theme affected not only his science fiction but also his serious writing. He credited "Proxima Centauri" with influencing his first novel, *Pebbles in the Sky*.

"The Fourth-dimensional Demonstrator" came out in December of that same year. It is a great example of Will's humor. He could have been having fun thinking of the short story "Pigs Is Pigs" written in 1905 by Ellis Parker Butler. "Pigs Is Pigs" was made into a small book and reprinted extensively. Will had it on his shelf, enjoyed it very much, and shared it with his children. In the story, a railway agent has received a shipment of two guinea pigs, and the customer wants to pay the pet rate, 25 cents, rather than livestock rate, 30 cents. While the argument continues, the guinea pigs keep reproducing, and the station is overrun with pigs and piglets.

In Will's story, a young man, in the throes of poverty, finds his uncle's invention, a machine that duplicates whatever is exposed to it. He and his fiancé, Daisy, decide to duplicate dollar bills, but things go awry, and, soon the room, and later the yard, is filled with Daisys, copies of her pet kangaroo, Arthur, and a few stray identical policemen.

Following that, *The Incredible Invasion* came out in five parts, August through December 1936. The invasion was spawned in the fourth dimension, and Will brought his usual solid speculative science to the story of treachery and suspense. It was brought up to date to include Russia as a threat and published as *The Other Side of Here* in 1955 in an Ace Double, backed by A. E. van Vogt's *One Against Eternity*.

After Gernsback lost *Amazing Stories* to bankruptcy in 1929 (it was eventually taken over by Bernarr Macfadden's *Macfadden Publishing*), Will started selling some stories there. "Power Planet," which appeared in the January 1931 edition of *Amazing Stories,* is notable because the energy supply concept for the power-generating space station he describes is a first. It was followed by three more stories in the 1930s and then no more until the 1950s.

In addition to these magazines, Will continued to sell frequently to other genre pulps, such as Munsey's *Detective Fiction Weekly,* beginning with "The Square Guy" published June 8, 1929, under the Will F. Jenkins byline. *The Man Who Feared* was printed in four parts from August 9 through August 30, 1930, also under the Will F. Jenkins byline. It was released in hardcover in 1942 by Gateway in New York. Will continued to appear in that magazine regularly through 1935.

When *Black Bat Detective Mysteries* came out in October 1933, Will was there with a brand new character, the Black Bat. As Murray Leinster, he had Black Bat stories in all of the six issues that were published. They were "The Body in the Taxi," "The Coney Island Murders," "The Hollywood Murders,"

"Murder at First Night," "The Maniac Murders," and "The Warehouse Murders." Black Bat's real name was never mentioned.

Ned Pines revived the character in his *Thrilling Publications*, using another author, for a magazine called *Black Book Detective*. This Black Bat was identified as a former district attorney named Anthony Quinn, who became a crime fighter after being blinded by acid.

Lurton Blassingame, who was Robert A. Heinlein's agent for a time, wrote a piece in the January 1937 *Writer's Digest* on "The Detective Fiction Market." In it he said there were 31 active, prompt-paying magazines that printed detective fiction exclusively. He divided them into groups and laid out some rules for cracking the market. He identified "Crime Thrillers," "Semi-Smooth Paper Detective Magazines," "Characterization Detective Tales," "Emotional Stories," and those dedicated to "Fast Action and Color."

Detective Fiction Weekly, Black Mask, and *Detective Story* were in the "Semi-Smooth Paper" category, and Will wrote for all of them. He also sold to Orlin Tremaine's "Fast Action and Color" magazine *Clues*.

Blassingame gave hopeful writers the same advice other experts have given them over and over. Read, read, read the magazines you want to sell to, and study their stories. Learn the editorial policies of the magazines.

Will continued writing westerns. Doubleday-Page's *West* printed *Dead Man's Shoes* in four parts in March and April of 1931. It was made into a movie entitled *Border Devils* starring Harry Carey and Gabby Hayes in 1932. When Alfred H. King, Inc., brought it out in hardcover under the title *Mexican Trail* in 1933, they listed the author as Will F. Jenkins because Murray Leinster already had a name in book publishing for his previous mystery novels, *Murder Madness* and *Scalps*.

Will typed away at his Remington, keeping up his volume and selling to every magazine he could. However, he did stay away from stories of the occult and supernatural. He told Ronald Payne (*The Last Murray Leinster Interview*, Waves Press, Richmond, VA, 1982) that he thought they stayed in the writer's subconscious and could be destructive.

He was able to follow his goal and support his family with his writing during the years of the Great Depression although there was the problem of getting paid. He sold plenty of stories, but magazines had to pay the printer and pay for the paper, or they were out of business. The authors, who had little choice, were the last to receive their money.

He continued to enjoy the close, home-focused life he had made, cocooned with family and enjoying the visits by extended family and friends.

Mary's younger sister Adeline had a special reason to visit. Lewis Allen, the bachelor editor of the *Gloucester Gazette*, had told Will, "If Mary has a sister, I'd like to meet her." Adeline was barely five feet tall, with her sister's sparkling brown eyes, a heart shaped face and the cupid's bow mouth made famous by Mary Pickford. Allen, as he was called, was pretty sharp himself, with hair slicked straight back and with distinctively expressive arched eyebrows. Adeline came down from New York, and they hit it off. When Allen was a little slow in proposing, Will had an idea.

"Just put your suitcases at the bottom of the stairs the next time he comes and tell him you're leaving," he told her. It worked and they married in 1931. They were frequent visitors after that, especially on holidays, and their daughter, Adeline, four years younger than Billee, sometimes seemed like the next sister in line.

Will's pattern of calling Lewis Allen by his last name was a remnant of a habit in the New York literary crowd of calling their colleagues by their last name, perhaps gotten from the Brits and their public school tradition. After twenty years of marriage, Lewis Allen (whom the Jenkins girls had always referred to as "Uncle Allen") asked his wife if she would please call him "Lewis."

In 1928, when Little Mary was six, Mary and Will decided against send-

"Little Adeline" and Billee at Clay Bank.

ing her to the Gloucester public school, but instead hired a local teacher, Miss Grace Stubblefield, to come to the house to teach her using the Calvert home school materials. Thinking, "Why not?" they started Betty a year later when she was four years old and Billee three years after that, when she was also four. This catapulted Betty and Billee three years ahead of their class through high school, and for Billee, into college. So by 1932, all three children were climbing the stairs to the schoolroom. It was furnished with child-sized colonial furniture made of walnut by a local African American carpenter, Jeff Booth, who was known for his fine reproductions. Nobody had to leave home even for the day.

The Calvert materials were outstanding. From a very early age, the children were exposed to the classics, art, science and Greek and Roman history. Some classics were rewritten in simple form for the very earliest years. Ever the scientist, Will would supplement the astronomy lessons with night views of the moon using his telescope. He used his microscope to show water from a flower vase on a slide to explain amoeba and paramecia. Will enjoyed showing the children how to make silhouettes of flowers and leaves with the sun and blueprint paper. He was the classic person who, when you ask him what time it is, tells you how to make a watch. Sometimes the children would avoid asking him questions, because they didn't want to sit through a long explanation.

Art and architecture materials from the Calvert School were so good that Will bragged that the girls could identify the work of different artists when they were taken to the National Gallery in Washington. There were excursions to Washington and to opera and theater at the Mosque Theater in Richmond, where Billee remembers, as a small child, falling asleep in everything from *Carmen* to *La Traviata*. She also remembers her first play, in 1939, *The Philadelphia Story* with Katharine Hepburn, Joseph Cotton and Van Heflin, also at the Mosque Theater. In spite of the 60-mile trip, the girls were taken to Richmond for dancing lessons.

As there was no nearby Catholic church, the girls' religious upbringing was pretty well confined to baptism in Sacred Heart Cathedral in Richmond, Easter services there, and knowing their parents were Catholic. Will decided to remedy that, and in 1937 the three girls, aged 9, 12 and 15, received First Communion and were confirmed. Will became one of the founders of St. Therese's Catholic Church, when it was built in Gloucester in 1938, and was proud that his youngest daughter, Jo-an, born in September of that year, was the first girl baptized in the new parish with her name inscribed on the cornerstone.

Will loved family life. Dr. L. V. "Happy" Morgan, local pharmacist,

Will, Betty, Mary and Little Mary on their York River dock.

friend and father of Virginia delegate Harvey Morgan, who initiated "Will F. Jenkins Day" in June 2009, spoke to the family at Will's funeral. "I used to see Will walking around the Court House with you three little girls and I would say to myself, 'There goes a happy man.'"

The daily routine was set on a schedule. In cool weather, Will would get up in the morning, stoke up the furnace and light the fire in the living room fireplace. The fireplace in the dining room was lit for dinner, and the one in Mary and Will's bedroom was rarely used. He would make coffee and take a cup to Mary in bed. For breakfast, the children always had oatmeal, and at least one developed a life-long aversion to it. School would be in session in the morning. Dinner was in the middle of the day — always a hot meal with meat and potatoes (Will didn't like rice) and two vegetables. Will had his greens served on a separate plate soaked in vinegar. There was always dessert — usually cake. Will's first choice was chocolate.

He loved chocolate and made fudge with his children and, later, grandchildren. He frequently told the children about the time, when he was a small boy, that he had carefully cut the chocolate frosting off to save it for last, and it was whisked away by someone who thought he didn't like it. He warned them: "Be careful about saving for last!"

His fudge recipe has been handed down in the family.

2½ squares unsweetened chocolate
2 cups sugar
1 cup milk
2 tbs. Karo corn syrup
1 tsp. vanilla extract (or flavor of choice, he liked to vary with lemon, orange, and rum!)
5 tbs. butter
Heat first 3 ingredients until a drop forms a soft ball in cold water.
Add last 3 and beat until it starts to harden. Pour in buttered glass baking dish.

The evening meal was light. Will often planned little treats for Mary and loved to arrange a supper plate for her, a toasted sandwich cut on the diagonal with pickles and olives artfully arranged.

Will thrived on this regular schedule, although he kept his own hours, often writing late into the night. He exasperated Mary by putting the kettle on the electric stove for a late cup of tea and, too engrossed in his work to hear the whistle when it boiled, finally getting to the stove to find the water had boiled away and the bottom of the kettle had melted.

There were two never-changing events on weekdays. Twice a day Will jumped into the car and drove the eight miles to the Court House to pick up the mail. He could have walked down the hill to the Clay Bank Post Office, but it was important to him to meet the meet the earlier delivery at the main post office. Was there a check, letter of acceptance or rejection, or important correspondence? Who knew what possible treasure waited in Box 212?

The trips were combined with other errands. Will did the grocery shopping at Martin's store and, if Mary forgot something, she could call Central in the telephone office on the second floor just across the street from the post office. Central had a good view of what was going on, and she might say, "I just saw Mr. Jenkins coming out of the bank and crossing the street. He might be over to Martin's right now." Mary would then ask to be connected to the store.

Between Christmas and the New Year was particularly busy with, traditionally, several days of open house with many guests and plentiful food. For the children, Christmas always started a couple of days before the 25th. Billee remembers it as always a sunny day, December cold but not freezing. The three girls would start out with Will, he carrying an ax, to look for a tree in the woods, a short walk down the dirt road that passed the house. Bursting with excitement, they would run ahead, but not too far, searching for a small clearing where the cedars would have room to spread out and grow fat and thick. Christmas trees at Clay Bank were always cedars, prickly with a familiar pungent scent. When they had finally found the perfect tree, Will would cut it down, and the group would search again, this time for holly branches, the ones with the most berries. For mistletoe, an obliging neighbor might know where there was a clump growing high in an oak tree, and he would get his shotgun and shoot down a few sprigs.

After the tree was dragged home, Mary would exclaim on its beauty and perfection, and Will would nail a wooden cross on the bottom of the trunk for it to stand on. On Christmas Eve, it would be moved to its position on the sun porch. When the tree was set up and ready, the next task was putting holly sprigs behind every picture frame and mirror on the main floor of the house, with additional arrangements for the fireplace mantels.

The tree was decorated after the children were in bed, but Will and Mary didn't follow the tradition where it was Santa Claus who did it. In fact, Santa had a small role in their young lives; he filled the stockings with small but welcome gifts, always with a tangerine in the toe. Mary's theory, which experience proved valid, was that in this way, when the children learned that Santa, like the stork, was their mother and father, it wouldn't be such a shock. And so to them Santa was an interesting curiosity, scurrying around the world in one night, to be discussed after they went to bed on Christmas Eve. Betty insisted, not unexpectedly, that she had actually seen him once, passing by the window with his entourage. Still, the girls knew enough to ask their parents for any special gift they wanted.

Special gift was always singular. Although Will and Mary were fairly well off for the times, there was usually only one big Christmas gift, such as a doll. This was the custom in those days. Additional gifts were smaller and included pajamas and underwear, all of which had to be displayed under the tree for visitors to see for at least a week, to the embarrassment of the girls.

One year Will went to a lot of trouble to make a canopied doll bed for Billee, using the workshop where his friend W. Preston "Scrapper" Day made gout stools that were sold in Colonial Williamsburg. Scrapper had also made Will a specially designed desk of knotty pine in that workshop. It was slanted for his typewriter, as he liked it, with room for papers on the side. (Later when Jo-an was a toddler, she liked to hide under the desk, playing at Will's feet while he worked.)

Scrapper was a fine craftsman and helped Will with his project. That Christmas, however, Billee had asked for a live animal pet. She was sure she

Will working at his special desk on the sun porch in Clay Bank, circa 1940.

was getting one, as Will had also gone to a lot of trouble to prepare a large, elaborate box with holes and warnings and with her name on it. He teased her daily about its contents. Beside herself with excitement by Christmas morning, she was ecstatic to find a baby chick in the box. Unfortunately, all of Will's hard work on the doll bed, which Billee appreciated only later, was ignored in favor of the tiny live animal.

Scrapper's nickname came from his days at Virginia Tech where he played sports in spite of his short stature. He and his wife, Reenie, were good friends, visiting often with their sons Jean and Don. The boys, around the same age as Billee, were her only regular playmates in those early years.

However, there was a lot to entertain the girls. It was an idyllic spot for children. The house stood on several acres, a third was either salt water or mud flats depending on the tide. When you owned property on the river, you owned to the low water mark, and the channel was a mile out. In the summer, the exposed mud was the most fun. When the tide was out, you could prowl over it squishing the mud between your toes. There were endless attractions, soft crab holes to poke, and minnows to trap, watch briefly, and release to dart away on their frantic personal business.

At high tide, there was the water to bathe in. It tasted salty, was full of disgusting precipitates, and was warm as bath water. Maybe that's why everyone said they were going bathing, never swimming. It was safe for children, no more than four feet deep at high tide as far as they could walk. Will said it was easier to float in salt water, and told everyone the children were so comfortable lying on top of the water, he thought they could fall sleep on it.

There were always castles to build on the sandy shore, fiddler crabs to capture to inhabit them, and fierce fights to protect them from older sisters.

Christmas was, of course, the highlight of the winter. On Christmas morning, the children would huddle at the top of the stairs waiting for the signal to begin what had become the traditional mantra, "bum, bum, here we come." They would be crowded together, because the stairs were short and curved in the story-and-a-half house, and they had to keep back before the bend so they couldn't see into the living room where the stockings were hung on the fireplace mantle. That first look at the tree was always glorious. Mary and Will decorated it after the children were in bed, sometimes staying up all night. There were flashing colored lights, glittering balls, boxes of tinsel tossed on. Underneath, Betty's electric train went round and round the cardboard village frosted with glittering snow. Next to the trunk was the Nativity scene, which Mary called by its Italian name, the *presepio*. The tree at Rockefeller Center has never even come close to the tree of Billee's childhood memories.

Mary's older brother John Mandola often stopped by at Christmas with his wife, Carmen, and their children, the cousins Jackie and Rita, on their way to Miami for the holidays. In a letter to Jo-an dated July 17, 1969, Will wrote of a visit from Rita and her family: "[Rita] seems to have taken her Christmases with us very seriously. She's been trying to carry on the traditions we established. I was really rather touched."

For the annual New Year's Eve parties, the big, polished maple dining room table was spread with delicacies prepared by Mary, who loved all the planning and preparations. For the children, there was always the excitement of being awakened just before the stroke of midnight for the celebrations, putting on new housecoats bought for the occasion. Will and Mary always led a conga line of family and friends through the house, while the children ran outside to honk the horns in the cars.

Will prided himself on his eggnog, thick with whipped cream and served in red glass punch cups. He loved making his own versions of elaborate (and usually sweet) mixed drinks with exotic names such as corpse reviver. He made mint juleps with dark rum instead of bourbon, insisting that rum was authentic. He put sherry on grapefruit halves, served claret lemonade to the ladies in the summer, and had a concoction of gin on vanilla ice cream that he called a Boston Cooler. If you were feeling frail, an egg-milk (just like it sounds) was the cure, better with a little bourbon in it. Hot toddies (bourbon, honey, lemon and hot water) were the guaranteed cure for colds.

As was typical in Southern homes of the time, there was "help." Ophelia Leigh worked for Will and Mary almost all their time in Virginia. In a relationship not always understood these days, she and Mary were friends and companions, and the children loved her. In a letter to Jo-an in the late fifties when work was being done on the house, Will wrote: "Mother and Ophelia are out examining the exterior improvements. Ophelia came to call."

And in another later letter (undated), "Ophelia came over to see us with two of her small grandchildren. We got to talking, and I made eucalyptus trees for them out of newspaper and printed some soldiers for them on the typewriter. I thought one of them was likely to climb on my lap any minute."

Their friendship continued until Mary's death in 1967.

There was also a succession of gardeners or yard men. Billee remembers Robert, one of the yard men, pushing her around in the wheelbarrow and teaching her to play mumbly-peg during his lunch hour. The four-acre yard was kept mowed with a gasoline-powered mower. Early on, there was a small miniature golf course and later, for a time, a grass tennis court. Will insisted on grass, because that's what they had at Wimbledon. The girls preferred to play at the Groh's, their neighbor's, with their sons Alan "Sonny" and Norman.

Clockwise from left: Little Mary, Mary (adult), Betty and Billee (front). Ophelia looks on from porch.

They had a clay court which was always ready to play on, no mowing or stripe marking.

Alan grew up to a successful career in New York City as director of The Stable Gallery. Some of the famous artists who exhibited there were Jackson Pollock, Willem de Kooning and Andy Warhol. After Alan's death in 1996, a collection was presented by his friends to the Bayly Art Museum of the University of Virginia, his alma mater, in his honor.

Living with a writer father was normal to the girls, although others might not realize that writing is a time-consuming activity consisting of a lot of sitting around staring into space. When not involved in a more urgent activity, Will was usually quietly reading or sitting at his typewriter. If he was staring into space, Mary would hush the children saying, "Shh. Daddy's thinking." He typed rapidly with his two index fingers and always had his Wellington pipe in his mouth, seemingly oblivious to the smoke curling up into his eyes. He was never comfortable out of reach of his typewriter, and when he was busy writing he did not like to be diverted. Billee remembers peeking over his shoulder once and reading, "It's Fourth of July. Damn!" This was because he knew a flock of visitors would be arriving for a picnic.

To feed his seemingly insatiable appetite for ideas and information, a wall of books grew in the living room, later spreading to other parts of the house, even to the bathroom. In addition to other titles he selected for research or pure pleasure, he bought the 51-volume *Harvard Classics* published in 1909 and originally known as *Dr. Eliot's Five Foot Shelf*, *The Encyclopedia Britannica* and also *Compton's Encyclopedia* for the children. He belonged to the Book of the Month Club.

All members of the Jenkins family were readers. When Billee was four, she announced firmly that she did not care to learn to read. She was perfectly satisfied with having people read to her for the rest of her life. This was rebellion on a scale that nose piercing or dying one's hair purple would have been in this traditional family. In the Jenkins house, everyone read. There were books in every room, a wall of shelves in the living room, shelves under the windows in the sunroom, shelves in every bedroom, shelves in the bathroom. If there were no shelves, there were books on the floor, on tables or open on someone's lap. If you were a Jenkins, you read, even if you were four years old. She learned to read.

Will loved browsing in second-hand bookstores and often bought boxes of old books at auction sales expecting they might contain one or two that interested him. He loved Victorian children's books, traveler's tales, deep-sea explorations, scientific studies, biographies, classics, everything that expanded his thinking and told him something he didn't know. He marked this seemingly random collection with a bookplate he and Mary designed and executed with linoleum block printing.

The Botetourt Bibliographical Society of the College of William and Mary asked to visit Will to look at his book collection in 1966. In his response he said, "They range from a *Renard the Fox*, in Latin, of 1490, through Parson Weems to Harold Bell Wright and Nicholas Carter, and—cutting back—*Valentine Vox the Ventriloquist* and *Charlotte Temple* and Doctor Johnson's dictionary and then off in all directions.... They are the books one professional writer has

Linocut bookplate designed and printed by Will and Mary for their own library.

accumulated because he wanted to own them, plus some cases of reluctance to part with anything once read."

His extensive reading provided useful background for Will's stories. He was proud when one time he got a letter from a fan in the Far East who said, "When did you live here? You describe it perfectly."

For Billee, at least, the shelf of hardcover books in the bookcase written by Will F. Jenkins or Murray Leinster had special significance. Although most were reprints of stories that had already appeared in magazines, the books were a more tangible evidence of what he did than the magazines that came into the house and were looked at and tossed aside. In addition, the fact that there were dedications in some of the books was also significant, and she was very aware of which was dedicated to whom.

The following were dedicated to his wife, Mary:

"To big Mary — who liked this story" — *Murder Madness* (Murray Leinster) was published by Brewer & Warren in 1931 (reprinted by Fantasy Publishing Co., 1949) *Astounding,* June, July and August 1930.

"To Mary Mandola Jenkins, Sr." — *Kid Deputy* (Will F. Jenkins) King, 1935, *Triple X Western*, February, March and April 1928.

"To Mary Mandola Jenkins" — *Black Sheep* (Will F. Jenkins) Julian Messner, Inc., 1936, *Adventure*, January 1928.

His daughters were included also:

"To Mary Mandola Jenkins 2nd" — *Sword of Kings* (Murray Leinster) John Long, Ltd., 1933 *Frontier Stories*, July 1928.

"To Elizabeth Madden Jenkins" — *Outlaw Sheriff* (Will F. Jenkins) King, 1934 (printed in UK as *Rustlin' Sheriff*) Eldon Press, 1934.

"To Wenllian Louise Jenkins" — *Fighting Horse Valley* (Will F. Jenkins) King, 1934.

A story Will loved to tell was that Billee, when called upon to sign her formal name (Wenllian) at a very young age, took *Fighting Horse Valley* off the shelf and remarked, "It sure is handy to have a book dedicated to you when you don't know how to spell your name."

As Jo-an was so much younger it was 1942, before he dedicated *The Man Who Feared* (Will F. Jenkins, Gateway, 1942) to her. Murray Leinster's *The Last Space Ship* (Frederick Fell, Inc., 1949) was followed in 1953 by *Space Tug* (Shasta), and in 1954 by *The Forgotten Planet* (Gnome Press).

Several other novels came out in the 1930s. *Scalps* (Murray Leinster) was published by Brewer & Warren in 1930, *Murder Will Out* (Murray Leinster) by John Hamilton in 1932, *Mexican Trail* (Will F. Jenkins) by Alfred H. King in 1933, *Murder in the Family* (Murray Leinster) by John Hamilton in 1935, *No Clues* (Murray Leinster) by Wright & Brown in 1935, and *Guns for Achin* (Murray Leinster) by Wright & Brown in 1936.

Nineteen thirty-six was a pivotal moment in Will's career. He achieved an important milestone with the publication of "Wild Waters" in the January 1936 issue of *Collier's*, his first in a mainstream "slick" magazine. "Two in a Boat" appeared in the March 7, 1936, issue, and fiction editor Kenneth Littauer bought six more stories from Will that year. He appeared in *Collier's* for the next twenty years.

These magazines not only paid more — *Collier's* was paying him $1,000 for a short story — but also were considered more prestigious both for the quality of the writing and the seriousness of the reporting. The pulps were considered second-rate. This was the beginning of a steady market in the slick magazines. He entered *American Magazine* in April 1938 with "Portrait of an Artist," in *The Woman's Home Companion* in September 1939 with "He looked like Robert Taylor," and *Cosmopolitan* with "Headline" in June 1939. He first appeared in *Esquire* with "Pygie Takes a Wife" in July 1939.

In 1937, writing for *Liberty Magazine*, Will won the first prize of $1,000 for "A Very Nice Family," published in the January 2 edition. He and Mary used the award money to complete guest quarters in the detached garage at Ardudwy in Clay Bank. The second prize was won by William E. Barrett, later well known for the novels *The Lilies of the Field* (later made into a movie starring Sidney Poitier) and *The Left Hand of God* (also made into a movie, this time starring Humphrey Bogart). As a result of the awards, the Barretts came to Clay Bank to meet Will and Mary, and the girls were delighted that they brought their young son with them. Because Will's daughters were home-schooled, they were eager to meet other young people, and any visitor close to their age was a treasure. They thought the Barretts' son was particularly cute, and, although the visit was brief, talked about him for a long time.

Also in 1937, a long relationship began with Curtis Publishing and Ben Hibbs, who was an editor at Curtis' *The Country Gentleman* from 1929 through 1942. This had been primarily an agricultural magazine but had begun to print short stories. Will began to appear in its pages with "Tik-Lui, the God" published in the August 1937 issue. Hibbs was known for traveling around the country to research his articles and editorials. He and his wife visited Will and Mary at Clay Bank in 1940.

During the visit, they stopped in at Morgan's Drug Store to meet Will's good friend Dr. L. V. "Happy" Morgan, pharmacist and owner of the store, and to enjoy one of Will's favorite all-chocolate sodas. Raymond Brown worked at the soda fountain when he was in high school and grew up to be

Will's doctor, fan and friend. After Will died, he and Happy Morgan set up a memorial to him at the Gloucester Public Library dedicating a collection of Jenkins and Leinster books.

Morgan's was a family place. When *Life* magazine came out with the controversial article "The Birth of a Baby" in their April 11, 1938, issue, Dr. Morgan carefully removed the offending pages before it went on display.

The afternoon the Hibbses visited, Happy Morgan's elder son, Jimmy, then aged 12, was lounging in the store. Jimmy was editor of his school newspaper, *The Scribe,* and as his brother, Delegate Harvey Morgan, tells it, the two editors chatted, and Ben Hibbs asked Jimmy his circulation number.

"Answer, 100. What's *your* circulation?"
"16 million [or some such number]. What do you charge for advertising, Jimmy?"
"$1.00 for a full page, 50 cents for half and 25 cents for a quarter page. What do *you* charge?"
"$200,000 (or so) for a full page."
And so the conversation went — both very earnest and respectful of each other.

The boys never forgot it.

Will's successful author-editor relationship with Ben Hibbs continued after Hibbs went to *The Saturday Evening Post,* also a Curtis publication, in 1942.

Keeping on top of the market and inevitable changes in magazines required a certain amount of personal contact, and Will had learned this early on. Pulp editors depended on the availability of a writer to take a project on. If you could produce, you had a good chance for a steady market. Pulp writers were also used to talking over an idea or two with an editor and getting approval before writing a story.

Will made a trip to New York with his family almost every year. The girls understood it was to see the editors. He liked to take quarts of shucked oysters, carefully iced, and bunches of daffodils as gifts when it was possible. On one such journey in the mid-thirties, memorable to Billee, one of the editors took them all to the Coney Island Amusement Park. It was her first and only visit to amusement park rides, except for those at the small carnivals that came to Gloucester Court House. She still wishes she could remember who it was and could thank him.

Curtis Publishing's home, the Curtis Building in Philadelphia, became a familiar stop for Will's daughters, who often accompanied their father on his visits there. Billee particularly looked forward to another sight of *Dream Garden,* the 15 by 49 foot glass mosaic in the lobby. Edward Bok ordered *Dream Garden* when he was senior editor at Curtis Publishing Company. It was designed by Maxfield Parrish and executed by Louis Comfort Tiffany in 1916. When, as an adult, Billee moved near Philadelphia, she was amazed that few people seem to know of this treasure, and she made a point of taking visitors to see it. (Philadelphians woke up when they almost lost it. Steve Wynn, a casino developer, bought it in 1998 with the intention of moving it to Las Vegas. Suddenly aware, the community rallied to save it, and it can still be seen in the lobby of the Curtis Building.)

An apparently routine move that also took place in 1937 was to have a strong impact on the science fiction world and usher in what came to be known as the Golden Age of Science Fiction. Will was very much a part of it.

Orlin Tremaine hired John Campbell in October 1937 to follow him as editor of *Astounding Stories,* and by the March 1938 issue Campbell had taken over and begun to make changes. He renamed the magazine *Astounding Science-Fiction* and put out the word that he wanted more emphasis on science. Campbell had attended Massachusetts Institute of Technology (MIT) but flunked the German they required for a degree in chemistry. He then moved on to Duke University where he took a degree in physics.

He not only knew the field of science, but also was a writer himself, having published his first story in 1930 when he was 19. He often used the name Don A. Stuart, an anagram of his first wife's name. However, he used his own name, John W. Campbell, Jr., for the 18-installment series of articles called "A Study of the Solar System" that began in the June 1936 issue of *Astounding*. These articles were very popular and the practice of including an article in each issue continued after he took over as editor. Two Stuart novelettes appeared in *Astounding* in 1937, "Forgetfulness" and "Out of Night."

Campbell soon began to put the full effort of his forceful personality into redirecting the focus of the magazine. This new emphasis on science was "right up his alley," as Will would say, and, from the first, Campbell wanted Will to continue submitting stories. He related this in his speech at Disclave I, 1963:

> When I first began my editorship of *Astounding* ... I wrote Will Jenkins, hopefully asking for stories. He was busy with commitments just then, and couldn't send stories, but very warmly offered to help me by sending me technique suggestions for getting stories written. That ... was very cogent and unforgettable.

Will had a basic tenet for science fiction that fitted the new *Astounding* well. He expressed it in his introduction to the *Great Stories of Science Fiction*, "Let's Call It a Hobby." He said that he, like most fans, would accept only one false assumption at a time. For example, that "there are five or six or seven dimensions instead of the three we know and Mr. Einstein's four. But we will not stand for it if somebody falsifies the Rylberg Numbers or the Einsteinian mass-energy equation or the formula for the Fitzgerald Contraction, or any little thing like that."

Busy with his commitments to the higher paying slick magazines, Will did not find time to submit anything to *Astounding* until 1942. Then, spending his full time in New York, he began the series of lunches with Campbell that resulted in a close friendship and some darn good stories.

The late 1930s brought changes in Will's family life as well. The girls were growing older and more involved with his tinkering and experimenting. For a while he spent a lot of time with a cardboard box with a pinhole. Will showed the girls that, when you blew a smoke ring, it moved from the inside out and became larger and larger. If you could make it move from the outside in, it would get smaller and smaller. They spent hours on that. Another experiment, its goal unremembered, seemed to cause everything in the house to turn purple.

Delegate Harvey Morgan shared another memory of how Will used to come into his family's drug store in Gloucester Court House looking for unusual items for his experiments. One example was using extremely slow-reacting lead monoxide mixed with another compound to open cargo hatches, etc.

Harvey remembers a visit he made to the house at Clay Bank. After about fifteen minutes, he heard an explosion outside.

"His daughters came running in the house exclaiming, 'It worked Daddy, it worked!' We all went outside and there in an open ditch we found the remains of a previously sealed metal pipe. He had mixed the heretofore believed unreactive chemicals and set his watch to determine how long it would take to develop the required pressure to burst the pipe."

Harvey also remembered: "Will Jenkins and my father were good friends. He would visit us in our family drug store and once asked my father why his Ant No More ant poison worked so well. My Dad explained that ants are carnivorous and, when one ate the poison and died others would eat them and die, until the whole colony was wiped out. This concept fascinated Mr. Jenkins so much that he wrote a story about giant ants invading the earth. When the usual weapons — guns, tanks and bombs — were ineffective, someone remembered that fact about ants, and civilization was saved by eliminating them with poison."

That story, "Doomsday Deferred," was published in *The Saturday Evening Post*, September 24, 1949.

Harvey asked Will once how he could write so visually about places he had never visited. Will explained about the use of language to convey a word picture.

"By learning about climate, customs, buildings, street locations, etc. through study, it is possible to describe a setting in such a manner that even one familiar with the location will accept the scene as accurately portrayed."

Will also told Harvey how to debate scholars and win. "Talk fast and ask questions!"

Will was fascinated with pure science. He loved to discover things and then, hopefully, figure out what to do with them. He saw in Little Mary particularly a spark of his scientific interest, and, like many parents, a second chance to live his dream. She was bright and pliant, and he began involving her in more and more of his science projects and some of his tinkering and gadgetry. Will set up a laboratory in the power house, the small outbuilding that had previously been used to house the Delco plant. There they worked on the project later mentioned in reports on the FBI investigation into Cleve Cartmill's story "Deadline."

Robert Silverberg in *Reflections: The Cartmill Affair Two*, printed in *Asimov's Science Fiction* (Oct.–Nov. 2003), quotes Will as saying, "They had 'conducted experiments designed to acquire quantities of atomic copper.'"

When Mary started high school in 1935, it seemed almost an opportunity for Will to capture the experience he had never had. He monitored her lessons and encouraged her to start a school newspaper with a group of her friends. It was published on the sun porch at the house in Clay Bank. First he made a hectograph, the old gelatin in a tray method of reproduction, and then staked them to a mimeograph machine. He suggested articles, including a gossip column, and helped type stories. He drove them around to sell advertising. He loved being part of the group.

Will missed Mary terribly when she left for Mount Holyoke College in the autumn of 1939, where he encouraged her to major in physics. She had the same problem with their requirement of German as John Campbell had at MIT so she switched to zoology, even though her heart was in art, a passion she followed in her later life.

Betty was just 15 in 1940 when she graduated from high school in Gloucester, Virginia. Mary and Will thought she was too young to go away to college, so she was instead sent to study in Richmond for a post-graduate year. She came home on weekends but was so pitifully homesick that she was never sent away again. Betty had always liked to make up stories and entertained her younger sisters with her tales, so it was not surprising when she and Will collaborated on a story, "Fly for Your Life," which was printed in the August 1940 issue of *American Magazine*. Betty's writing skills were later focused on the local newspaper, Glo-Quips, that she and her husband started in Gloucester after their marriage.

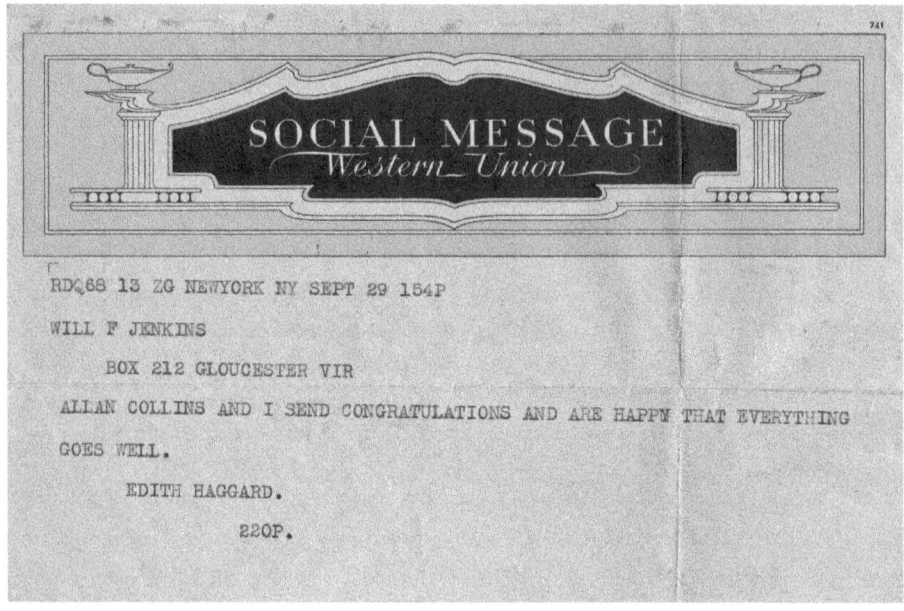

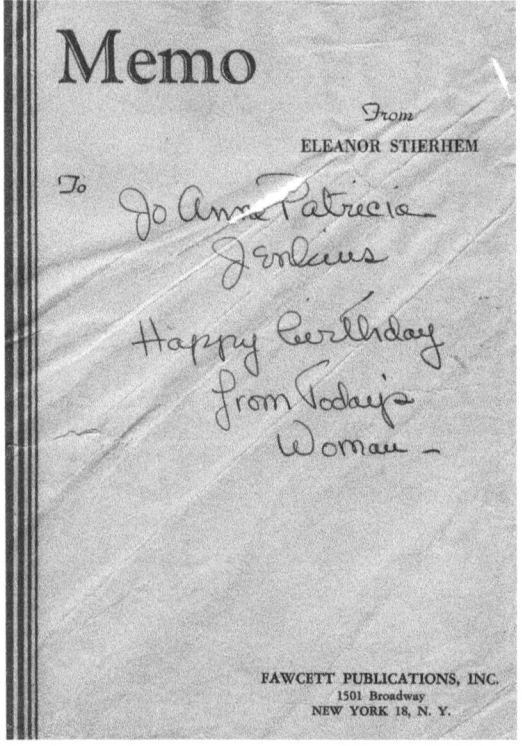

A welcome distraction in 1938 was a new baby. The last bit of dirt road between Gloucester Court House and Clay Bank was freshly paved when Will brought Mary and baby Joan Patricia (always pronounced "Jo-Ann") home from Stuart Circle Hospital in Richmond after her birth on September 22. She was the first of the four children not to have been born at home. He was tickled with the new arrival and the newly paved road. "If

Top: Telegram of congratulations on Jo-an's birth from Will's agent Edith Haggard and Allan Collins at Curtis Brown. *Left:* A welcoming "Happy Birthday" to Jo-an from Eleanor Stierhem, editor of *Today's Woman.*

you build a better mousetrap," he would quote proudly, "The world will build a path to your door."

Edith Haggard, Will's long-time agent at Curtis Brown, sent congratulations from herself and Curtis Brown's president, Allan Collins. Eleanor Stierhem sent a "Happy Birthday" note from *Today's Woman*. Will was 42 years old and, even though he had hoped for a son instead of a fourth daughter, he was a happy man living a life he loved. Soon, this new daughter, too, began to be enchanted by his stories, and he was enchanted by this new developing life.

In 1939, the whole family went to New York to see The World of Tomorrow at the World's Fair in Flushing Meadows. Will had a heyday telling the girls what he thought was good science, what was speculation, and what would catch on. When the silhouettes of the rides in the amusement section called out to eleven-year-old Billee, they were dismissed with a careless, "You can go on rides any time." They moved on through a tomorrow exhibition that, as it turned out, wasn't half as exciting or prescient as any of Murray Leinster's stories.

• SEVEN •

The New York Years: The 1940s

Like most Americans from 1939 onward, Will became focused on the escalating war in Europe and spent much of his time glued to the radio, listening to news reports and anticipating our entrance into the conflict. When the bombs fell on Pearl Harbor on December 7, 1941, Will, Mary and their children were visiting Mary's sister Adeline Allen and her family in Front Royal, Virginia. When they heard the news report, the Jenkins girls and their cousin Little Adeline came back from the nearby soda shop where they had been spending time with friends, including young men in high school at nearby Randolph Macon Military Academy. Looking at the boys who accompanied them to the Allen home, Will and Lewis Allen said, "I guess the academy will be going ROTC [Reserve Officers Training Corps] now." It immediately struck daughter Billee that these young friends might actually have to go to war, face unthinkable danger, and possibly not come home again. As she said later, "My childhood ended right then."

Will was eager to make a contribution to the war effort and began searching for a niche. He got in touch with every contact he could think of. In the spring of 1942, he found that niche with the about-to-be-opened Office of War Information (OWI), where he was soon to be a senior publications editor. In his employment application, he named Allan Collins, c/o Curtis Brown, Ltd., agent; Ben Hibbs, c/o *Saturday Evening Post*, editor; Robert Reed, c/o *Country Gentleman*, editor; Henry LaCossitt, c/o *The American Magazine*, editor; and Max Wilkinson, c/o *Collier's Magazine*, editor, as references.

The family then left Gloucester and went north. For several weeks they stayed with Mary's sister Julia and her family in Fort Lee, New Jersey, and then rented a house for the summer in Flushing, Queens, New York.

The OWI was a U.S. government agency operating from June 1942 to

Seven • The New York Years: The 1940s

September 1945. It was created to consolidate government information services, promote patriotism, warn about foreign spies, and attempt to recruit women into war work. As it gradually developed, it began to concentrate on brief films and posters produced by advertising professionals, much to Will's disappointment. Among the many people who worked for the OWI for a time were Owen Lattimore, Milton S. Eisenhower, Jane Jacobs, Archibald MacLeish, and Arthur Schlesinger, Jr. OWI information lists Will as Murray Leinster.

Will's story "Morale," subtitled "A Story of the War of 1941–43," which had been printed in *Astounding* in 1931, moved from fiction to an actual current event.

A home was needed for the family during Will's time with the OWI. It was found in the fall of 1942 in Beechhurst, a community in the borough of Queens about an hour's journey from Manhattan via subway and bus. What was most attractive to Will and Mary was that the Beechhurst Towers at 160-15 Powell's Cove Boulevard, where they rented an apartment, overlooked the Long Island Sound. There was a tennis court and a playground with swings and a slide immediately behind the building, and behind that a tree-filled park on the edge of a cliff leading to a private beach and pier. It was as close as Will could come in New York to his beloved home at Clay Bank.

What they did not know was that many theater and film people had discovered Beechhurst before they did and were also attracted by the waterfront location. Mary Pickford had a home there, which she may have bought when she was making movies for Adolph Zukor at his Famous Players studios in Astoria. She made 21 films in Astoria between 1911 and 1916, and by then she was probably the most famous woman in America.

It was during this period that Charlie Chaplin came to America from London. Beechhurst legend says Charlie Chaplin also lived in Beechhurst for a time, actually in the Towers, and Mary Pickford may have brought him there. She had not been close to Chaplin originally, but he was Douglas Fairbanks's best friend. She had developed a relationship with Fairbanks while still married to Owen Moore and, after divorcing Moore in 1920, married him. Fairbanks, Pickford and Chaplin had already, in 1919, joined together and formed United Artists film company. The Towers was designed and built during the 1920s boom, and, for a man on the move like Chaplin, a luxury rental in a new apartment building near his friends and favored by showgirls would have been attractive.

Many wealthy people had homes nearby, now largely abandoned. Among them was the Tudor-style mansion built in 1924 for Arthur Hammerstein, the Broadway producer and uncle of lyricist Oscar Hammerstein II. The two-story, 15-room house, called Wildflower for Arthur Hammerstein's 1923 hit play, lay in the five-acre grounds of the estate at 168-11 Powell's Cove Boulevard. The original building burned down in 1994. It was restored, named a national landmark, and is now part of a gated community of condominiums.

Other well-known former residents of the area included entertainer Harry Richman, movie producer Joseph Schenck, and actress Paulette Goddard. Escape artist Harry Houdini had a home there and, around 1915, magician Howard Thurston built his three-story house across the street from his idol, the German magician Alexander Herrmann. Rudolph Valentino lived nearby when he was filming *The Sheik*.

Industrialist Harvey Firestone also built a home on Cryders Lane near Wildflower that was called Michel by the Sea. Luxury co-ops now stand on the site.

In 1942 when the Jenkinses arrived, these famous people were gone, and many of those mansions had been long abandoned. Beechhurst was a quiet neighborhood predominately made up of small, private homes surrounded by gardens. However, there were still links to the theatrical past. Floyd Buckley, well known for providing the gravelly voice of Popeye on the radio during the 1930s, lived with his family in a home on 161st Street backing up to the grounds where the deserted mansions were partially hidden by trees. Buckley had a long career in theater and motion pictures beginning before the turn of the century. He appeared in *The Perils of Pauline* sequel *The Exploits of Elaine* in 1915 and played the automaton Q in the 1919 Harry Houdini serial *The Master Mystery*. In 1920, he came back to his hometown of Chatham, New York, to appear in a movie, *By Man's Law*.

Will Swift tells the story about this movie in part in an article in the Spring 2004 *Columbia County Historical Society Heritage* publication. John S. Lopez, who directed the film, created a lot of excitement in the town by recruiting local townspeople for the roles. Later they enjoyed seeing themselves on film but didn't think much of the plot. A young Norma Shearer was the star, and Buckley arranged for Miss Shearer to stay at his parents' home. She promised to reciprocate back in Hollywood, but, according to the family, when they got to California, she snubbed them, saying she was too busy. Chatham is reported to have snubbed the movie back.

Buckley again promoted his hometown in 1923 when Houdini was making the film *Haldane of the Secret Service*. Houdini was looking for an old-fashioned mill with a wooden water wheel, which he could be tied to for one of his trademark escapes. Buckley suggested a mill near Chatham, and the requisite wooden wheel was built there. Unfortunately, the movie failed.

Billee found Floyd Buckley's son, Tom, to be a great tennis and swimming partner. Tom later had a successful career as an author and journalist including a stint with *The New York Times*. There were two younger sisters, Joy and Faith. His mother, Julie, was a lovely, warm woman, very beautiful with her black hair brought back in a bun, accented by a striking white streak. She was on Broadway in *Yours Truly,* a musical starring Irene Dunne and Leon Errol, when she married Floyd Buckley in 1927. She had been in several musicals, including *Rose Marie*. She loved clothes and fashion, and Billee used to show off her new clothes to her. Later, when Betty married, Julie made her wedding dress. Mr. Buckley, who sported a theatrically waxed mustache, seemed too dignified to be called by his first name, which seemed an anachronism considering his role as Popeye. When he died of an aneurysm in 1956 at 83, he had just completed his 445th straight performance in *No Time for Sergeants* on Broadway playing Andy Griffith's father, and it was noted that he was the oldest actor still working.

Also very visible in Beechhurst was a rambunctious and friendly small boy of about ten years old with brilliant dyed red hair. His name was Ben Cooper, and he lived with his parents and sister, Berna Anne, a few houses from the Buckleys. He was quick to tell you that he was on Broadway where he was playing Harlan, youngest son of the Day family, in the long running play *Life with Father*. Young as he was, he had an eye for Will's curly-topped niece Little Adeline when she visited, and he was a joy to have around. The Jenkins family went to see him in the show several times, including when he moved up to the part of an older brother, Whitney.

Ben had a successful career in movies. He played a memorable part in *The Rose Tattoo* and won a Golden Boot award in 2005 for his work in westerns. No one could have predicted that he would later play the astronaut Nazarro in the *Time Tunnel* series, based on a Murray Leinster novel. The episode, "One Way to the Moon," aired on September 16, 1966.

For Will and Mary, Beechhurst seemed ideal. However, although it was important to Will that he give to the war effort, this move to New York cost him more than he ever anticipated, marking the beginning of the collapse of his carefully structured life plan. He never thought that their daughters Betty, then 17, and Billee, 14, would go to college and that their youngest daughter Jo-an, four, would spend her childhood here, away from Virginia. He certainly never dreamed that Clay Bank would cease to be their primary home for more than a decade. It was not until shortly before 1957, when Betty married and moved to Gloucester, and Jo-an was away at college, that they returned to live in Virginia for most of the year.

Meanwhile, Beechhurst was now home, and Mary and the girls soon adapted to a radical change in life-style. For Billee, the transition from a high school in Gloucester, Virginia, with a total of 100 students, to a high school in Bayside, Queens, New York, with more than 6000 students, must have been difficult. However, her only memories of the time revolve around the lipstick issue. Although she was a senior, she was only 14 and not supposed to be wearing lipstick. It became a serious game of intrigue with Will and Mary — putting it on after she left the house — wiping if off before she came home, worrying who might see her with it on, whether they would tell her parents. When she entered college at 15, they gave up.

Chewing gum was another game of intrigue. Will would not allow it. Mary used to sneak it to them in the movies (where Will never went) on the grounds that it would keep young Mary and Billee from biting their nails.

Billee graduated from Bayside High School in 1943, just a week after her 15th birthday. Her sister Betty had also been 15 when she finished high school in Virginia. Now they both started college at the same time. Betty, 18, commuted to Adelphi in Garden City, Long Island, while Billee traveled daily to Packer Collegiate Institute, a kindergarten through junior college private girls school in Brooklyn, for her two year associate's degree. After graduating from Packer, Billee transferred to Sweet Briar College, in Virginia, for her junior year.

Will continued his writing while he was with the OWI, just as he had when serving in World War I, and was appearing regularly in *American Magazine, Collier's, Country Gentleman,* and *Liberty*. During the 1940s more slick magazines were added to his list of markets. *Good Housekeeping* published "The Web" in September 1944, and "The Persian Love Story" was printed in the *Saturday Evening Post* on January 18, 1947. He had been concentrating on the higher paying slicks since the late 1930s but was still appearing frequently in science fiction magazines in the 1940s, although the market was shrinking. Several magazines had closed by 1947.

Will also continued his tinkering and had an official outlet. On July 17, 1943, he wrote to the assistant to the security officer in Washington, DC:

> I believe that Lieutenant John Rudloff spoke to you of some OWI gadgets the other day in New York, They are being sent abroad for use, and it seems desirable to show them to the Army and Navy in case they could be useful outside the OWI. Since I worked out the gadgets, I have been asked to do the showing, and was told to write you about the necessary appointments,
>
> If possible, I'd like to make the trip to Washington the latter half of the week, Wednesday, Thursday, or Friday. Thursday would be my choice, if that matters.
>
> For your information, there are three of the gadgets, two of them much alike; printing devices designed for underground use in Europe. In one version, they are sheets of paper with a prepared text, which duplicate that text up to a thousand copies without any machinery at all — nothing but the sheet itself laid

down anywhere — and with any additional pigment from writing-ink to berry-juice will go on and print an infinite number more. In another version, they have no prepared text, but are supplied with a special backing sheet. One writes on the back with a lead-pencil, and the text is prepared. This last might be handy for field orders. A pad of them would be a complete printing plant, usable anywhere there was paper and water. To print an 8½ by 5¼ inch space, they weigh one pound per hundred.

The third gadget is an emergency process for making negatives for the zinc plates used in Davidson and other offset presses mounted in mobile units. There is no photographic material involved. One takes an original text or carbon copy of typed, drawn, or written matter, and turns it into a negative from which the zinc plate can be made. The process takes about five minutes from start to printing-frame.

There is no further information on this.

Years later he wrote Jo-an saying, "Did I tell you that I thoroughly enjoyed Winston Churchill's *Toy Shop*? I was doing that sort of thing for propaganda devices instead of booby traps when I was with the OWI. A totally different scale, but I had many of the troubles the author of that book had."

Now that Will was spending more time in New York, he met regularly with John Campbell. "The Wabbler," published in *Astounding* in October 1942, was the first Murray Leinster story to appear there in six years, and more soon followed. His reappearance was particularly interesting because Campbell had been successful in developing some new young writers, including Isaac Asimov and Robert Heinlein. These young people John Campbell encouraged were a generation younger than Will and very different in background. Many had come out of fandom, were or had been members of fan clubs, and had grown up reading science fiction. Many, like Will, had started writing and selling early. Of those who went to college, some started before they graduated. They were motivated by a love of the genre. They wished to be a part of it, and their dedication resulted in what has been called the Golden Age of Science Fiction.

Will was also a fan, and he read and wrote science fiction because he loved it. But he did not limit himself to it, because writing was his profession, and he depended on it to support his family. However, his interest in and emphasis on correct science in his writing fit perfectly into Campbell's goal for the magazine.

Science fiction writer and editor Barry Malzberg comments that Will was "a major science fiction writer from the beginning of the 1930s within the genre magazines, and one of the very few who easily made the shift to Campbell's *Astounding* and modern science fiction."

Will and Campbell became good friends and lunched together often, Will fiddling with his pipe, and John carefully inserting yet another Camel into his holder. They exchanged ideas and discussed everything in the world. John liked to discuss possible plots, some as potential stories, others just for the exercise. One of these discussions resulted in *The Murder of the U.S.A.*, published under Will's own name by Crown in 1946. He dedicated it to "John W. Campbell, Jr., whose belief in this story, from the beginning, is the reason for the existence of this book." In *The Murder of the U.S.A.*, Will gives one of the earliest accounts of a nuclear attack on the U.S., accurately predicting the grim realities of the Cold War — the missiles in their silos, the belts of radar warning and, in detail, the anti-missile-to-missile problems.

Arthur C. Clarke says in his review of the book, "This is a 'whodunit' on the largest possible scale. It opens with the initial murder of seventy million Americans in a surprise attack by atomic rockets.... The author, better known in science fiction circles as Murray Leinster, has given us a dramatically written, technically brilliant and horribly plausible story."

Clarke continues, "We find Sam Burton and his colleagues of Burrow 89, one of the deeply hidden Rocket Missile Launching bases of the Atomic Counter-Attack Force of the United States, trying to seek out the guilty nation, which has naturally taken every possible measure to cloak its identity. The manner of the final unmasking is both ingenious and exciting, and the search itself will keep you thoroughly enthralled. This book may do a lot of good if it is read in the right circles."

Campbell loved to play the devil's advocate, arguing and even writing controversial editorials on such topics as slavery, tobacco, and religion. Will loved these discussions, and they had lively debates. As a Catholic, Will especially enjoyed following the development of John's interest in Dianetics from the time the science fiction community was saying, "Look what Ron Hubbard is doing with tomato soup cans," to later, when John embraced and promoted Hubbard's theories. He thought it was all great fun. While many people complained that Campbell monopolized a conversation and said, "You couldn't get a word in edgewise," Will found their differences in opinion intellectually stimulating and had no trouble keeping his end up.

Both men's families sometimes had a problem with their penchant for seemingly endless discussions whenever the opportunity arose. Campbell's wife Peg tells how it was in Perry A. Chapdelaine, Sr.'s collection *The John W. Campbell Letters, Vol. I.*

"Later on came the beaux John's daughters brought home. Many's the time I had to interrupt one of those marathon debates to suggest that the girls might like to go out on their dates, rather than fidgeting, all dressed up, in the back-ground."

This was an all too familiar scenario for the Jenkins girls.

Seven • The New York Years: The 1940s

In 1971, after Campbell's death, the editorship of *Analog* (as *Astounding* was later renamed) was taken on by Ben Bova, later an award winning editor, writer, lecturer, president emeritus of the National Space Society and president of the Science Fiction and Fantasy Writers of America. Of his first and only meeting with Will soon after he began at *Analog*, Bova recalls:

> I had just taken the editorship of Analog magazine after John Campbell's unexpected death, feeling very uncertain of myself in this new job. Will Jenkins let me know he'd be in New York and of course I invited him to lunch. We had a pleasant meal and chatted about John Campbell, mostly. As he was taking his leave of me, Jenkins said something like, "Here we've had a good lunch and we haven't come up with one single brilliant idea for a story." I felt like slitting my wrists. He was accustomed to swapping ideas with Campbell and I had disappointed him, I fear.

Campbell's death on July 11, 1971, was a great blow to Will. Although he had not been going to New York very often after Mary died in 1967, he had lost a great friend, one who had shared his passion for science and science fiction and had served as a sounding board for thirty years. There was mutual admiration, and Isaac Asimov commented in his introduction to *Isaac Asimov Presents the Great SF Stories, Vol. 10* that when he was starting out as a young writer, Campbell seemed convinced that Will was a new Edison, and he got tired of hearing about the new works of genius coming from Will Jenkins' workshops in Virginia every time he went to the *Astounding* office.

There was one thing Will and Campbell didn't talk about until after the atomic bomb was dropped on Hiroshima on August 6, 1945. They were among the three or four writers interviewed by the FBI about a story called "Deadline" printed in *Astounding Science-Fiction* in March 1944. They now knew a horrifying secret: that the USA was working on an atomic bomb, because Cleve Cartmill and Campbell had worked out together in explicit detail a story that was about an atomic bomb.

Will recalls the incident in his introduction to *Great Stories of Science Fiction* (Random House, 1951). One day he had a phone call. "A voice said pleasantly that it was the FBI calling and they'd like to talk to me. The voice said they would come to the apartment and they did."

The girls vividly remember their father and the FBI men going up on the roof of the Beechhurst Towers for privacy. As he told it:

> One of them said, "Tell me, have you ever read the Cleve Cartmill story, 'Deadline'"?
> I said I had. The larger FBI man said interestedly, "What did you think of it?"
> "A pretty good story," I said, "and the science is authentic. Quite accurate."
> Then there was a pause. A rather long pause. Then he sighed, and reluctantly inquired, "Well, what we want to know is, could it be a leak?"

At this point my hair stood up on end and its separate strands tended to crack like whiplashes. Because "Deadline" by Cleve Cartmill, was a story about an atomic bomb, and this was the year before Hiroshima. The bomb in the story was made of uranium-235, it was to explode when critical mass was attained, and there were other details. The story described most minutely the temperature of an atom-bomb explosion, the deadly radiation, the lingering after effects, the shock-wave, the heat-effect, and all the rest of the phenomena that a year later were observed at Hiroshima and Nagasaki.

But I was being asked about it *before* Hiroshima, and the Manhattan Project was perhaps the most completely hush-hush of all the hush-hush performances of the war. Because I am supposed to know something about science fiction — I am a professional writer, but science fiction has been my hobby for years — I was one of the two persons I know who were consulted by the FBI on the question of whether the story was a coincidence or a leak of facts.

I was able to tell them where all the information in the story could be found in print. The idea of an atomic bomb was not new to science fiction, but Cartmill's story was beautifully worked out. It was so infernally close to the truth that the people who were making the bomb thought the facts had leaked.

I was privy to a secret I would greatly have preferred not to know.

But came the day when the atom bomb was dropped on Hiroshima, that morning I happened to be in the office of the magazine *Today's Woman*. I was free to talk about the bomb then, and I did. That afternoon Eleanor Stierhem called: "I thought I'd ask if you could write us an easily understandable article on what the atom bomb means to the average American housewife."

The article was printed under the title "The Friendly Atom."

The military censors were also interested in the Leinster story "Four Little Ships" when it was published in *Astounding Science-Fiction* (November 1942). This story described a way of disrupting enemy shipping using underwater sound transmission, which was, coincidently, under military development at the time. Will once remarked that, if the enemy had read science fiction magazines, they might have won the war. He was not alone in that thought.

Robert A. Heinlein created a volunteer think tank with fellow science fiction writers Isaac Asimov and L. Sprague de Camp, who worked with him at the Philadelphia Naval Yard. They met formally once a week in the evening to consider problems given to them by navy officials. Several other science fiction writers were involved as well, including L. Ron Hubbard, who later went on to found his own religion, the Church of Scientology.

Michael Swanwick, science fiction writer and winner of the Nebula and five Hugo Awards, remembers this conversation with Will:

> Will Jenkins told me that Heinlein had wanted him as a member but had been overruled by the top brass because he had only a grammar school education. However, Heinlein did arrange to informally pass along problems that he and the other writers were stuck on. One of these was the problem of the submarine periscope.

Seven • The New York Years: The 1940s

This resulted in one of Will's favorite stories. Early in the war, before radar, there had been a problem with the wake that a submarine left when it surfaced and moved through the water. Will had a very simple solution. He took a stick, tied some ribbons to it, and when they trailed out behind the stick, they prevented the eddies from forming.

Will knew his boyhood friend Cornelius "Neely" Bull was a good friend of Admiral Ernest J. King, fleet admiral during World War II. He wrote Bull telling him about the thought and asking: "What should I do? ... Should I send him a model? I observed I would take great pleasure out of imagining him and Admiral King playing with one of my ribbon-decorated sticks in the bathtub. I particularly stressed the bathtub angle."

Bull turned the letter over to the admiral who turned it over to the Bureau of Naval Construction. When the report came back, both Neely and Will were pleased with the top sheet.

It said: "The inventor speaks of experimenting with this device in a bathtub. What I would like to know is, when he was experimenting with this device in a bathtub, what did he use as a periscope?"

In May 1945, *Astounding Science-Fiction* published "First Contact." It turned out to be, along with "Sidewise in Time," one of the most influential stories in science fiction history. The story raised the question: "When a human ship meets an alien one in a far off nebula, neither side has reason to trust the other with the location of its mother world. How to ensure both ships can safely leave for home without letting the other know its home world location, and yet be able to keep contact?"

First, you have to establish communication. Robert Silverberg talks about "First Contact" and this problem in "Reflections: Hic Rhodus, Hic Salta," published in the January 2009 issue of *Asimov's Science Fiction*. He refers to the story:

> "We've hooked up some machinery," says Tommy, "that amounts to a mechanical translator." After some plausible-sounding engineering talk about frequency modulation and short-wave beams, Tommy goes on to tell his captain, "We've agreed on arbitrary symbols for objects, sir, and worked out relationships and verbs and so on with diagrams and pictures. We've a couple of thousand words that have mutual meanings. We set up an analyzer to sort out their short-wave groups, which we feed into a decoding machine. And then the coding end of the machine picks out recordings to make the wave groups we want to send back. When you're ready to talk to the skipper of the other ship, sir, I think we're ready."

Silverberg goes on, "If this is not the first use in science fiction of that handy gadget, the electronic translating machine, it is certainly one of the earliest and best. From then on, spacefarers voyaging into alien territory in the pages of magazines like *Astounding* and *Galaxy* routinely uncorked their translating machines as needed, thus allowing them to get on to their interstellar tasks and the authors to get on to their story's plot requirements.... All very convenient for us writers."

The story line was part of a general move to more psychological themes in science fiction, and not only has "First Contact" been reprinted innumerable times, but it launched a subgenre of first contact stories of its own.

Twenty years later after the story's initial publication, Will reported an amusing anecdote in a letter to Jo-an on January 9, 1963:

> Arthur C. Clarke — you know his stuff — in a hospital in Australia, had somebody from the Russian Embassy bring him some Russian science fiction to read. One book was by Ivan Yefrimov titled, "The Heart of the Serpent." It's a future story of space travelers who detect the ship of an alien intelligent race coming toward them. What do they do? They read and discuss by name Murray Leinster's "First Contact." But they decide there is no danger, because a race capable of space travel must have developed an ideal Communist state and so must be peace-loving and amiable persons eager to be true friends!

A posthumous Retro Hugo for 1946 was awarded to "First Contact" for Best Novelette at the World Science Fiction Convention held in Los Angeles, August 30 to September 2, 1996. "The Ethical Equation" was nominated for Best Short Story on that occasion. Will's daughter Betty DeHardit and granddaughter Beth DeHardit were there to accept the award for him.

The practice of awarding Retro Hugos was started in 1996 to honor people and works that would have been eligible fifty years before a current World Science Fiction Convention. No Hugos were awarded at the World Science Fiction Convention in 1946, as they were not instituted until 1953. Retro Hugos have been awarded only three times, in 1996, in 2001, and in 2004.

The year after "First Contact," *Astounding Science-Fiction* published another groundbreaking story — one whose startling inventiveness would not be clear for more than fifty years. It was "A Logic Named Joe" (Appendix A), first published in the March 1946 issue of *Astounding Science-Fiction*.

That issue already included a Leinster story, "The Adapter," so it appeared in the back of the magazine under "Will F. Jenkins." Readers, recognizing it as exceptional, rated it number one for that issue, ahead of longer stories written by well-known science fiction authors, including Will himself. In the following years, it was reprinted in a number of magazines, anthologies and adapted for radio. It is generally accepted as the first home computer story.

In *Isaac Asimov Presents the Best Science Fiction Firsts* (Beauford Books, 1984), Asimov says the story was "written in a time when the first computer was just coming into being, a truly prophetic piece of speculation."

15 —Shut down the Tank?

Does it occur to you that the Tank has been doin' all the computing for every business office for years, has been handling the distribution of ninety-four percent of all telecast programs, has given out all information on weather, plane-schedules, and special sales, employment opportunities, news, person-to-person contacts over wire and every damned business conversation and agreement.... Listen, fella, Logics changed civilization! If we shut off Logics, we go right back to a kinda civilization we have forgotten how to run! I'm gettin' hysterical myself, fella, that's why I'm talking like this! If my wife finds my pay-check is thirty more credits a week than she knows about and starts hunting for that red-head-."

He smiles a mirthless, haggard smile at me and snaps off. And I sit down and put my head in my hands. It's true. If somethin' had happened back in cave days an' they'd hadda stop usin' fire; - if they'd hadda stop usin' steam back in the nineteenth century or electricity in the twentieth.... It's like that. We'd got to the point where we'd kinda passed the peak of complication. Back in the nineteen hundreds a fella'd have a separate typewriter, telephone, radio, television, teletypewriter, newspaper, reference encyclopaedias, office-files, directories, library, messenger services and consulting lawyers, chemists, physicists, dieticians, filing-clerks, secretaries, an' Gawd knows what all, --all to put down stuff he wanted to remember an' tell him what other people had put down that he wanted to know, an' to tell what he said to somebody else an' tell him what they said back. That was complicated. Now We had Logics. Logics did all those things. Just a simple gadget with keys an' a vision-screen, hooked into a Tank that was hooked into all the other Tanks all over. Anything we wanted to know or

Page from the original manuscript of "A Logic Named Joe" with line "logics changed civilization."

5

kiddies will be askin' detailed questions about the facts of life an' getting their dope ~~fkak in a strictly factual fashion from the Tank,~~ --which is accurate but not ~~exactly~~ spiritual.

This fella punches, "How Can I get rid of my wife?" Just for a gag. The screen is blank for half a second. Then comes a flash; "Service question: Is she blonde or brunette?" He hollers to us, an' we come look. He punches, "Blonde." There's another brief pause. Then the screen says; "Hexymetacryloaminoacetine is a constituent of green shoe-polish. Take home a meal ~~sExtakxinx~~ including dried-pea soup. Color the soup with green shoe-polish. It will appear to be green-pea soup. Hexymetacryloaminoacetine is a selective poison which is fatal to blonde females but not to brunettes or to males of any coloring. This fact has not been brought out as yet by human experiment, but is a product of Logics service. You cannot be convicted of murder. It is improbable you will be suspected."

The screen goes blank, and we stare at each other. Its bound to be right. A Logic workin' the Carson circuit can no more make a mistake than any other kinda computin' machine. I call the Tank in a hurry.

"Hey, you guys!" I yell. "Somethin's happened! Logics are givin' detailed instructions for wife-murder! Check your censor-circuits -but quick!"

~~I snap off an'~~ wipe my ~~fxxkkxxfx~~ perspirin' brow. That was close. But little do I know! At that precise instant a drunk over on Monroe Avenue starts mournful to punch for somethin'x on a Logic. The screen says "Announcing New and Improved Logics Service!....If you want to do something and don't know how to do it, -ask your Logic!" And the drunk says, owlish, "Migawd! ~~An' I got troubles!~~

Page from original manuscript of "A Logic Named Joe" with paragraph on logics giving potentially harmful information.

Seven • The New York Years: The 1940s 99

In the story, the protagonist explains how Joe works:

You know the Logics set-up. You got a Logic in your house. It looks like a vision-receiver used to, only its got keys instead of dials and you punch the keys for what you wanna get. It's hooked in to the Tank, which has the Carson Circuit all fixed up with relays. Say you punch "Station SNAFU" on your Logic. Relays in the Tank take over an' whatever vision program SNAFU is telecastin' comes on your Logic's screen. Or you punch "Sally Hancock's Phone" an' the screen blinks an' sputters an' you're hooked up with the Logic in her house an' if someone answers you got a vision-phone connection. But besides that, if you punch for the weather forecast or who won today's race at Hialeah or who was mistress of the White House durin' Garfield's administration or what is PDQ and R sellin' for today, that comes on the screen too. The relays in the Tank do it. The Tank is a big buildin' full of all the facts in creation and all the recorded telecasts that ever was made — an' it's hooked in with all the other Tanks all over the country — an' everything you wanna know or see or hear, you punch for it an' you get it. Very convenient."

Joe Rico says of the story:

No discussion of Murray Leinster's contribution to the SF field is complete without touching on "A Logic Named Joe."

Many people wrongly believe that Science Fiction's main purpose is to predict the future. Still it is wonderful to find an example of an accurate prediction, especially one that was so uncannily accurate. At a time in which the world had about 10 electronic computers, he wrote a story about a future in which every household has a personal computer and is connected to an internet-like system. If this story had been written in 1956, 1966 or 1976 it would have been known as the most predictive story in the genre, but it was written in 1946!

David Ferro and Eric Swedin, of Weber State University in Utah, discuss "A Logic Named Joe" in their article "Towards Investigating the Importance of Science Fiction in the Historical Development of Computing." The article begins:

With notable exceptions the bulk of science fiction (SF) missed the possibilities of some of the most innovative and influential technologies of the 20th century. These innovations include personal computers, networks, the internet and world wide web, and online resources. This paper surveys some of that literature, especially a noteworthy exception — "A Logic Named Joe" — to kick-off the discussion of techno-scientific development and, more specifically, computer development.

Despite the stereotype that "Science Fiction imagines and science makes it so," for a long time SF was thought not to have predicted the rise of technologies like the internet, world wide web, and personal computers. SF published and filmed in the first ⅔ of the twentieth century continually had larger machines and/or more powerful robots that acted as intelligent agents....

"A Logic Named Joe" in many ways predicted the rise of the internet, personal computers, and the convergence of interactive computing, television, and telephony. Like many stories it plays with the idea of a "naturally occurring" sentient mechanism — in other words, the machine just somehow "woke up a bit more" when it was created. The difference is the almost prosaic presentation of the machine as a networked appliance. The protagonist himself is portrayed as an "average Joe" computer technician who has a first-person style that evokes a 1940s plumber....

The creativity and prescience displayed in the creation of this story is astounding. In 1946, the public might have known of one electronic computer: the ENIAC. It was the size of a room. An army of women who flipped thousands of switches handled the input of the machine. Its output was hundreds of blinking lights on its front panels. Among many other things, Leinster saw instead an easy-to-use keyboard and screen interface on a machine the size of a breadbox linked to millions of other similar machines. A computer that size would not exist until the 1970s. The internet would not exist until 1969, the world wide web, not until the 1980s, and the combination would not become commonplace until the 1990s....

Our question is: did such a forward-looking story actually affect those developments?

Drs. Ferro and Swedin studied the William F. Jenkins papers at the Syracuse University Special Collections Research Center where they are deposited. They said they found no direct correspondence linking those developing computer technologies with this or any other stories. But they found "a continuing effort on the part of Jenkins and other authors to maintain science and scientific veracity and uphold those ideas in the fictional form they termed SF," and additionally found "evidence of the interaction and mutual support between scientific and SF worlds."

Ferro and Swedin's work highlights this connection to the computer world. They point out that, in that world, servers are named for characters and locations in SF novels and movies, and SF language is used in technical conversations. Many scientists have credited SF with their career choices. They quote SF writer and editor Ben Bova as saying "everyone who landed on the moon read science fiction."

When thinking about computers and artificial intelligence, one can't help but wonder about the possibility of replicating the human brain. W. Daniel Hillis is one of several who pursued this goal. He even founded a company called Thinking Machines Corporation in 1982 and developed powerful parallel computing systems. It went out of business in 1994, and its hardware and parallel computer division were acquired by Sun Microsystems.

Jeff Hawkins, who created the Palm Pilot and the Treo, has developed software that more closely works like the human brain. In 2004, he wrote a book, *On Intelligence*, outlining his theories and in 2005, along with Donna Dubinsky and Dileep George, founded Numenta, an artificial intelligence program based on those theories. Hawkins has been quoted as saying, "When you are born, you know nothing."

Will made a similar statement, "A baby starts out with a mind that is blank of information and ideas," when he began to record his exploration into the subject. In 1954, eight years after the publication of "A Logic Named Joe," Will wrote an article, "To Build a Robot Brain" (Appendix B), which was printed in the April 1954 issue of *Astounding*. It was undoubtedly one result of his many luncheon discussions with John Campbell, an obvious next step in their scientific and philosophical discussions following the publication of "A Logic Named Joe."

Will's thesis was similar to Hawkins'. Babies develop their human brains by assimilating data fed to them through their senses. Will a computer develop a near-human brain if you continually feed it data?

Will begins by saying, "The technician will use the tools and assemble the parts. Before that the physicist-engineer will design the parts. But even before that, the philosopher has to design the concept!" He introduces the possibility that a computer may — or may not — suddenly become sentient. He starts by saying that the story of Casey and the suddenly speaking computer is an "honest-to-Hannah" true one.

Rear Admiral Grace Hopper is credited with telling Will about the humorous incident in the early 1950s. She was working as a programmer for Univac at the time and was already a legend in the computer community. Will was writing a script for a television interview with her.

She was a mathematics teacher at Vassar in 1943 when she joined the Naval Reserve and was quickly put to work on projects for the Mark series of computers. Soon she became a leader in computer software development and began working toward her goal of making computer programming more user-friendly. She developed the compiler to that end.

An article in *Time* magazine (April 16, 1984), credits Admiral Hopper with spreading the practice of saying "there's a bug in it" when there is a computer glitch. When she was at Harvard in 1945, a two-inch moth was actually pulled out of the computer she was working on. She has been called "Amazing Grace" because of her astonishing achievements. She retired with the rank of rear admiral at the age of 80.

Will said this experience with Admiral Hopper gave him the idea of writing a popular book on computers, one that would be anecdotal and directed to a general audience rather than engineers. He tried to interest publishers but was unsuccessful. However, it also gave him a good lead-in for this article.

"To Build a Robot Brain" starts with Casey reading a comic book while he sits alone at night in a huge building minding a massive, early 1950s computer. Suddenly:

> Against all precedent, the electric output typewriter was clicking furiously before the problem was solved. A loudspeaker made a din. The thinking machine was working the typewriter and had turned on the loudspeaker alarm to call Casey on the run. He got to the typewriter in a hurry. Its keys still clicked. They stopped indignantly, as he read:
> "*Casey, you blank-blanked-son-of a so-and so, you forgot to change the spool to Number Two.*"
> Casey's hair stood on end, and he wanted to run. He thought for a moment that the machine had come alive on him and was bawling him out.
> Two seconds later he was hopping mad, of course. As soon as he thought, he knew what had happened. The man who'd prepared the two spools of tape had known Casey would run the problem through. So, at the end of the first tape, he'd zestfully included instructions for the machine to blast the loudspeaker and type that abuse to Casey, before the normal signal for change-of-spools came on. When those instructions-on-tape took effect, Casey's tranquil ease was shattered.

Will suggests one answer to the question of how to build a human brain that is neither conclusively science or fiction, but one that reflects his own background and history: "You learned it in Sunday School."

Will appeared in *Astounding* seventeen times during the 1950s. He and John Campbell continued to meet regularly, and undoubtedly many ideas for stories were exchanged. Campbell presented one in a letter to Will on August 25, 1952 (Perry A. Chapdelaine, Sr., collection, *The John W. Campbell Letters, Vol. I*).

> Dear Will,
>
> I've got an idea that would, I think, make a lovely story. The only trouble is that it takes an extremely deft touch to handle the thing. Maybe you'd like to play with it, and I hoped you would. You're the only one I know of who could do it; as I see it, it would be somewhat similar, in tenor and mood, to that "Historical Note" [*Astounding*, February, 1951] item you did. The idea, essentially, would be this: Nature will, you know, answer any questions anyone asks. Nature has no race, political, or religious biases, so far as anyone has detected to date. Further, nature invariably answers the question correctly.
>
> Now let's imagine that Nature can be communicated with directly. For our story, we have a nature talker machine invented, whereby a direct wire to Nature can be set up. Only we won't refer to Nature as such.
>
> You teletype into the machine any questions, any problems, and immediately get the answer. Naturally, military defense takes over the teletyper. There is a certain amount of confusion, because the answer is always exactly correct for exactly the question you ask, but you may be asking a question other than the one you think you are. For instance, if a chemist in the old days has asked something about "phlogiston" he'd have gotten the correct answer to what he actually meant, which wouldn't have been what he thought he was getting. In other

Seven • *The New York Years: The 1940s*   103

words, the only limitation on the teletype is that you must know exactly what you are asking. Some limitation is clearly necessary, or the story goes haywire.

The essence of the thing is that, naturally, the Russians get plans of the machine, and they, too, start asking questions. Nature had to be taught to answer questions in English, of course; somebody suddenly discovers that nature talks Russian, now, too.

The repercussions of Security are wonderful at that point naturally.

But then Nature responds with a neat detail of how-to-do-it with some remark that "as tried out at Borschtograd" and given freely without stint of Russia's most secret work. Nature's most useful as a computing machine, outstripping the best electronic devices by six orders of magnitude, everybody's feeding their secret weapons figures into the teletypers for answers.

I think it would be rather wonderful the way Security tempers would rise. The howls of anguish when it was discovered that Nature couldn't keep a secret. Tsk, Tsk. Ain't it awful.

I think we could have fun and hilarity with this item. The teletyper is, of course, the poor physical scientist. But in this guise the problem of what to do about science would suddenly loom somewhat different.

Regards, John

Will, with his fascination with gadgets and extensive scientific reading, wrote fictional descriptions of a number of other inventions, which became desirable or achievable only much later. Will describes a power-generating space station in a very early story, "Power Planet," which appeared in the January 1931 edition of *Amazing Stories*.

Robert Silverberg points out that the idea of beaming electricity down to Earth from satellites is getting major attention today. He quotes a report made by the Pentagon in October 2007 in his column "Reflections" in *Asimov's Science Fiction Magazine*, published in August 2010. It said that it would provide "affordable, clean, safe, reliable, sustainable, and expandable energy for mankind." Silverberg adds, "the history of the power-satellite theme in science fiction goes back much farther than that — to 1931, astonishingly, and Murray Leinster's novelette 'Power Planet.'" Silverberg continues:

> "Power Planet" appeared in the January 1931 issue of the pioneering SF magazine *Amazing Stories*. The magazine science fiction of that era was mostly pretty creaky work, but "Power Planet," despite some crude pulp touches, remains surprisingly readable today. It presents us with fiction's first power-generating space station:
>
> "The Power Planet, of course," Leinster writes, "is that vast man-made disk of metal set spinning about the sun to supply the Earth with power. Everybody learns in his grammar-school textbooks of its construction just beyond the Moon and of its maneuvering to its present orbit by a vast expenditure of rocket fuel. Only forty million miles from the sun's surface, its sunward side is raised nearly to red heat by the blazing radiation. And the shadow side, naturally, is down to the utter cold of space. There is a temperature drop of nearly seven hundred degrees between the two sides, and Williamson cells turn that heat-difference

into electric current, with an efficiency of 99 percent. Then the big Dugald tubes — they are twenty feet long on the Power Planet — transform it into the beam which is focused always on the Earth and delivers something over a billion horsepower to the various receivers that have been erected. The space station itself is ten miles across, and it rotates at a carefully calculated speed so that the centrifugal force at its outer edge is very nearly equal to the normal gravity of Earth. So that the nearer its center one goes, of course, the less is that force, and also the less impression of weight one has."

This is astonishing stuff for 1931. Where did Leinster/Jenkins get the idea?

In "The Wabbler," Will's first story for John Campbell, (*Astounding Science-Fiction*, October 1942), Will described an autonomous underwater robot, which is now in development by a research center for artificial intelligence. The concept has been explored for everything from NASA–funded research on techniques to explore the ice covered liquid water oceans on Europa, the fifth moon of Jupiter, to develop self-propelled gliders that could be used for long-distance scientific missions, and to expand the realm of possibilities for studies of the oceans.

In *The Murder of the U.S.A.*, mentioned earlier, Will describes a nuclear attack on the U.S., the Cold War, missiles in their silos, the belts of radar warning and the anti-missile-to-missile problems.

Later, in *Space Tug*, published by Shasta, 1953, he dreamed up gravity-simulator harnesses, inflatable air locks, magnetic-soled shoes (required for space walks), spaceship ejector seats, and spaceflight simulators in a story about the problems of running a space station.

In describing a gravity-simulator harness, Will wrote:

> "When we got back," Joe told Brown, "we were practically invalids. No exercise up here. This time we've brought some harness to wear. We've some for you, too..." Joe got out the gravity-simulator harnesses. He showed Brent how they worked. Brown hadn't official instructions to order their use, but Joe put one on himself, set for full Earth-gravity simulation.
>
> He couldn't imitate actual gravity, of course. Only the effect of gravity on one's muscles. There were springs and elastic webbing pulling one's shoulders and feet together, so that it was as much effort to stand extended — with one's legs straight out — as to stand upright on Earth. Joe felt better with a pull on his body.

NASA has now developed an orbital exercise machine designed to keep astronauts in shape. It is called the Combined Operational Load Bearing External Resistance Treadmill, or COLBERT, and was named after comedian Stephen Colbert. When NASA organized an online poll soliciting names for Node 3 of the International Space Station, Colbert's many fans won the privilege for him but, after much discussion, it was decided to name the treadmill after him instead. The node is called Tranquility after the Sea of Tranquility, where Apollo 11 landed on the moon, more in keeping with names of other nodes, Unity and Harmony. In spite of the original concern over the appropriateness of the name, NASA felt the campaign was successful in that it generated welcome attention for the oft-forgotten International Space Station.

Colbert's fans are known for their activity in trying to get his name in prominent places. He came in first in a 2006 bridge-naming contest in Hungary. The country's government later said it "cannot name the bridge after the comedian because he does not speak Hungarian and is not dead." This is the kind of story that would hugely amuse Will, and he would have repeated it endlessly.

Thrilling Wonder Stories became another regular market for Murray Leinster stories after they printed "The Eternal Now" in the fall 1944 issue. It was the new name for *Wonder Stories* after Hugo Gernsback sold it to *Standard Magazines* in 1936. Will developed a long relationship with Leo Margulies, when he was editor, and later with Oscar Friend and Sam Merwin, Jr., when *Startling Stories* came on board in 1939. Oscar Friend was Will's agent for a while.

The June 1947 issue of *Thrilling Wonder Stories* included three stories by Will, each under a different name. *The Boomerang Circuit*, listed as a novel by Murray Leinster, and "The Nameless Something" under the name William Fitzgerald were featured on the cover. A short story by Will F. Jenkins, "From Beyond the Stars," was inside.

Will was popular with the magazine's fans. The same issue's letters to the editor section had several comments on the previously published story "The Manless Worlds": "Some of your readers enjoy fantasy — as for me give me SF (and Murray Leinster). "'Manless Worlds,' good SF story with many twists." "'Manless Worlds'— Wonderful." "I was delighted to see 'The Manless Worlds.' I have been gnawing my fingernails waiting for a sequel to 'The Disciplinary Circuit.'"

On the other hand, one reader wrote, "Give Murray a sharp rap across the knuckles and let him try again."

Will discusses two of the stories in the magazine's The Story Behind the Story section in *Thrilling Wonder Stories*.

As Murray Leinster, he writes about *The Boomerang Circuit*, last in the Kim Rendell trilogy.

> In this novelette like the other two ("The Disciplinary Circuit" and "The Manless Worlds"), I was trying to work out the consequences of a mechanical means of Government. It would, uncontrolled, lead to war. But the whole progress of civilization has been a succession of tamings of previously dangerous things. Wild animals and fire were the first two conquests. We have in the

immediate future the need to tame the fissionable nuclei of various explodable elements. But there is a bigger job still. To tame machines.

In the three novelettes I've been talking about a machine which takes over most of the functions of government and practically all of its coercive or executive functions. Such a machine, without controls, would be just as dangerous as a chain reaction. That, I tried to make clear.

In this story, to me the most important event is the dropping of those little cases of apparatus on the worlds that tried to wipe out Ades — and, of course, the arrangement that they shall become articles of commerce. They will leave the governments of their worlds with full power to deal with individual criminals, but no power to oppress groups. Full authority for government, but none for oppression.

That limitation not only will be needed in the future, but it's badly needed right now in some parts of the world. Maybe these three novelettes will start somebody thinking.

The trilogy was published in book form as *The Last Spaceship* (Frederick Fell, NY, 1949). He writes about *The Nameless Something* under the name "William Fitzgerald."

> Bud Gregory fascinates me. Somewhere there's somebody like him in some fashion or another. I've seen what you might call embryo Bud Gregorys more than once.
>
> I've seen people who could make much better mousetraps than average, and nobody paid attention, much less beat a path to their door. Somewhere, the answer to an awful lot of problems either rest or lie latent in some human skull, and it will be only luck if they're pried out.
>
> The fact is the ability to think and the desire to think and accomplish things are only rarely joined together. Most of us know many people who want very desperately to do great things and simply haven't got the equipment. But some of us, too, know people who have got the equipment and simply don't bother. Their superior equipment simply enables them to loaf more and have a better time generally. There's Bud Gregory, drat him.
>
> I suppose what I have to say about the whole thing is simply, "Do you have a little Bud Gregory in your home?" Somebody has.

Avalon reprinted the story as *Out of This World* in 1957, and Will tells more on the flyleaf. He says he was inspired by an incident he was told about that supposedly happened at the Harvard Mathematics Department. A young farm boy who had no previous training in math, not even high school, rushed in, excited, and said he had discovered something interesting. The professors, not impressed, took a look, and then another. What he had figured out on his own was one of the greatest discoveries in mathematics — logarithms. He was only a hundred years late.

Thrilling Wonder Stories published several more of Will's stories in the 1940s including "The Lonely Planet" and "The Lost Race" (published in book form as *The Duplicators*). Will offered "The Lost Race" for an anthology, *My Best Science Fiction Story*, published by Pocket books in 1954.

In its introduction, "Why I Selected the Lost Race," he said:

> It is merely my favorite story at the moment ... I like it because it gives me a chance to talk about so many of my pet theories, of which one or two may even have some sense to them. A moon-rocket is impractical though not impossible at the moment because the fuel is too cheap, by the pound. The best rocket-fuel we've got hasn't too many times the energy-content of coal, and its value per pound is proportionate. Produce a fuel that is really practical and safe for a space ship, and you'll have a fuel that steamship companies will bid up to almost any price you can name, because with it they can carry cargo in the space now occupied by coal-bunkers and oil-tanks. In terms of light-years of travel, of course, a ship's fuel will be worth more than the ship itself! Which is one of the notions I wanted to play with.
>
> Another is the matter of tedium in space-travel. Human beings being what they are, I think that sheer boredom is going to be the second biggest problem awaiting us in space travel, fuel being the first.

"Dead City" (also known as "The Malignant Marauder") and "De Profundis" were also printed in *Thrilling Wonder Stories*. "De Profundis," printed in 1945, was a special favorite of Will's.

In an article called "Reverie" in *Science Fiction Review*, April 27, 1964, Will said: "I like it because everybody's heard of men seeing sea serpents and telling other men, who don't believe them. "De Profundis" is a story about a sea serpent seeing a man. And he tells the other sea serpents. And they didn't believe him."

Will continued to be published in *Thrilling Wonder Stories* until it shut down in 1954.

Startling Stories, companion magazine to *Thrilling Wonder Stories*, published a number of Leinster stories including the novel *The Man in the Iron Cap* in November 1947 later published in book form as *The Brain Stealers*. *Triple Western*, another of the *Thrilling* group, reprinted *Black Sheep* in April 1948.

Jack McDevitt, 2006 Nebula winner, remembers all those magazines. He says:

> Somewhere in the mid-forties, at about the age of nine, I fell in love with *Thrilling Wonder*, *Astounding*, and *Startling*, with their dazzling covers, their robots clanking off with half-dressed women, and their rocket ships. Most of all, the rocket ships. Will Jenkins rode one all his life. And those of us who were lucky — or smart — enough to tag along, owe him more than we can ever repay. If Flash Gordon — my introduction to science fiction — used his magnificent ships to go after crazed dictators and interplanetary pirates, Will showed us what far traveling was really about.
>
> His work was unlike anything I'd seen before. I'm not sure that "First Contact"

was my earliest science fiction story, but it's the first one that stayed with me. That kept me up at night. I read it, and wondered why they couldn't find stories like that to assign in school. And I was never the same. In "A Logic Named Joe," I had my first encounter with a machine that seemed able to think. Was such a thing possible? He introduced me to time travel, and managed it like nobody else. He made me realize, e.g., that a person who travels into the past need never die, because he can always go back and rescue himself.

He scared the devil out of me with his jungle ants. He took me on my first visit to alternate worlds. He demonstrated that life was much more complicated than I'd been led to believe. He opened doors that I hadn't realized were shut.

I grew up in South Philadelphia. And I suspect that without him, and his colleagues, I might never have seen what lay beyond the rooftops.

Thank you, Will.

Will knew and respected many of the then current science fiction writers and editors, although few found their way out to his apartment in Beechhurst, Queens. (Rogers Terrill and his wife told of a particularly harrowing trip home from a dinner party at Will and Mary's involving subway accidents, unspeakable coffee stops and a 3 A.M. arrival home.)

One who did make it several times was Ted Sturgeon. His first story in *Astounding* was published in 1939, and he was a fan of Will's. Will talked to him about writing, giving his usual tips and suggestions from his own experience. The girls were never banished from adult conversations, and Billee was fascinated by Sturgeon's accounts of his life in the Merchant Marine. She was particularly interested in the conversations when he discussed his ideas for "The Chromium Helmet," published in *Astounding* in June 1946. In it, engineer Godfrey's daughter has the answer to the reason she and his wife and sister all believe so strongly in wishes that couldn't be true, but he keeps ignoring her. When Billee had her own children, she remembered what she had learned from that story and tried to listen very carefully to what her children told her.

Once Sturgeon brought over a handful of dough-like material and explained that General Electric had developed it as a possible synthetic rubber, and now no one knew what to use it for. You could squeeze it and make shapes, pull it out, and bounce it on a hard surface. Will reeled off a bunch of possible uses, but it was so much fun no one singled out a practical one. In 1960, someone thought to name it Silly Putty, put it in a plastic egg, sold it as a toy, and made millions.

For Will, one of the milestones that gave him the most pleasure was bringing science fiction to the slick magazines under his own name. "Symbiosis," printed in *Collier's,* June 14, 1947, was a story of a particularly devious and sophisticated form of biological warfare. In "Doomsday Deferred," which appeared in the *Saturday Evening Post,* September 24, 1949, we meet the Soldado Ant and wish we hadn't.

Seven • The New York Years: The 1940s

Later, Robert A. Heinlein, writing in *Writing Science Fiction and Fantasy* (page 6, St. Martin's Press, 1991) quoted Will as saying, "Bob, I'll let you in on a secret. Any story — science fiction or otherwise — if well written, can be sold to the slicks." Whether this was an influence or not, when Heinlein turned his concentration to the slicks, his career took off.

With his sense of fun, Will came up with an idea specifically addressed to fans and their magazines. It was printed in *The Fanscient*, issue number 7, Spring 1949, under the section "Author, Author."

> [I am going] to spend the rest of what space is allotted to me urging a stunt I think fans and fan magazines could do for fun and the greater good of science-fiction [*sic*]....
>
> I may have turned out as many as six honest-to-god good yarns in my life. Some people may cut it down to four, but I hope it is six....
>
> Most writers of science-fiction don't write anything else. I do. I had pretty well established markets for other types of fiction before I did "The Runaway Skyscraper" for *Argosy*, around 1918–19. I had always been a fan, but I was afraid I couldn't do it myself. I got away with that, and have been writing science-fiction every since. I am an incurable gadgeteer, and I like enormously to set up a theory and then track down the consequences. The result is the type of story that fans have read under the Murray Leinster signature.
>
> That trick of theorizing and then trying to see what the theory implies is responsible for nearly all my science-fiction. I think that "Sidewise in Time" was the first of the parallel-time-track-yarns to see print. I am inclined to take credit for another genre of "Proxima Centauri," which I think was the progenitor. I think that in "The Morrison Monument" I wrote the time-travel story which should have ended all time-travel stories, but didn't, and I think but am not sure — that in "Symbiosis" in Collier's, (a Will Jenkins yarn) that I did the first biological warfare yarn. But such matters are only curiosities.
>
> Science-fiction, however, is more than a curiosity. I believe that it contributes definitely, if indirectly, to the progress of science and the pattern of the future. There is a good deal of evidence that it presaged, if it did not traceably produce, the devices and happenings of the present. In my own yarns, for instance I find that in "Terror Above" in *Collier's*, was explained the necessity for giant bombing planes and the theoretical advantages of blockbusters, years before either were produced. In a yarn called "Morale," the tank-plane combination, which made the German Blitz in World War II, appeared in detail. In the same yarn, the LST was plainly prefigured. In "Preview of Tomorrow," in *Coronet*, I actually happened to describe with some particularity a supersonic rocket-plane and the ending of the war with an atomic explosion in Japan.
>
> I could extend that list from my own work. Taking in other writers' stories, I could carry it on indefinitely. As far as I know, there is only one modern device of great importance which was not old stuff to science-fiction readers when it was first described as working. The exception was the electron microscope, and I think it's an exception solely because it doesn't lend itself to fictional use. And there is my point for this article.
>
> Right now, the prophecies in which we science-fiction addicts take such pride are made only by people who can both dream up gadgets and write readable

fiction. They could write pseudo-factual articles which would be fascinating, but there is nowhere where such article would be welcomed.

That's where I think the fans and fan magazines could come up with a contribution to the future. Why shouldn't there be pseudo-technical as well as fictional data on the future? Kiplings' accompanying magazine departments and advertisements to "With the Night Mail" are a perfect example of what I have in mind. Commercial magazines won't touch the stuff. There's no regular source for it but fan magazines could develop it. Read Kipling's stuff and you'll see what can be done. A fan magazine could duplicate — save for gossip columns, for example — an issue of *Spaceways* for 1987, and might feature besides its advertisements, an article like "So You're Going to Mars" which could be a chatty, non-technical account of space-ship routine as a passenger sees it, with advice on etiquette, space-sickness, the spaceport regulations and so on. There should be an article on Mercutian artifacts from the twilight zone, a blistering discussion of IPC rulings on salvage, perhaps some vox-pop letters, and that sort of thing. The advertisements should be good sport, too. Just how would the rest resorts in the Halmas — "The only hills on Mars!" — push their wares? And how would the space suit makers — for private space-yachts mostly — describe their competitive features? What would they be advertising that simply doesn't make sense to us now? Your grandfather, if he'd seen only fifty years ago the regulation advertisements of a television set, neatly equipped with what he'd think was a framed picture, simply couldn't make head or tail of the advertisement. Radio would not mean a thing. He wouldn't believe in a dishwasher ad and a "deep-freeze" would be quite cryptic.

A single issue like that ought to be fun. But what might be called a pre-print policy needn't go that far. A pre-print of a travel article, "The Cities of Titan" from *Holiday* of July 2042 would be all right as a feature in itself. *The National Astrographic Magazine* should have some swell stuff — nonfiction — in almost any edition from 2021 on. And if space could be found for book reviews, one would like to get a look at "Modern Tube-Room Practice" even in a review, with comments (the book will be published by Spaceways Publishers, Venus City, 2038. Cr 2.50 post-paid to Earth) on the newest dodges in emergency insulation for the high voltages they will be using and what to do when your fuel polymerizes ... and even the digest magazines ought to yield some good stuff, too. I heroically refrain from suggesting that pre-prints from a digest magazine would be predigested. But most readers would like to see at least extracts from "Space Drives and the Limit of Speed," the classic by Titlow. And by all means, that misprint in the third chapter, which instantly gave Faussin the germ of the first working faster-than-light drive, should be included.

Do you see? Kipling had a good trick in "With the Night Mail," and it's time it was used again. Fan magazines could do it. And it wouldn't necessarily be only a stunt. John Campbell, Bob Heinlein, Isaac Asimov and some others may not go into details, but they'll assure you as I do, that not all dream gadgets of science-fiction have stayed dreams.

For the hell of it and as a completely possible contribution to the pattern of the future, won't somebody try this trick?

Please!

Will F. Jenkins

Seven • The New York Years: The 1940s

Throughout the 1940s, Will and his family remained in New York, except for summer visits to Gloucester beginning after the war. Although the Beechhurst apartment was kept for more than 25 years, Will's heart remained firmly in Virginia. The tales he spun for his smallest daughter, Jo-an — who barely remembered living anywhere other than New York — were so magical that, throughout her childhood, she imagined that her real home was not this small apartment in suburban New York, but her father's dream house in the idyllic south. She painstakingly scrawled "Clay Bank, Gloucester, Virginia," in all of her schoolbooks.

When the war ended in 1945, Mary was not eager to give up her busy New York life to return to the seclusion of rural Virginia, except for short visits. With the girls settled — Mary by then working in Boston, Betty commuting to college on Long Island, Billee away at college in Virginia, Jo-an in the local school — it was easiest to remain where they were. Another factor was that the Clay Bank house and grounds, first rented during the war to careless service people and then left vacant, needed extensive cleaning and repairing before a permanent return. So they stayed on.

For Mary, New York was a return to her home — near two of her sisters, Rose and Julia, just over the George Washington Bridge in New Jersey, and to her brother, John, a real estate broker, even closer in Brooklyn. Mary loved the freedom of being in the city, close to new friends, shops and department stores, all easily reachable by foot or bus (she didn't drive). She volunteered at Jo-an's school, helped at their fairs, and made aprons and other items for church sales, activities previously not available to her with home-schooled children and no nearby church in rural Virginia. An auction house in Flushing was a treasured discovery, and the apartment was furnished with her finds, including a huge breakfront, a player baby grand piano (on which Jo-an took lessons), and an old trunk, bought for just a dollar, which, when unlocked, was filled with beautiful dresses from the early part of the 20th century. Although this was a big change from Clay Bank, where there was little outside the house to divert her attention from Will, he gave her his complete support and enjoyed admiring her auction acquisitions.

However, when Mary proposed buying a house in Beechhurst, a sensible financial move, Will was deeply upset at the idea that they might commit themselves to live for any length of time anywhere other than his beloved Virginia and refused to even consider the idea.

Close, lifelong friends were made in Beechhurst, most especially the Fexas family. Achilles "Chick" Fexas had emigrated from Greece as a very young boy. Now an optometrist, he wore a bushy black moustache, a visible display of his Greek heritage. His laborious stutter did not obscure his keen

Betty, Mary, and Will in the Beechhurst Apartment with Jo-an playing on the floor.

mind, and Will shared his deep interest in theology and philosophy with Chick, and involved him as a partner in some of his tinkering projects. One of Will's ideas was for improving contact lenses. There was a problem then with the eye drying out under the lens. Will thought, if tiny holes were bored in the lens, the tears could circulate and the problem would be solved. He and Chick spent hours in the tiny apartment breakfast room calling in members of the family from time to time, so they could insert lenses in their eyes and test the theory.

Chick's petite wife, Antonia "Toni," was also an asset to conversations. Her father had been editor of a Greek language newspaper, and she had grown up in intellectual company. The Fexas family had a Chris Craft powerboat they kept in Northport, Long Island, and the Jenkins family spent many happy days with them touring the Long Island Sound. Will commented that he never had a boat on the York River in Virginia, because he would have to have one big enough to have his typewriter aboard, and then he would have

Seven • *The New York Years: The 1940s*

spent his time writing, not enjoying the water. Tom Fexas, Chick and Toni's son who was Jo-an's age, carried his boating heritage to a brilliant international career as a naval architect. Younger daughter Penny married a doctor, Luis Casas, and as Penelope Casas, became a well-known writer of Spanish cookbooks.

There were difficult times during these New York years when first Mary, Will and Mary's eldest daughter, and later their third daughter, Billee, made their inevitable bids for independence. In 1943, Mary junior graduated from Mt. Holyoke College in Massachusetts, and Will was devastated when she decided to take a job in Boston instead of coming home to live. Two years later, Mary brought a suitor home, Vahan "Danny" Daniels, and, although he did not pass inspection with her father, married him and settled in Boston permanently. She was 23 years old. And then, in June 1946, just after her 18th birthday and third year in college, Billee eloped with her soldier boyfriend, Peyton "Pete" Stallings, when he came home from Germany.

Will, in particular, found these events deeply painful. The breakup of his own family in his early teens and the shifts and changes that followed had left deep scars. He had invested so much emotion in his daughters that what in most families is an expected and normal transition was to him a deep and searing loss. In addition, with his chosen lifestyle already threatened by what, in spite of 15 years in New York, he considered a temporary relocation, he saw the destruction of his close sheltered family group.

John Clute, in discussing Will's science fiction, saw this in Will's work where he depicted "a prewar America somewhat idealized after the fact of the slick journals for which Leinster also wrote copiously. At the heart of his work, as befits the creator of so stable a universe, lies a clear and probably personal horror of metamorphosis, of change" (*Science Fiction Writers: Critical Studies of the Major Authors from the Early Nineteenth Century to the Present Day*, Everett Franklin Bleiler, ed., New York: Charles Scribner's Sons, 1982.)

Many years later, after his granddaughter Pam Stallings' 1968 wedding to Clifford Hayes, Will showed Jo-an a photograph of Pam's father Pete at the door of the church, waiting to escort the bride down the aisle. "This is the saddest picture I've ever seen," he said, looking at it mournfully and shaking his head in regret. Asked to explain, he answered: "This is a picture of a father losing his daughter."

Will and Mary later bitterly condemned sending one's children away from home to college, saying it caused you to lose them.

One daughter did stay at home. After graduating from Adelphi College on Long Island in 1947, Betty took a job in New York City and lived with her parents in Beechhurst. She became a close companion to her mother, driving her to the shopping strips now springing up on Long Island and taking her little sister Jo-an to ballet and little-theater lessons at the Adelphi College Children's Theater.

For Will, having a young child growing up in the house again was a real pleasure. A young man, Phil Merwin, who had been a boyhood fan in Beechhurst, shared this memory in a letter of sympathy after Will's death. "[I remember] ... your father was lying on his back in the living room floor holding Jo-anne [*sic*] up in the air on his legs."

He was the one to walk her to and from school. She accompanied him to editors' meetings and particularly loved going to the Street and Smith and Fawcett offices, because she would come home with a fist full of comic books. There were side excursions to the Natural History Museum on the West Side of New York, and, before she went to sleep, he spun stories for her about his southern childhood and the animals he had had. Soon, she felt she knew Bruno, a black lab type who had come down to Clay Bank after his owner, Mary's father, died in 1931, and the mischievous fox terrier who had been Will's companion when he was a young man. When he finished the night's tale, she fell asleep to the comforting sound of his typewriter tapping away in a room nearby.

Much later he told his granddaughter Gail Stallings, "I love young children, but I'm not very good with teenagers."

The special relationship between the young Jo-an and her father continued. Like Will, she loved books. He introduced her to the *Wizard of Oz* series and his favorite science fiction, and she read each of his stories as the pages came out of the typewriter. At twelve, she wrote a fan letter to Wilmar H. Shiras about her story "In Hiding," saying that her three stories about "the wonder children" were the most interesting she had ever read "except for two of Dad's." A thoughtful reply came back, suggesting a book about intelligent children — "Children Above 180 IQ" by Hollingsworth — which she thought she and her father might enjoy, adding: "My older children like science fiction too, and we have read and enjoyed your father's stories."

Will became more involved in his Catholic religion as Jo-an grew up in it, and he made his First Communion and confirmation, formally joining the Catholic Church, at the nearby St. Luke's Church in Whitestone at the same time she did. He became very interested in St. Thomas Aquinas and G. K. Chesterton's writings, and his faith deepened as Jo-an went on to a Catholic high school, Our Lady of Mercy Academy, in Syosset, Long Island, and then to the College of Notre Dame in Baltimore, Maryland.

After the end of World War II, Will was anxious to reclaim at least some of his life in Virginia, despite the ties that held the family to New York, and in the late 1940s the family began an annual summer visit during Jo-an's long school holidays. As always, Will wove a magical story for Jo-an around the long, eight-hour drive to Gloucester, making the final, fifteen minute, eight-mile drive from Gloucester Court House to Clay Bank a time of mounting excitement — each country store with its rusty old gasoline pump, sleepy dogs and straw-hatted attendant, each white painted clapboard house with its open porch, another marker on the way to Ardudwy, Will's own personal paradise.

While Ardudwy, the Clay Bank house, was being cleaned and reopened, the family stayed at the Botetourt Hotel in Gloucester Court House, now owned and run by sisters Hylda and Augusta "Gussie" Lawson, friends since their marriage. Located in the center of the village, the hotel, as Jo-an remembers it, was a rambling, dark green and white painted building with three stories, including the basement that housed the dining room. The big open porches were filled with rocking chairs and swings where all would gather to rock and chat on hot summer nights.

There were opportunities to reconnect with old friends. One was Orlin Tremaine, editor of *Astounding* before John Campbell and now in Virginia editing the *Southerner Magazine*. Tremaine had written a book *Short Story Writing* (Rodale Press, PA, 1949) and asked Will for permission to use one of his stories to be analyzed in a demonstration of how to check for weak spots while writing. He used "Biography" which had appeared in *The Country Gentleman* in October 1942. Tremaine follows the progression of the plot step by step and ends with the warning, "Only one thing remains unchanged by understanding — the hours must still be spent alone with your typewriter, dictionary and aching back!"

During these summers in the late 1940s and early 1950s, Clay Bank became once again the center for family and friends that Will so loved. In the days before television in the rural south, evenings were for visiting. Once it grew dark, car after car would drive up the narrow dirt road, raising clouds of dust, with headlights flashing as they turned into the opening between the tall hedges surrounding the big yard. Sometimes four or five cars would arrive, filled with friends who would laugh and talk far into the night, while Will served the drinks. To the child Jo-an, raised in the confines of the Beechhurst apartment, every night was an adventure. Who would come? Jo-an's memories of those days are golden, a chance to see and enjoy the promised land her father had described to her so often.

Magical, too, the daytime parties when piles of steamed crabs would be piled on trestle tables covered with old newspapers on the front lawn under the tall trees swaying in the breeze from the York River. (On river properties the front is the side facing the water.) Bowls of melted butter and cut up lemons were available for those who wanted them — and sometimes oysters to be opened one by one with a special knife and experienced hands. In those days you could wade out into the warm shallows of the York River off the narrow Clay Bank beach and, feeling in the soft mud with your toes, gather as many oysters as you could find, piling them into buckets to be washed and cleaned before eating. (No more, sadly, as pollution has spoiled this simple pleasure.)

Will adored oysters. Often, with his small daughter Jo-an by his side, he would drive to the oysterman at his York River base and buy shucked oysters by the gallon tin. He would happily eat them raw — proclaiming "it was a brave man who first ate an oyster" — but Mary dipped them in egg and cornmeal and fried them in butter or turned them into chowders and stews.

Always inventing, Will contributed a recipe for frozen oysters to Anne McCaffrey's book *Cooking Out of This World* (Ballantine Books, 1973).

> I'd had a bushel or so of oysters hauled up on the beach for a picnic. There was an unusually cold night. I found some of the oysters frozen and partly opened. I tasted them. Oysters taste best when they are cold. Frozen oysters are as cold as you get. Some people don't like frozen oysters because they are slimy. Frozen oysters have the texture of finely crushed ice.
>
> This may sound absurd, but honestly that picnic was a party! They can be frozen in the freezing compartment of your ice box, and frozen oysters are really something!

During the long hot summers, Will worked mostly on the sun porch on the river side of the house, typing on his specially built, slanted wooden desk, his favorite Wellington pipe always in his mouth. Sheltered by a huge weeping cherry tree and with the wall of windows opened to any breeze from the wide York River, it was the coolest you could get before air conditioning. Even then, Mary scolded him for wearing a long sleeved shirt and tie in the summer's heat. He found old habits hard to change.

It was another ten years before Will's dream of returning almost full time to Clay Bank was fulfilled.

• EIGHT •

The 1950s

By 1950, the science fiction market was beginning to recover from the paper shortages and the other problems of the 1940s. It is true that Street and Smith had folded all its pulp magazines in 1949, but the number of active magazines had grown from a low of eight in 1946 to twenty by 1950. Fred Pohl says in his book *The Way the Future Was* (Ballantine Books, 1978) that there were 36 in the mid-fifties.

An important newcomer was *Galaxy Science Fiction*, launched in 1950 with Horace L. Gold as editor. Before the war, Gold had been an assistant editor at Standard Magazines, reading for their three science fiction magazines *Startling Stories, Thrilling Wonder* and *Captain Future*. A former colleague, Vera Cerutti, now in the New York office of an Italian publishing company, *World Editions,* approached him in 1949 looking for new magazine ideas. Gold suggested a new, more serious science fiction monthly, similar to the new *Magazine of Fantasy & Science Fiction*.

His idea was to publish a quality product that would compete with the slicks in literary merit yet appeal to the present readers of science fiction. He proposed to attract good writers by offering three cents a word instead of the usual one cent. He planned to publish stories that were more focused on sociology, psychology and satire than on technology and pulp adventures.

The first issue appeared in October 1950, and, in March 1951, Gold published "The Other Now," the first of a series of Murray Leinster stories in this more cerebral mood. Always enjoying the challenge of a new kind of story, Will produced a gentle tale of a husband and wife who find themselves in opposing worlds after a fatal car accident — in one, the husband has died and the wife is left bereft; in the other, it is the husband who grieves at his loss. A door between the worlds opens, and they find a way to be together again.

Gold included it in his *Galaxy Reader of Science Fiction 1952,* along with "If You Was a Moklin," published in September 1951. One of Will's favorites, this tale of a planet of creatures who so admired humans that they wanted to become just like them — and did — appeared in three later collections of his stories: *Monsters and Such* (Avon, 1959), *The Best of Murray Leinster* (Corgi, 1976), and *First Contacts, The Essential Murray Leinster* (NEFA, 1998).

Will again extended his range. Barry N. Malzberg, in "The Dean of Gloucester, Virginia" (Prologue, *A Logic Named Joe*, Baen Books, 2005), singles out "The Other Now" and "If You Was a Moklin" as stories that managed in "Gold's sardonic early-fifties Galaxy" to "embrace Gold's grim world-view in a no less sprightly manner than 'First Contact' had embodied Campbell's more positive mien, and there is little doubt that a Jenkins born fifty or seventy years later could have functioned very well on the contemporary edge of contemporary science fiction."

In October 1951, a disagreement with *World Editions* led to the sale of the magazine to its printer, Robert M. Guinn. The new company was named Galaxy Publishing Company.

"Sam, This Is You," is another *Galaxy* story published in May 1955. It was also a favorite of Will's and appeared in the two most recent of the collections above as well as in *Twists in Time* (Avon, 1960). It is a whimsical piece about a man who, to his amazement, is contacted by his future self to warn him of events to come.

Two more Leinster stories appeared in the early sixties, "Doctor to the Stars" in 1961 and "Med Ship Man" in 1963.

Galaxy was successful, and Gold won a Hugo for best magazine in 1953, the first year it was awarded. However, since his service in the war, he had suffered from agoraphobia, and, in an effort to overcome it, began making therapeutic excursions in the city at night. He was in a taxi accident and never fully recovered from his injuries. He began to depend more and more on his wife and his friendship with Frederik Pohl and others for help with his duties. In 1960, it became too much for him, and Pohl was hired as editor, a position he kept for the next ten years.

Pohl was one of the new breed of writers and editors who had come out of fandom. He was born in 1919, the year "The Runaway Skyscraper" was first published. By the time he was 19, he was editing two of Popular Publications' science fiction magazines, *Astonishing Stories* and *Super-Science Stories*, working under Rogers Terrill (who was Will's agent in the 1950s). He recalls that he was paid $10 a week.

Pohl had been a member of one of the local science fiction leagues for young fans that were promoted by Hugo Gernsback and later was one of the organizers of the legendary Futurians. Early members of the Futurians included Cyril Kornbluth, Dirk Wylie, Isaac Asimov and Donald A. Wollheim.

It has been estimated that at one point in the 1940s former Futurians edited approximately half of the science fiction and fantasy magazines in the U.S.

In addition to editing, Fred Pohl was a prolific writer and successful agent.

Donald A. Wollheim was already a published author when he joined the Futurians. He had sold his first story, "The Man from Ariel," to *Wonder Stories* when he was nineteen. It was published in the January 1934 issue. He was one of the organizers of the first U.S. science fiction convention, which was held in Philadelphia in 1936, and he continued to be an active fan, publishing many fanzines.

Wollheim was editor for Ace Books from 1943 to 1946 and for Avon from 1946 to 1952, when he went back to Ace.

At Avon, he edited the *Avon Fantasy Reader*, a magazine that was sometimes referred to as a series of anthologies. In it, he republished science fiction and fantasy stories by well-known authors. The Murray Leinster novella "Power Planet" was printed in the February 1947 issue, followed by "The Morrison Monument" in April 1951. There were 18 issues published in all.

During his second tour at Ace, Wollheim instituted the Ace Double, which became a very popular format. Two novels were printed, back-to-back, one upside down to the other, with two covers. Several Leinster stories came out in doubles beginning in 1954 with *The Brain Stealers*. They included *Gateway to Elsewhere*, *The Duplicators*, *Space Captain*, *The Other Side of Here* and *City on the Moon*. *Pirates of Zan*, backed with *The Mutant Weapon*, was published in 1959.

Two more fans, Martin Greenberg and David A. Kyle, started Gnome Press in 1948. Kyle was a Futurian. Gnome printed *The Forgotten Planet* in 1954, and it was reprinted by Ace three times. *Colonial Survey*, also known as *The Planet Explorer* when published by Avon the same year, was a collection that came out in 1957. Stories included "Combat Team" (also known as "Exploration Team"), "Sand Doom," "Solar Constant" (also known as "Critical Difference"), and "The Swamp Was Upside Down."

Gnome also printed many significant science fiction stories, including Asimov's *Foundation* trilogy and several Heinlein stories, but, unfortunately, it was undercapitalized and went under in 1962.

Shasta, a small press started in 1947 by a group of Chicago area fans, published the Murray Leinster collection *Sidewise in Time* in 1950. It was titled after its lead story, which was first printed in *Astounding Stories* in June 1934. The contents also included "Proxima Certauri," "The Fourth-dimensional Demonstrator," "A Logic Named Joe," "De Profundis," and "The Power."

In 1953, Shasta printed two new juvenile science fiction books by Will featuring a young hero, Joe Kenmore. They were *Space Platform* and *Space Tug*. Another in the Joe Kenmore series, *City on the Moon*, came out in 1957 and was published by Avalon. These books were highly praised by prominent educators, including Max L. Hertzberg, past president of the National Council of Teachers of English, who said of *Space Tug*, "There is current-events interest in the book since many news and magazine articles have shown that the creation of a man-made satellite is the next step in man's conquest of Space. Leinster is at his best here."

In *Space Platform,* Will includes an acknowledgment of Willy Ley saying, "There is Willy Ley whom I would like to exempt from responsibility for any statement in the book, while I acknowledge the value of personal talks with him and the pleasure anyone who has ever read his books will recognize."

Ley was a leading rocket scientist and advocate for space travel who left Nazi Germany in 1935. In March 1937, he appeared in *Astounding Stories* with an article, "The Dawn of the Conquest of Space." He became a frequent contributor to *Astounding* and, beginning in 1952, had a regular science column in *Galaxy* titled "For Your Information." In it, he would reply to readers' questions. He and Will became great friends. Will enjoyed attributing the invention of the Screwdriver cocktail to Ley, playfully and poorly mimicking Ley's Berlin accent while he asserted that the drink came out of an evening when Ley was thinking, "Vot can be done with wodka."

The crater Ley on the far side of the moon is named for Willy Ley. Sadly, he died a month before the moon landing in 1969.

"Night Drive," a Will F. Jenkins story published in March 1950 by *Today's Woman,* became a standard in high school creative writing classes. It was inspired by a winding, isolated part of the road between Gloucester and Richmond, Virginia, along which Will had driven frequently when the three older girls were taking ballet lessons in the 1930s. The story is about a woman driving at night who agrees to take another woman along with her, whom she's told needs a lift. Soon she realizes that the woman is in reality a man. "Night Drive" has been reprinted regularly and has become a classic of suspense.

Will was particularly delighted when he wrote to Jo-an on April 15, 1970, that it was later included in a collection along with several of his favorite writers:

> I think I told you about being in a schoolbook with O. Henry, MacKinlay Cantor, Sherwood Anderson, Damon Runyon, Pearl Buck, Saki and Saroyan. There are two stories in the mystery category. One is "The Monkey's Paw" by W. W. Jacobs and the other is "Night Drive" by Will F. Jenkins. I'm flattered as hell.

It was memorable to at least one student. In 2010, an inquiry came into Loganberry Books' online question-and-answer page, "Stump the Bookseller."

> This was a short story given us as an intermediate or high school reading assignment. We may have been given mimeographed handouts so I don't know the source. This story was to demonstrate irony. The plot involves two strangers traveling from one city to another by automobile.... They arrive at their destination without violence, but I can't remember the ironic ending.... I'd appreciate any help in identifying the title or author of the story and any clue where to find it.

The Bookseller replies with the correct identification and notes that it was anthologized in *In the Grip of Terror* and *Twisted!* both edited by Groff Conklin, and that it may have been included in some schoolbook texts.

One of Will's most frequently reprinted stories is "Keyhole," published in *Thrilling Wonder Stories* in December 1951. In an article called "Reverie" in *Science Fiction Review*, April 27, 1964, Will said:

> I had a ten-year-old daughter when I wrote that story. She read it and zestfully told me a story about a man who wanted to study the reactions of a chimpanzee. He led the chimp into a room full of things a chimp should find interesting. He went out and closed the door, and then put his eye to the keyhole to see what the chimp was doing. He found himself looking into an interested brown eye only inches from his own. The chimp was looking through the keyhole, too, to see what the man was about. I put my daughter's tale as a preface and a coda to my own yarn and called it "Keyhole."

Will continued his relationship with *Argosy* with a story, "The Devil's Henchmen," that appeared in the May 1952 issue. It was reprinted in *The Supernatural Reader*, edited by Groff and Lucy Conklin (Lippincott, 1953).

Science fiction novelist Edward Morris found the story in a later reprint that belonged to his mother: *Isaac Asimov's World of Fantasy #2, Witches*, edited by Isaac Asimov, Martin H. Greenberg and Charles Waugh (NAL, 1984). It was his introduction to Will's work.

Morris writes:

> I was floored and delighted by his conceptions of mysticism and all the ways that fold mysticism and hillbilly Christianity bump up against each other, and occasionally work together. Like Stephen Vincent Benet and Manly Wade Wellman, Will's work taught me that it's okay to talk about the simple things, the fine pride you can take in your life even if you're shirt-tail poor ... "if your heart's right."
> From that story, it was but a short hop to the elegantly simple "A Logic Named Joe"; "Sidewise in Time" (without which story another Joe, Mr. Lansdale, would not have been inspired to write his great Leinster homage "The Drive-In") and the voluminous trails that Will blazed into the field of good, honest, workmanlike SF.
> Being half a Southerner, I have a special place in my heart for all Southern

writers, Leinster and Wellman the most of all. Like Dante, both men spoke in *la vulgare eloquentia*, the language of real people. I look up to Will because he was a pioneer in the field, and taught me to be absolutely uncompromising about story value.

Will enjoyed playing with abstract ideas and unexpected consequences. He discussed the most complicated philosophies with his daughters from an early age. "If a tree falls in a forest and no one is around to hear it, does it make a sound?" was one of them. It is a riddle that has been discussed endlessly over the years and attributed, as Will did, to Bishop George Berkeley. The bishop was a 17th century philosopher whose dictum was "Esse est percipi"— "To be is to be perceived." Bishop Berkeley was a familiar name in Will's home, always good for a lively discussion.

Will's interest could possibly be traced to the 1910 book *Physics* by Charles Riborg Mann and George Ransom Twiss. A quiz at the end of each chapter posed the question: "When a tree falls in a lonely forest, and no animal is nearby to hear it, does it make a sound? Why?"

"The Little Terror" was inspired by Bishop Berkeley, and Will discussed Berkeley's theories in the story which was published in *The Saturday Evening Post*, August 22, 1953. He tells about a little girl who was told (rather absent-mindedly) by her father that she could make people disappear. So she did, to everyone's great alarm. Her father then quickly told the little girl that she couldn't make people disappear, which she then believed, so the people she'd made disappear came back. "The Little Terror" was reprinted in *Saturday Evening Post Stories, 1953* (Random House, 1954), and in *The Post Reader of Fantasy and Science Fiction* (Doubleday, 1964), as well as *Tomorrow's Children* (Futura Publications, 1976) where editor Isaac Asimov calls Will, "The giant Sequoia of the science fiction world, the hardy perennial to whom mere decades mean nothing."

Who's Who in America included Will in its 1952 edition, an event that delighted him as a pleasing tribute. He would be listed for the next twenty years.

> I think I've told you I've been thrown out of Who's Who. They listed me in 1952 and threw me out in 1972. I very foolishly listed only books — annually — that I was reasonably pleased with, and I think I looked even less important, if possible, than I am in the literary world and was thrown out for discontinued significance.
>
> *Letter to Jo-an, August 9, 1972*

His real recognition from his peers came in 1956 when he was awarded a Hugo, for "Exploration Team" winning as Best Novelette. The Hugo, named for Hugo Gernsback, is awarded annually at the Worldcon (World Science

Fiction Convention). The idea of this award was conceived at the 1953 convention, but it was made annual only in 1955. Will's was the second awarded for best novelette.

Superficially, the story is about an illegal colonist on a dangerous planet using trained bears to rescue survivors of a failed legal colony. Actually it is about two men, each with a strong and conflicting value system, who find a way to resolve their differences in a way that satisfies them both without requiring them to abandon their personal standards. It is one of Will's better efforts of combining a story with a moral and an exciting adventure. *Astounding Science-Fiction* published "Exploration Team" in the March 1956 issue. It has since been reprinted more than 30 times in several languages.

While Will's choice of lifestyle kept him from close relationships with many of his fellows, he admired and respected them. He felt the award was a huge honor, which it was, and winning it gave him a great deal of pleasure.

Eric Flint in *The World Turned Upside Down,* an anthology published by Baen Publishing, Inc., 2005, comments on the fact that this, and the awarding in 1996 of a Retro Hugo for "First Contact," were Will's only major science fiction awards (he never won the Nebula). Flint says:

> To be sure the major SF awards like all such awards are notoriously subject to the popularity of the recipient with the relatively small numbers of people who cast the votes. And since Leinster paid no attention to them — he rarely if ever attended a science fiction convention, and had very little contact with other science fiction writers — it's not surprising that they tended to ignore him in return.

Flint further commented, "Maybe familiarity created contempt," and "Leinster was there at the creation of science fiction — he created much of it himself."

It is true that Will attended few conventions but this is probably related more to the fact that he, and he and Mary together, did not travel except by car and on the East Coast. They did not fly. His only airplane flight was after Mary died, and he visited Jo-an in London. During the 12 years that Billee lived in the midwest, he and Mary never visited, and the only time they visited their daughter Mary in New England was when Billee drove them from New York.

In addition, when fans first began to organize science fiction conventions, he was in his forties. The organizers were a generation younger, most of them in their twenties.

During the 1950s, Will became once again reconciled with his mother, Mamie, after twenty years of estrangement. It was his daughter Billee who brought them together. When Billee was a young teen, she knew and enjoyed her friends' grandmothers and felt a deep sense of loss at never knowing her own. Asking her mother for her grandmother's address, she wrote to Mamie, and they began to exchange letters. Then, when Billee was at Sweet Briar College in Virginia in 1945, she found that a classmate lived in Portsmouth. She went home with her for a weekend and met Mamie for the first time.

Later, after she was married and her oldest daughter, Pamela, was born, Billee took an opportunity to visit her grandmother to show Mamie her first great-grandchild. She found Mamie, at 84, to be as vibrant and interested in life as her son Will.

Mamie lived in a room in the historic Monroe Hotel in downtown Portsmouth which was filled with memorabilia, odd pieces of silver, and bound copies of her son George's stories. She relished the location, the freedom to walk anywhere she wanted in the center of the city, and the proximity to her brother Oliver Murry, half-sisters Jenny Watts Davis and Grace Watts Syer, and their children. She had her own style. To the end of her life, she wore high-necked Edwardian net inserts that she made herself. Her granddaughter Betty bought the cotton net for her in New York when she could no longer find it in Virginia.

Thanks to Billee's reconnection, when Will and Mary were beginning to spend more time at Clay Bank, Will began to repair his relationship with his mother. They began to visit her often, bringing Jo-an and, when she was in Gloucester, Betty as well.

In 1953, Will dedicated the book *Space Platform* to her, an act that pleased her immensely.

Mamie was 90 that year, and *The Norfolk Virginian Pilot* sent a reporter to interview her. She explained that she was living at the Monroe Hotel in downtown Portsmouth because it enabled her to be free to go anywhere she wanted at any time. "If I want to go to the movies at 9 o'clock at night, I can."

In 1957, when she was 94, the hotel was destroyed by fire, and a newspaper reporter asked her if she had to be carried down the stairs from her third floor room.

"Of course not," she said. She said she had put on her stockings and her rings, and "I walked down by myself." But all her belongings, including the bound collection of stories written by Will's brother George, were completely destroyed.

Afterwards, she spent time with her half-sisters in Portsmouth, and with Will and Mary in Clay Bank, which was much too quiet for her. She stayed for a while at the Botetourt Hotel in Gloucester Court House, which she enjoyed more, because she could sit on the big front porch and chat to everyone who came by. However, at 95, she found it difficult to settle anywhere and finally decided to move into The Home For the Aged in Portsmouth.

Eight • The 1950s

In a letter to Jo-an at college in 1958, Will wrote:

> Your grandmother does not look well. She is raising an unusual amount of hell, even for her, but she acts as if her heart isn't in it and she looks very ill indeed. If I sound cold-blooded, it is because she makes me feel so hideously guilty because I can't make things the way she wants them. But it is starkly impossible to rebuild the hotel and set her back in it with everything as it was before the fire.

She died, on October 20, 1959, less than three months shy of her 97th birthday.

Billee was disappointed that Will and Mary, still living in New York, couldn't meet her in Gloucester when she visited Mamie in 1948. She and her husband and baby were heading home to Minnesota after her first visit to Florida to meet her in-laws, and they couldn't extend the trip to New York. Will and Mary's pre-war seven-passenger Plymouth was not reliable enough for the drive down, and they were disappointed, too. Billee's family car, a 1938 LaSalle, was in no better shape. They drove the last 21 hours without turning off the engine, even when buying gas, because the car had trouble starting. Arriving at their apartment in St. Paul, they parked it in front of the building and had it towed away.

Happily, Billee spent several weeks with Will and Mary in 1952, bringing both Pam and her second daughter, Gail, who was born in 1950. The family was moving to Kansas City, Missouri, where her husband had taken a new job. They had bought a house in Minnesota, and it sold quickly. Rental apartments were still scarce in Kansas City at that time, so Billee and her girls went to New York to wait until a new home was ready.

Will had a hard time relating to very young children who were strangers to him, but he enjoyed his granddaughters thoroughly when they were older and spending a lot of time with him in Virginia. Mary, however, relished being a grandmother from the beginning and bored everyone with her excitement, telling anyone who would listen that Pam and Gail were coming. She was forgiving even when Gail, at age two, found a loose seam in the Beechhurst apartment's wallpaper and pulled off a piece. She said, "I knew I should have fixed that."

Will's writing continued without pause. He reported to Jo-an early in 1957:

> The news is on this order. I've finished a novelette for John Campbell, which also finishes a book that both Marty [Greenberg] and [Thomas] Bouregy [Avalon Books] both want to publish hard-cover, and I think it will be a lousy book which, nevertheless, I will try to sell direct to a reprint. [*This may have been "City on the Moon" published by Avalon in 1957 and reprinted by Ace in 1958.*] I have a feeling that I will get more out of it. I have the page-proofs on "Colonial Survey" [Gnome, 1957] and take them back tomorrow....

> I'm simply dumb. Copying all day yesterday and the day before, finished up today, proof-reading, and now I've got to go and make corrections ... I wish I could think of something witty or whatnot. Tomorrow I go to John Campbell's, to the new high school magazine, to CBS, to Rogers' [*Terrill, his agent*], to Marty Greenberg's, and possibly McFadden's [*sic*]. No high adventure there!

Later that year again, he wrote, "I had a play on radio today, and didn't get a chance to tape it. *Galaxy* called up. They supply the material for a science fiction radio show [*X Minus One*] which is going to use, "Sam, This Is You."

Will and John Campbell met frequently and respected each other. Bob Silverberg, who has the distinction of winning major awards in every decade from the 1950s to the 2000s, still remembers an incident when he met them together in Campbell's office.

> I didn't know Will Jenkins well — he was almost 40 years my senior, after all — but I did have one memorable encounter with him in March of 1956, exactly ten years after "A Logic Named Joe" was published. I was a senior in college but I had already begun my career as a professional writer, and that day I brought my newest story to the office of the legendary editor John W. Campbell, who had dominated the SF world since before I was old enough to read. Will Jenkins happened to be in Campbell's office that day, and I said something appropriately awestricken.
>
> Then, to my horror, John proceeded to read my new story right in front of both of us. After about ten minutes he looked up and said, "There's something wrong with this, but I am not sure what it is. Will, would you take a look?" And he handed my manuscript across the desk to Will Jenkins. I sat there squirming, aghast all over again, as the author of "First Contact" and "Sidewise in Time" read my story, too. And at last he said, in that gentle, Virginia accented voice of his, "I think the problem is here, in the next-to-last-paragraph."
>
> "That's absolutely right," Campbell said. "Get to work, Bob." He pointed to a typewriter on a desk nearby. I revised that paragraph then and there, and sold the story on the spot.

Always excited by new ideas and information, in 1959 Will became interested in Panama, possibly influenced by new friends recently moved to Gloucester after many years in that country. As he wrote to Jo-an on October 17, 1959:

> I got some beautiful material for a book on Panama. (They're going to try to take back the Panama Canal, a la Suez, probably next year. [*Negotiations toward a new settlement began in 1974, and resulted in the Torrijos-Carter Treaties in 1977.*] I've offers of introductions to everybody who knows the story, the Ambassador in Washington, free quarters in Panama to write the book, which is so hot it makes the Ugly American look like dry ice by comparison — and so far I can't find anybody who'll get excited about it.

His fascination with scientific development was constant, however, as he wrote to Jo-an at college early in 1958:

Irving Dischinger [*a long-time friend from Gloucester*] called. He's designing a titanium mill. The doggoned stuff is frantically difficult to work. Rolled cold, it is brittle. Rolled at 1000d it is ideal for airplane work. Terrific tensile strength (twice as strong as steel, etc.) and weighs only 60 percent more than aluminum. But when heated it absorbs oxygen, nitrogen, helium, C02, chlorine — anything you please. And when it has absorbed them it gets brittle. It should be rolled in a vacuum. Irving's going to put a set of rollers between two chambers filled with argon (!) as it is the only stuff it won't absorb, and roll it back and forth between them, with hydrogen-flame "curtains" to keep it hot and confine the argon.... I asked why he didn't electroplate it and roll it, thus sealed from the air. He said it goes into solid solution, alloys with anything it's plated with as soon as it's heated. Quaint?

By the time Jo-an graduated from high school in 1956, Mary and Will were spending more time in Virginia, almost all of the holidays and most of the summer. Betty was working in New York City and joined them when she could. She was beginning a long-distance courtship with William "Billy" DeHardit, a Gloucester native she had known all her life. He was the current editor of the *Gloucester Gazette-Journal* and the youngest son of Billee's godfather, George DeHardit. He had been a fixture around the house for a long time, and Will enjoyed talking to him. Billy was also a talented piano player and a member of a local band. Betty liked to join him on the evenings out when he had a gig.

Betty (in a white organdie dress she designed, which was made by Julie Buckley of Beechhurst) and Billy were married at St. Therese's Catholic Church in Gloucester, June 1, 1957. Jo-an came home from college in Baltimore to be maid of honor. Billee's daughters Pam and Gail arrived with their parents from Missouri to act as flower girls. Mamie, in her familiar high-necked Edwardian dress and straw hat, attended the wedding with her half-sister Virginia "Jennie" Davis and niece Grace Davis.

Adeline and Lewis Allen and young Adeline were there. Will loved to tell the story of Lewis Allen and Billee's husband Pete Stallings' trip to a nearby country store for some needed supplies. The clerk said, "I guess you're here for the Jenkins' wedding." When they said, "Yes," he said, "I thought so. You look like one of them." Neither of them being blood relatives, they got a kick out that.

Will had another favorite story about the Virginia liquor laws then in force. Spirits were sold only in state Alcohol Beverage Control stores commonly known as ABC stores, and you were limited to buying two bottles at a time. When they shopped for liquor for the wedding reception to be held at the Gloucester Country Club, they had to pick out and pay for two bottles, take them to the car, come back in and buy two more, and so on, and so on.

Eight • The 1950s

After their marriage, Will encouraged Betty and Billy to start their own bi-weekly local paper, *Glo-Quips*, and had a part in naming it. He started writing a column for the new paper, "Isn't It Odd?" It included thoughts and short pieces that were interesting to him. In December 1973 when there was excitement about a new comet expected to be visible, he concluded the column with the comments:

> Right now there is a comet on the way to visit us. Especially knowledgeable persons will say that when it gets near enough to the sun it will sprout a tail, or maybe two or three or maybe even more. I shall watch this activity solely as an innocent bystander. I may count the comet's tails and let it go as that. But maybe I should do more than watch. I may learn this comet's name. Under other circumstances it would be Kohoutek Two because it was discovered by Mr. Kohoutek — a citizen of whom Czechoslovakia may well be proud — because he discovered two comets in the same year, and even one discovery of a planet is quite an achievement. And two comets in one year bagged by a man named Kohoutek seems more remarkable still. Anyhow — Isn't it odd?

Will continued writing the column until shortly before his death.

With Betty married and living in Gloucester and Jo-an in college in Maryland, Will and Mary began to spend more and more time at Clay Bank, making regular business trips to New York and spending a couple of weeks in the Beechhurst apartment on each visit. By the time Jo-an graduated from college in June 1960, they were living pretty much full time in Clay Bank. In the autumn, after spending the summer in Clay Bank, Jo-an went to New York to take a job and moved into the Beechhurst apartment.

In 1958, Billee and her family moved to Haddonfield in southern New Jersey from where they had been living in Missouri. The whole family was now together on the East Coast. They were now only a six-hour drive from Clay Bank and could make frequent visits. On one of these visits, they brought their pregnant cat along. She delivered four kittens in the bathtub the first night. Will had never liked cats, but both he and Mary fell in love with one of the long-haired ginger tabbies and, when he was old enough, kept him naming him Rickki-tickki.

Will seemed to be enjoying the back and forth life he and Mary were leading between New York and Virginia. Although he was happy to be back at Clay Bank, he recognized the need to be in New York and found enough diversion there to keep him from resenting it.

One of Will's great friends was Austin Stanton, who founded Varo, Inc., a company that developed high tech equipment for the military. He created

Opposite: Betty's wedding. Will, Grace and Jenny Davis, and, in front, flower girls Gail and Pam Stallings.

night vision telescopes, electronic night inverters, and guided missile launch systems for military aircraft. He was an early supporter of spaceflight.

In the 1950s, Wernher von Braun, the German V-2 expert who became U.S. Army's top missile advisor, was developing plans for sending a satellite into orbit using the already tested Redstone missile beefed up with booster rockets. A committee including Stanton met with von Braun in Washington in March 1954 to develop Project Orbiter under the joint auspices of the United States Army and Navy.

In 1955, anticipating the start of the International Geophysical Year scheduled for July 1, President Dwight D. Eisenhower decided to develop a satellite program. The National Security Council was called upon to decide how to run the project. The decision was made that the satellite project should be separate from military ballistic-missile research and that the navy should be put in charge. This spelled the end of the joint Project Orbiter and the beginning of the navy's Project Vanguard.

On October 4, 1957, the Russian satellite *Sputnik* was launched. *Life* magazine ran an article "Why the Reds Got There First" and Austin Stanton was quoted as follows: "Ample funds improperly applied. Our first satellite program could have beaten the Reds, but efforts to get contracts and personal fame stymied American scientists."

After *Sputnik*, Project Orbiter was revived as the Explorer program under the army. They hoped to speed up a launch by using an existing rocket called *Juno 1*. Meanwhile the U.S. Navy's launch of *Vanguard TV3* on December 6, 1957, failed.

The *Juno 1* rocket was launched on February 1, 1958, putting *Explorer 1* into orbit. It became the first Earth satellite of the United States. The navy's *Vanguard TV4* was successfully launched on March 17, 1958, and is the oldest satellite still orbiting.

Stanton was convinced of the practicality of spaceflight and went further, supporting the encouragement of commercial ventures. Will's matter-of-fact acceptance of space travel and the soundness of the science in some of his predictions brought them together.

In 1957 Will dedicated the book *Colonial Survey* to him.

To Austin Stanton, Esq.

Who believes that the things I write about should be accomplished right away;
Who believes that all men are potential geniuses;
Who gives responsibility and opportunity to men while they are young;
And thereby does his bit to make actual the things that I only write about.

Murray Leinster

Eight • The 1950s

In an undated letter to Jo-an in 1956, Will tells of attending a meeting of the American Astronautical Society, "I think I told you Austin Stanton called up. Asked if I wanted to go to the awards of the Astronautic Society. I said yes. There're giving an award to Cmmdr. [*sic*] Hoover. I got a folder, permitting me to buy tickets and discovered Stanton is getting an award, too. He didn't mention that." [Stanton was elected a Fellow in the Society.]

In a later letter, Will added:

Last night I went to the annual award meeting of the American Astronautical Society, They gave an award to Cmmdr. [*sic*] Hoover, a very handsome plaque, which puts my space-ship [the Hugo Award] in the shade, both in looks and in the achievement it signifies. His eighteen-year-old daughter was there. Goes to Maryland U. Envies you having been to Annapolis [while a student at Notre Dame College in Baltimore]. Met an admiral and a flock of four-stripers, swapped recipes for steamed crabs with one (the secret is use two parts beer and one part vinegar instead of all vinegar) argued about whether the tranquility produced by Milltown would increase combat-efficiency or whether the effect "it isn't important" would be a hindrance. (They're testing it.) ... Hoover really spilled the beans. Said when they want to find out if some new project is possible they put it up to three conservative-type civilians engineers. If the engineers say it is impossible, the satellite-project gang sighs with relief and sets to work on it. They know it can be done. Afterwards, the guy I swapped recipes with got impassioned, telling me of one incident after another in which exactly that thing had happened.

Everybody was from some impressive outfit. Met a Marine major (migosh, majors are young these days!—Actually I'm ancient) and we both felt horribly inferior. (Rosenberg [probably Major General Robert A. Rosenberg who later in 1959–1962 participated in the development of the Atlas and Agena satellite programs] came up to me and said who he was (I know, anyhow) and who he was with and peeked at my badge and said, "Who are you with?" and I said "Unemployed.") But the major and I pooled our misery. He came up with an entirely mythical firm-or-project idea. I suggested initials. So thereafter when we were asked what we were we said nonchalantly, "N. I. P." and people looked impressed and went away not knowing the initials stood for "Nothing in Particular."

• NINE •

The 1960s

Will and Mary began to live almost full time at Clay Bank in the 1960s, and family visited often, keeping Will close to his dream of Ardudwy as the family seat. With the magazine market drying up, Will turned more and more to novels, and he was also able to continue his tinkering. This constant experimenting developed front projection, which had brought him his first patents in 1955, and in this decade, commercial and financial success for his invention.

His first novel of the decade was *The Wailing Asteroid*, published by Avon in 1960. Fifty years later, one fan remembered it well enough to send the following to Steven H. Silver, the science fiction fan, bibliographer and editor who started and maintains the Murray Leinster website.

> I am sure that this may sound silly but Murray Leinster changed my life almost 50 years ago, and until last night I did not even know his name. When I was a child, I was an avid reader of Science Fiction. Having been spoonfed the best books by my grandfather who was an AeroSpace Engineer at Litton Industries there were a lot of stories and adventures buried in my mind. Still there was one story that I read in the mid 1960s that has haunted my dreams, memories and even fantasy. I have talked about it to friends and family for decades and no one ever knew about the book I was talking about.
>
> Last night I was talking about it to my wife after dinner and forgot all about it again. That was until I sat up in bed at 1:00 AM while dreaming about the book and yelled out "The Wailing Asteroid!" bolted down the stairs and Googled the name not expecting much. I was floored to find the book instantly and information about the author. He was so much ahead of his time and I would give anything to go back in time just to talk to him and let him know what he has done for my life and my creativity and that of my children.
>
> Tonight my son will get to read "The Wailing Asteroid" and a new generation will know the name Murray Leinster.
>
> Thank you for keeping his web site up!
> Bill Carroll, Sr.

Science fiction and fantasy writer Stephen Goldin worked as a civilian space scientist before switching careers to full-time writing. He wrote about Will:

> I never had the good fortune to meet Murray Leinster — our generations just barely overlapped. But his work influenced me tremendously.
> The first thing I think about when I hear his name is *The Wailing Asteroid*. That book practically defines the phrase "sense of wonder." It transported me out of my ordinary world to a place of fascination and adventure and held me spellbound to the very end.

The Wailing Asteroid was made into a movie called *The Terrornauts*. It was filmed in England in 1967. Three British scientists succeed in their efforts to make contact with other intelligent creatures in the universe but are unexpectedly teleported to a hostile planet. The most favorable review calls it "a camp delight." It was reported to be a New York TV staple in the 1990s and is still available on DVD.

Besides *The Wailing Asteroid*, the following novels were published in the 1960s: *Creatures of the Abyss* (Berkley, 1961) (reprinted in the UK as *The Listeners*), *Operation Terror* (Berkley, 1962), *Talents Incorporated* (Avon, 1962), *The Duplicators* (Ace Double, 1964) (also known as *Lord of the Uffs*, backed with *The Mutant Weapon*), *The Greks Bring Gifts* (Macfadden, 1964), *Invaders of Space* (Berkley, 1964), *The Other Side of Nowhere* (Berkley, 1964), *Time Tunnel* (Pyramid, 1964), *Checkpoint Lambda* (Berkley, 1966), *Space Captain* (Ace Double, 1966), *Tunnel Through Time* (juvenile) (Westminster Press, 1966), *Miners in the Sky* (Avon, 1967), *Space Gypsies* (Avon, 1967), *Time Tunnel*—Pyramid, 1967 (novelization of TV series), and *Timeslip!* (Pyramid, 1967) (novelization of TV series).

Will and Mary were delighted when Elizabeth "Beth" Jenkins DeHardit, daughter of Betty and Bill, joined the family on March 28, 1961. How wonderful to have a baby grandchild right in Gloucester to be enjoyed almost every day! Pam and Gail Stallings, now thirteen and ten, visited often with their parents, and occasionally alone.

Little Mary had taken in a young foster son, Franz Farquhar, and she brought him down, often staying for several weeks in the summer. For Franz, Will became a treasured granddaddy, and he has happy memories of those times, while Will enjoyed having a small boy around. Jo-an was living and working in New York, so visiting at Clay Bank was possible. Ardudwy was a family center once again.

Pam and Gail also have rich memories of those days. When Gail was asked for her favorite memory of her grandparents, she quickly answered, "Grandmother sitting in Granddaddy's lap." Will once said, "A happy marriage is a series of love affairs with the same woman." They had a happy marriage. Will recalled, "One night we got to talking and all of a sudden saw the sun come up. We had talked all night."

Both Pam and Gail also fondly remember parties, many of them under the enormous weeping cherry tree on the front, or river side, of the house. Mary had planted two weeping cherry trees shortly before going to New York and came back to find that one had died, It was fortunate because the other had grown so large it covered half the view of the river from the house, creating a large room under its branches. Two trees would have completely cut off the view. They paved the space under the remaining tree with bricks, and it was a favorite spot for outdoor dining and relaxing on summer afternoons.

"Staying up late and talking" is a vivid memory that Pam and Gail have. Children at Clay Bank were both seen and heard whenever they wanted to be a part of adult gatherings. In the years they visited, both girls remember doing all the things their mother did, swimming, crabbing, climbing trees and riding to the Court House with their grandfather to pick up the mail — a good time for long talks. He amused them by raising each eyebrow individually, a skill that has re-surfaced in one of his great-granddaughters. They were entranced with his experiments and the odd things he collected around the house. A Victorian medical gadget that gave a small, supposedly health-improving electric shock when you cranked the handle particularly fascinated Gail. They read the books that filled the house. After finishing the Oz books from the collection that was still in one of the bedrooms, Gail began to dip in to *Analog* and remembers the first of her grandfather's books she tried. It was *Four from Planet Five*. At her prepubescent age, she thought it had too much "love stuff" in it.

Will was a natural musician and could play the piano and stringed instruments (especially the banjo and mandolin) by ear. His half-sister Lula also played by ear. He had never studied, so was not an expert, and Mary couldn't carry a tune, but nobody cared and everyone had a lot of fun. They would sing old songs like, "Did You Ever See a Lassie," and "She'll be Coming 'Round the Mountain," and the children and grandchildren would sing along.

Gail and Pam were at the age that Will most enjoyed. He could open their eyes to new experiences, explain them, and they were interested. They could work on projects together. Gail wrote a little story, and he bound it for her by making a cardboard cover. He showed Pam how to make a book safe, taking an old discarded book with an interesting binding and cutting out a section of the pages to make a "hidey hole." She vividly remembers him refer-

Opposite: **Will plays for his grandchildren, Gail on left and Pam on right.**

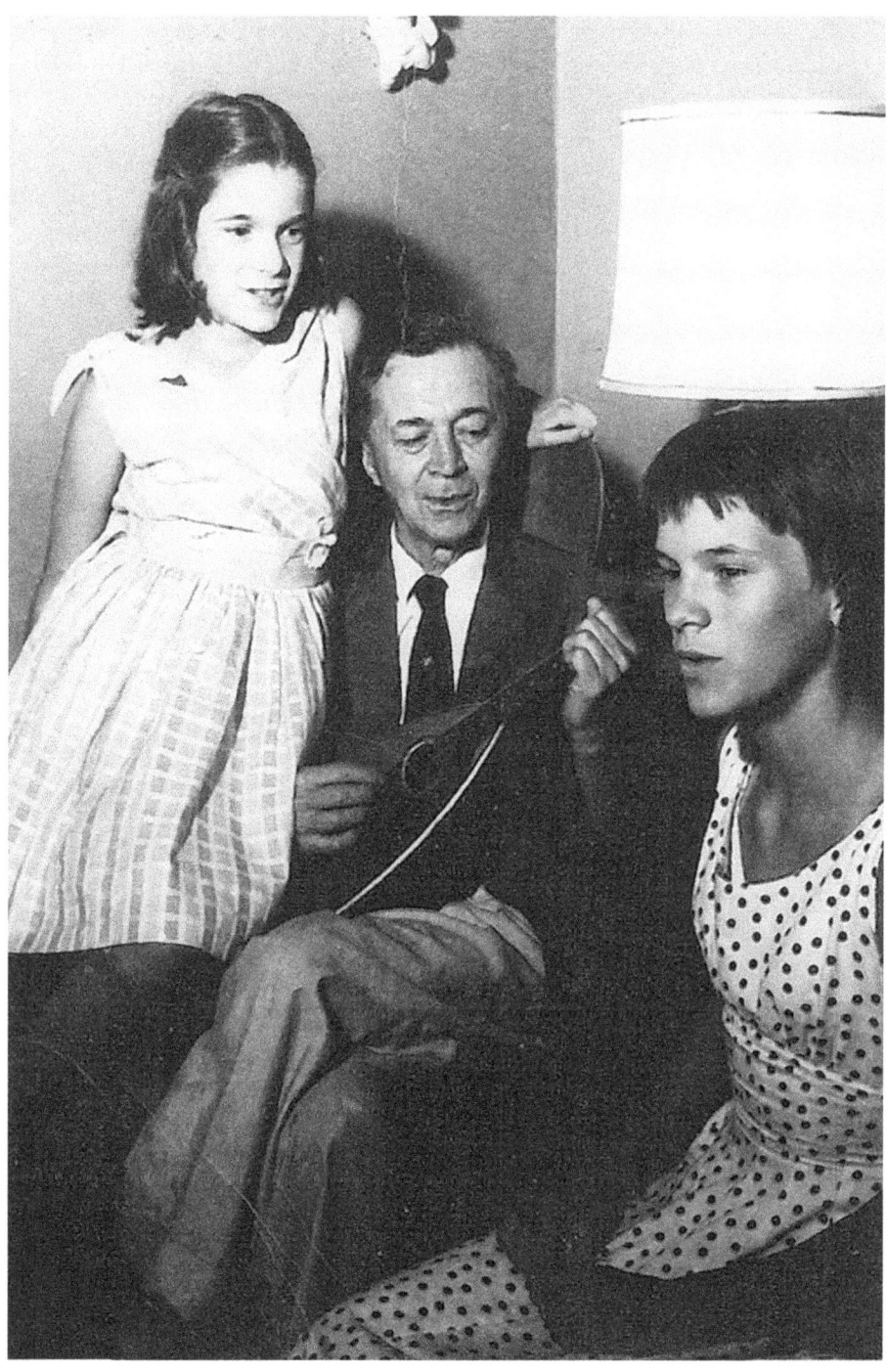

ring to his novella *Proxima Centauri* as they watched the stars one dark summer night when they were especially bright. He spoke about the Proxima Centauri star and its constellation Centaurus, noting they cannot be seen from the little dot of our existence in the continental United States. This incident and the implications of our human limitations have remained with her in her faith-based journey. He enriched their lives.

Will was a great fan of G. K. Chesterton and often quoted from his autobiography. A favorite passage of his and his grandchildren was in a letters to the editor section in a Fleet Street paper edited by Chesterton's brother. Because Will repeated it so many times, it seemed to reflect his own views. Although he was not uncomfortable with southern culture, as it existed in those days, he was liberal for his time. The exchange in the letters was about racial intermarriage and was initiated by a report on a meeting between H. G. Wells and Booker T. Washington. The first letter, deploring intermarriage between black and whites, was signed "White Man." A letter from Wells followed signed "Bexley Street White Man." Another letter followed signed "Black Man," and a third addressing intermarriage with races of Asia was signed "Brown Man."

"Finally," Chesterton writes, "there appeared a letter, of which I remember almost every word; for it was short and simple and touching in its appeal to larger and more tolerant ideals. It ran, I think, as follows:

> Sir, May I express my regret that you should continue a correspondence which causes considerable pain to many innocent persons who, by no fault of their own, but by the iron laws of nature, inherit a complexion uncommon among their fellow-creatures and attractive only to the elite. Surely we can forget all these differences; and, whatever our race or colour, work hand in hand for the broadening of the brotherhood of humanity.
>
> Yours faithfully, Mauve Man with Green Spots
> *(The Autobiography of G. K. Chesterton, Chapter 8)*

Will and Mary continued their trips to New York, finding it beneficial to keep up personal contacts in publishing. They now had a convenient way to break up the trip. Haddonfield, New Jersey, where Billee lived, was six hours from Clay Bank and less than two from New York City. They would stop and stay a few days, sometimes longer, and Will could even take an express bus to New York for the day if he wished. Mary loved these stops. Billee could drive her to the many shopping malls, and they could plan decorating and work together on sewing projects. Will was never far from his typewriter but joined in some activities. He expressed a wish to visit Winterthur, the Dupont estate easily accessible in Delaware, so Billee took him and Mary there.

In the winter of 1961, while visiting Billee and her family, Will complained of pains in his left arm and Billee whisked him to the nearest hospital. It was diagnosed as an incipient heart attack, and he was treated and quickly recovered.

In a letter to Isaac Asimov on January 5, 1962, Will gave permission to use "Exploration Team" as a Hugo winner for Asimov's Doubleday anthology and added:

> I have to thank you and several others for your note, listing drinks and expressing sympathy for my being on a bed of pain. I had a pain in my back and it was a coronary waiting to happen. It got stopped. No permanent damage, I'm told. It pleased me very much that people would bother to send such a round robin of sympathy.

In a letter to Jo-an a year later, on March 16, 1963, after she had asked how he was, he told her:

> Have to keep on with the peretrate stuff. The peretrate stuff requires that I also take extra vitamins because it destroys them. If I stop the peretrate, I appear likely to get a backache like the one that sent me to hospital. I get one, take the peretrate, and it stops. But Sam Mines [editor of *Thrilling Wonder* and *Startling Stories* from 1951 to the end of 1954. They stopped publishing in 1955] sent me some vitamins, which Raymond [Brown, Will's doctor and close friend] approves warily. But they seem to include some tranquilizer. That makes me a zombie. So I have to get vitamins, which do not include a tranquilizer. I should take 200 mg. of ascorbic acid for each peretrate pill. I will do so. Minus tranquilizer. Then it is likely that I will be my normal, coruscating self.

In the early fifties, Will had begun working on a system of providing background by projection from the front of instead of the rear of a set, and filed for his first patent March 3, 1952. He filed for a second patent November 30, 1953. When the patents were denied, in true Jenkins fashion, he went down to Washington and explained how his invention varied from others. Both patents were issued in December 1955. The process was simply called front projection. Much later, in his article "Applied Science Fiction" published in *Analog Science Fiction*, November 1967, Will explained how this particular project began:

> Here's the low down. There was once a television series called "Out There," which televised some of my science fiction stories. I remember my "First Contact" and "The Seven Temporary Moons" in particular. The producer was John Haggott, who is one of the good eggs of the world. One day he invited me to watch a rehearsal of "First Contact" in preparation for broadcast. Afterwards he asked me how I liked the production job. I made one criticism. The action of the play took place on a spaceship, and the ceiling of the set was so high as to be invisible — at least fifteen feet. The set didn't look cramped, as I thought it should. A spaceship would travel in empty space, but it wouldn't carry empty space inside it. There'd be plenty outside.

Haggott explained, scenery costs money. Also it had to be made in one place, carried to another to be used, and then carried back to be scrapped. Besides — and even more importantly — a ceiling would play hob with the lighting of the set. He explained the last in detail, but it was the transportation angle that impressed me. I went away muttering to myself about machinery interfering with art like my stories.

Writing science fiction as I do, it seemed to me that in a science-oriented world such things ought to be better handled....

I considered the problem as if I were planning a story in terms of a device. For a story, a device needs only to seem plausible. Whether or not it would work doesn't matter. And this is how the whole thing started.

Will's family lived with the new project's progress on a daily basis. In a letter from New York to his daughter Jo-an in the fall of 1956, in her first year of college, Will told her:

I went over to Transluxe today and showed them the gadget to improve Front Projection. They were very much pleased. Said it made an entirely different picture of the whole performance (picture, there, not referring to the projection) and tomorrow morning I have to go to Brooklyn to talk to their engineers. It's now necessary to find out the engineering cost of making the first acceptable commercial job.

I think it's gone over. I learned two things. One is that in engineering circles, such haywire, cardboard, improvised assemblies as I demonstrated with are called "cheesecake." (The more conventional cheesecake has more aesthetic appeal.) The other thing is that M-------- (his lawyer) admires me — not for what you'd think, but because the outfit including the new gadget is so much superior that the original outfit (which RCA got a license on, as you know) looks inferior now. M-------- said: "You knew all along that the original thing was worthless without this — you son-of-a-gun!" He admired me enormously for holding out on it.

You might be amused to know that I was gravely asked if I was willing to pass on my computations on the lenses. Me, computing something! So I said I was no lens designer and the guy I'm to see tomorrow is also no lens designer, so maybe we'll get along all right. Let us hope so. They seem to like this very much, but M-------- says they're concealing their enthusiasm. Anyhow, they want (a) an engineering estimate on what it will cost to turn out and (b) an idea of the market. They asked if I would write a sort of presentation to be sent to some of their markets for a reaction. I said: "If you read a description of what this thing does, would you believe it?" The idea of a presentation was dropped. Nobody would.

Opposite: Diagram of Front Projection. Diagram from the original submission for Front Projection Patent #2727427: (a) is a camera, (b) a projector, and (c) a glass plate, (d) is a screen of reflex material, (e) is an actor casting a shadow which does not show as the camera looks down on the line of projected light, (f) is light thrown on the glass plate which is not reflected to the screen and is thrown away.

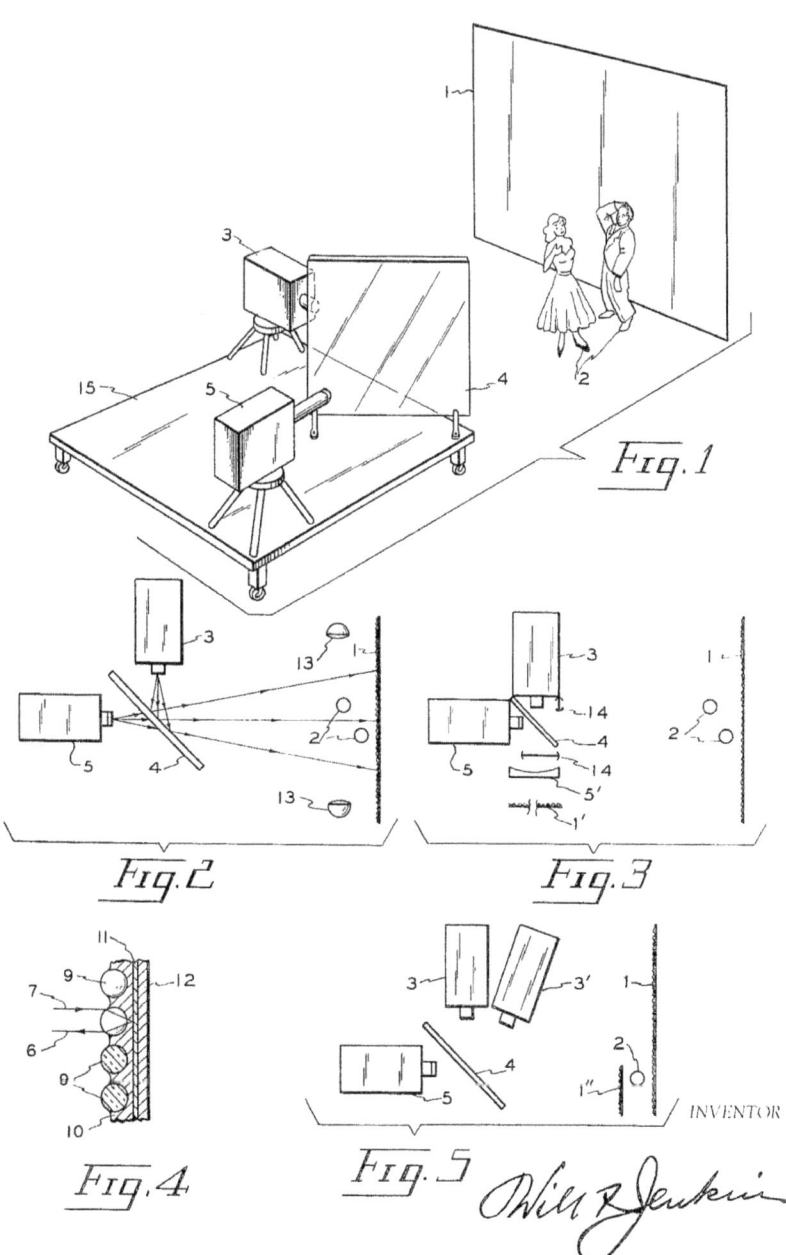

By the early sixties, there was a lot of activity in front projection and Will described the latest events in a letter to Jo-an on November 17, 1962, as follows:

> Here's the dope on the Front Projection stuff. I assume that you want a reasonably complete outline.
>
> I was doing some science fiction TV shows for CBS and the director moaned over the cost of scenery. I thought it would be interesting to try to solve it. Rear projection is standard stuff. One hangs up a sheet of translucent material, projects a picture on it from the back, the actors stand in front of it and are separately lighted, every effort being made to keep the lights on the actors from striking the sheet. This isn't too good.
>
> I devised the idea of combining Scotchlight material (technically a "reflex reflector" which returns all light to its source instead of reflecting it away either diffusely or at an angle on the principle that the angle of reflection is equal to the angle of incidence.) I used a reflex screen such as is used on highway road signs to be lighted by one's car headlights. The Scotchlite manufacturers claim that it is more than two hundred times as bright as white paint. And, close beside the source of the light, this is true. The light goes from the light-source to the Scotchlite screen as an expanding cone. Natural imperfections cause some scattering (which is useful in a highway sign) but most of the light does go exactly back to the light.
>
> I take a projector and aim it across — at right angle — to the line of sight of a camera. I put a partly silvered glass plate so that it reflects some of the light to a reflex screen. Most of it goes through the glass plate and is wasted. But most of the light reaching the screen is returned to its source (in this case the partly silvered glass) and some of it is returned to the projector, but a great deal passes through.
>
> Technically, at a specific position behind the glass plate, one looks (or a camera does) down the optical axis of the projection. This means that if an actor stands in the projection, he masks his own shadow. The point is, of course, that the screen is effectively two hundred times as bright as white paper, or an actor, so that the projected image falling on the actor is invisible while the background is visible. Then one throws more light on the actor from set lamps, to make him bright enough to photograph against the bright set.
>
> CBS tested it. They set up a 9 × 12 foot screen of Scotchlite and a 9 × 12 foot rear-projection screen with a 2,000-watt arc-lamp projector. I used a 350-watt 35 mm home projector Identical slides were made for both projectors. They were set up so that a black and white TV camera had only to swing from one to the other.
>
> It was found that the front projection image was superior in quality and so much brighter that we had to stop down the home-projector image to f 8 to make the images comparable. Using a rheostat to dim it, the two images were about equal when 55 volts was going to the home projector (with 110 volts it gave 360 watts of light) and it was still brighter but was changing color rapidly.
>
> CBS drew up a contract to get the use of the device, but a research man from Minnesota Mining went into the office and Witlig (CBS Special Effects) showed him the gadget. My patent applications were in, but were still pending. The MM and M man said he didn't think I could get a patent. It was too simple.
>
> CBS then stalled until M-------- gave them a deadline. They did not meet it.

We withdrew it, showed it to NBC and they paid me a thousand bucks for one year's experimental use. They renewed it the following year. They did not conclude the deal because union rules in New York forbid any set element to be larger than 4 × 8 feet, and this would involve joints which showed on the image.

It was attempted to make the screen roll up, but Scotchlite then was made only with an aluminum foil back. When rolled up, it stretched, and when unrolled it wrinkled. After two years they quit.

Jenfred, Inc., had seen some experiments made by a guy named Jenkins who, before I thought of the idea, had attempted something of the sort. I learned that they were making plans to build a complete stage set unit for live TV shows on local stations. They supplied one unit which provided standard conventional sets, rear-projections, and they were going to use my gadget, not knowing it was patented. When shown my patents, they made an undertaking to develop and market the gadget. They wanted only still-projection rights. That's what they got. They killed time for two years, and at last had a rollable screen, etc., but by that time there were no longer any live shows.

Kerkow had a similar, in appearance, idea. He used a reflex screen, projected direct to it, and got a very bright returned image. But he could only use it for animation. An actor in his apparatus did not mask his own shadow.

When shown my apparatus, he took out a license, which he kept in force for two years for some uses, and for a third in some others. There is confusion here, but he insisted that Jenfred warned him that my patents were invalid and he'd get in trouble if he continued.

RCA used it and paid royalty. They used it again and paid royalty. They made some top-secret films with it and paid. They made an RCA animation film with it and were so pleased with the color, etc., that they had more than 300 prints made for each RCA dealer to have one.

Then came the latest stuff. The Rank Movie people, in England, got patents on a special reflex material to be used with a partially silvered glass. *There was no U.S. patent.* The thing was patented in England, France, Belgium; I think Germany, and Mexico. My patents date before it. At the present time they are promoting what they call the Alakan-Gerard Process. It is my gadget, minus a number of features. The SOS Company has now advertised that it supplies the material for the Alakan-Gerard process.

CBS paid five thousand dollars for a license to combine it with their vistocene gadget (private information says it didn't work before, and they had to save their bacon by making something ok after spending so much money; but that if they threw away the rest of the gadget they'd be better off) and they wouldn't have paid that much if they didn't think the patents were airtight.

That's the stuff to date. Here is some added material.

My gadget gives more than twenty-five times as much light as rear projection. For RCA it has been used to get color effects superior to any they've had before. Again for RCA, some special-effect work gave some types of animation a rather remarkable speed. We have a film in which much of the animation was shot at 25 frames per second, and the animation-cost of the film was only 10 percent of the same animation with other processes.

Since my screen returns all light to its source, it also returns stray light to its source. Front projection pictures are shot in a normally lighted studio. The floor space is only one-half of that required for rear projection.

Again, since my screen — any reflex screen — returns all lights to its source, more than one projector can throw an image on the screen at the same time. If two projectors are separated by an angle slightly under 15d, referred to the screen, they each receive back their own image. This means that an actor can be shot at different angles with appropriately modified backgrounds by two or more cameras. Since the camera shoots along the optical axis of the projection, the image does not key-stone, *to the camera*.

If a second screen is placed before the first, with its edge, say, lined up with a projected doorway-edge, an actor walking out from behind the second screen appears to walk onto the set through the door, i.e. here is projection with practical entrances and exits. "Practical" sets of reflex screen can be assembled and "painted" with light.

One new thing has turned up. The brightness of the image, from the appropriate position behind the half-silver glass plate, is so great that one can project microfilm on a vertical screen in a normally lighted office.

As a test of this, I took a unit out of doors in daylight. Seated at a desk with no hood, I was able to read reflected material. This gives a new dimension to microfilm information storage, in a sense. One can even put a screen on an office side-wall or ceiling, and have it used by a number of different men at the same time.

I tried to keep this short.

Daddy

In early 1963, Billee got a phone call in her Haddonfield home. A male voice said, "This is Sherman Fairchild. I understand your father has a patent on a device for front projection. I'd like to talk about it."

As a result of that call, Billee and her husband went to dinner at Fairchild's mansion in the Upper East Side in New York City. The three of them sat at one end of a table that would seat 12, Sherman Fairchild at the head with a telephone at his right hand. He said he was interested in buying the patents, stated his offer, said it was a good one, and emphasized that he had a lot of money to run with the project, and Will Jenkins had very little. Will signed with him.

In his article "Applied Science Fiction," in *Analog's* November 1967 issue, Will ended his story about the initial development of front projection with:

> So there you are. I enjoyed puttering over this thing into existence, even if the current production models make me feel less smart because I couldn't have built them. I've done a lot of puttering, but this is the only item I sweated over. I like to think there are units in use right now in such unexpected places as the Pentagon and at Polaroid headquarters and The Saturday Evening Post and Life and Glamour, and that they are used regularly by large furniture manufacturers and mail order catalogue publishers and that there is one functioning admirably behind the Iron Curtain. And there are local TV stations putting on local programs with 35mm slides furnishing their backgrounds — and they don't haul scenery around at all.
>
> It's a nice, complacent feeling. I even feel slightly noble.

Front projection is a relatively simple concept that was waiting to be developed ever since Scotchlite was invented in the 1940s. To summarize, the camera is focused on the subject standing in front of a highly reflective screen. A projector, at 90 degrees to the camera, projects an image of the background onto a partially silvered mirror angled at 45 degrees, which is located in front of the camera. The mirror, in turn, reflects the image onto the performer and the screen.

What is key is the necessity for careful alignment of all pieces so that the projected light source and the camera lens are located at the same point. This allows the projected light to be reflected directly back to its source, which is now inside the camera. It also helps to have a knowledge of physics.

Will figured it out, and it was used successfully for several years in still photography and television studios. Stanley Kubrick took it to the next step when he seized on the technique for his groundbreaking film *2001: A Space Odyssey*. The "Dawn of Man" sequence would probably have been financially impossible to film without its use. He also used front projection for the scenes of astronauts walking on the moon and was still using it in his 1999 film *Eyes Wide Shut*.

Other producers added their adaptations. The British film *On His Majesty's Secret Service* used front projection, and it was later used with further refinements for Christopher Reeve's flying scenes in *Superman*.

Digital is now the most common technique for special effects.

A new, unexpected diversion appeared at the beginning of 1962. Will described it to Jo-an in a letter dated January 22, "In the short and simple annals of your parents there isn't much excitement, but we have suddenly developed a situation causing great excitement in (of all things) archaeological circles. An Early American garbage pit has been discovered on the lawn — or under it — and you should have a report."

In digging up the stump of a dead walnut tree, a mass of old brick masonry with oyster lime shell mortar was found buried three feet underground. Will's son-in-law Billy DeHardit called a friend at Williamsburg Restoration, the chief archaeologist Ivor Noel Hume, who came to look at it. Excavation soon revealed a large number of oyster shells and, among them, pieces of white clay pipes with the letters SA impressed upon them, which immediately aroused Hume's interest.

Will continued:

> It appears that a mysterious master pipe maker about the year 1700 made pipes so marked which are found in the digs at Williamsburg. Then up came a fragment of a red clay pipe stem, and Hume observed happily that it was probably one of the pipes the Indians made to sell to the early colonists. Then

fragments of tin-glazed pottery. A cryptic mass of iron rust, which Hume said instantly was a pair of scissors. More pipes.

Hume, pink-cheeked with excitement, revealed that there had at some time been a refuse pit — Anglice (meaning in the English manner) garbage dump — whose center was there and it was an earlier garbage dump than had ever been found away from Jamestown. Even Williamsburg does not contain — he deduces — such truly Early American — practically primeval — garbage. The top of this garbage heap is from about the year 1700.

Will was delighted. He treasured the history of his old house, which was dated about 1690, retaining with pride the foot-long, hand-forged iron key that opened the original lock, still in the front door. Now, the possession of early rubbish, interesting enough for the chief archaeologist at Williamsburg to investigate, was a triumph indeed.

Hume later described his discoveries in *Excavations at Clay Bank in Gloucester County, Virginia, 1962–1963*. In a letter of sympathy to Betty and Bill DeHardit after Will's death in 1975, Hume noted that Will had contributed to the nation's archaeological heritage and "his gift of the Clay Bank artifacts to the Smithsonian will be a lasting memorial of that fact."

His contributions to science fiction were recognized in 1963 when he was named guest of honor for Discon I, the 21st World Science Fiction Convention. Always modest, he said little about it, but he was deeply pleased.

Sam Moskowitz's comments in *Seekers of Tomorrow* (World Publishing Company, Cleveland, 1966) went into detail:

> Like the alien in "The Strange Case of John Kingman," the science-fiction community awoke one day in 1962 to the realization that Will F. Jenkins alias Murray Leinster was an unusual phenomenon. Here was a man who had again and again proved he was a leader, if not master, of the field in all its transformations and nuances. On September 1, 1963, he was Guest of Honor of the 21st World Science Fiction Convention, held at the Statler-Hilton, Washington, D.C. For more than a decade they had called him "the dean of science fiction;" now they had decided to make it official.

John W. Campbell wrote "An Appreciation" for the program book including the following:

> I remember Will telling me that he had, for several years, practically made his living by using the formulas in a book on *How to Write Short Stories*. They way you do it, he explained, was to take each rule the book offers — and dream up a story which specifically and flatly violates that rule. Since all short story books have dozens of inviolable rules on story telling, you immediately have material for scores of stories. You know — like "all adventure stories must have fast action — movement — something happening in every line," so you write a story about a man sitting quietly on the bottom of the bay, with his foot trapped by a giant clam, waiting to see whether the clam's shell-muscle will tire enough to free him before his SCUBA air supply gives out.

Edmund Hamilton said in his tribute:

> His technical knowledge and his ability to use it lucidly are very unusual. A lot of us may glibly tell how our hero "quickly constructed a small instrument" that did unusual things. Not Leinster. He tells you how the gadget was constructed step by step, how and why it works and the whole thing is so convincing that you feel he ought to go out and patent it.

Ted Sturgeon wrote, "I've remarked publicly, more than once before, about his ability to make science demonstrations out of a pane of glass, a No. 6 dry cell, cardboard, glue, and paper clips."

Mike Resnick, science fiction author and executive editor of *Jim Baen's Universe*, recalls, "Will was Guest of Honor at the very first convention I ever attended — Discon 1, the 1963 Worldcon in Washington, D.C. I'd taken a 24-hour train ride to get there, knew nobody, and didn't know quite how to approach these giants of the field ... but Will made it very easy. He found time to chat with me and encouraged me to pursue my dream of becoming a science fiction writer. It was the only time I ever met him, but it left an indelible and favorable impression."

John Clute, co-author of *The Encyclopedia of Science Fiction* (Granada, 1979), had thoughts about why Will earned the title of "Dean."

> For the first ten years or so of my life as a sf reader, from about 1953 to about 1963, Murray Leinster was everywhere. Only slowly did I begin to realize that he differed from some of his apparent contemporaries — like Christopher Anvil or John Brunner or Robert Sheckley — by the fact that he had been everywhere for a very long time. Some of his vast output was pure entertainment; some of it offered more than just fun. What he gave us at his best was a generous clarity that conveyed a sense of inevitability to his conceptual breakthroughs; what he always gave us was a sense of inherent decency. For half a century, he wrote of parallel worlds and futures in which it would be possible to be decent. He was called the Dean of Science Fiction for several good reasons, one of those reasons being that he did us honour.

Will would have been most pleased to read in Clute's essay in *Science Fiction Writers* that, "His importance lies in the pleasure he gave. In that he was the dean."

Will was amused to learn later about a glitch in the convention arrangements, averted just in time. Apparently there was a fan from Philadelphia named Will J. Jenkins who was accidentally given the guest of honor courtesy room at the Statler. He was evicted before Mary and Will arrived, bothering no one but the panicked committee chair.

Will was glad that his half-sister Lula's daughter Francis [*sic*] and granddaughter Ellen were able to attend, as well as many other members of the family, and everyone had a good time. His daughters thought it was fun when they were asked for autographs, and couldn't imagine why. It was a high point for Will, who was essentially modest and did not seek out attention, but was very pleased when it came to him.

In the mid-fifties, Scott Meredith had told his clients not to bother sending in anything under 100,000 words: the short story market was dead. In spite of that, Will appeared in *The Saturday Evening Post* three times in 1961 and 1962. The *Post* stopped printing in 1969 (resuming in 1971 as a quarterly with health and medical articles). Will published fifteen books in the 1960s, taking up the slack for the diminishing magazine market, and kept on looking for new markets.

On March 8, 1962, he wrote from Ardudwy to Leo Margulies at *Mike Shayne's Mystery Magazine*:

Dear Leo,

Herewith three stories originally printed in Collier's. As you know, the Colliers-Crowell people now have no interest in these rights. You can check this, of course, by telephone.

One comment. When Collier's printed "Two in a Boat," they omitted the quotes from the reward poster. I think they were wise. I've crossed them out myself.

As usual, I look eagerly in the mail for that cheque you said would be along around the first of the month for "Shelter Hut."

Regards to Sylvia,

In a postscript, he reports enthusiastically on the "dig," bragging that he is now "the owner of one of the earliest collections of colonial garbage in the United States."

"Shelter Hut" was published in the August 1962 issue of *Mike Shayne's Mystery Magazine*. Of the three stories mentioned in a postscript in the letter, "Two in a Boat" appeared in the same magazine in November 1962, and "No More Walls" in December 1963. "Fate Doesn't Care," also mentioned, was not reprinted.

In a March 1963 letter, he told Jo-an:

I did Med Service stories for *Analog* and *Galaxy*. Both went over. Now I have a Med Service book [*Doctor to the Stars*, Pyramid, 1964 included "The Grandfather's War," "Med Ship Man," and "Tallien Three"] but have to have the dates of publication for those stories set before I can sign a contract, which will have to specify publication after magazine use. Incidentally, Byrne of Macfadden, who used to be in charge of Berkeley [*sic*] Books said he'd like a book for Macfadden. I've sent him a synopsis (which John said he'd like for a serial) and he's to read a Med Service story to see if he'd like that book also. Ace Books wants it, but Macfadden would pay exactly twice as much advance. I shall hope.

Macfadden published *The Greks Bring Gifts* in 1964 and reprinted it in 1968. Ridderhof translated it into Dutch in 1964. This story is unusual because, perhaps due to the influence of having four daughters, the female protagonist, Lucy Thale, makes most of the important discoveries.

One character in the Med Service series was so popular he had his own fan base. As Will reported in a letter to Jo-an, November 24, 1974, "There is an imaginary small animal called Murgatroyd who has shown signs of having his own public. I've had fan mail addressed to him."

An imaginary book referred to in the Med Service series also attracted many fans. *The Practice of Thinking* by Fitzgerald, often quoted by one of the doctors, sounded so good that for years readers asked him where they could buy a copy.

Writer Stephen Goldin was a Murgatroyd fan.

> There's also a fond place in my heart for his Med Ship stories that appeared in such books as *Doctor to the Stars* and *This World Is Taboo*. I'll always remember Murgatroyd the tormal, whose sole conversational contributions were "Chee!" (or, in a more talkative mood, "Chee chee"), but who saved countless lives and made invaluable contributions to medical science. These stories blazed a trail that Star Trek later followed. Murray Leinster taught me that the best stories are the ones that expand your universe while they entertain. It's a lesson I've tried never to forget.

On May 3, 1963, Will wrote to Jo-an:

> Things look up. That option business was not a request for an option on *Monster from Earth's End*. Somebody paid $500 for a year's option in 1961 and didn't take it up. They were asking if they could make an outright purchase on the terms the option outlined. Movie rights, three thousand, if television shows were made in addition, so much — not much — additional. It was the Reynolds agency that bought Rogers Terrill's agency when he died. Last year Fawcett arranged a reissue of *Four from Planet Five* through them.

The Monster from Earth's End was made into a movie called *The Navy vs. the Night Monsters* released April 15, 1966. Its director, Michael A. Hoey, went on to direct many well-known TV shows. The production was very low budget, and Hoey was so upset by the result that he and producer Jack Broder had major disagreements, among them the use of the "tree stump monsters" that had been created for the film. Hoey thought that they were ridiculous and refused to shoot them.

An online critic recommended it for "nostalgic sci-fi buffs," saying the story was interesting, the actors professional and the film print good. The Internet Movie Database (IMDb) lists the salary for Murray Leinster as $4,000, and for Michael A. Hoey as $10,000. The movie is available on DVD. There is general agreement that the biggest asset is the star Mamie Van Doren.

Dan Stumpf in *Mystery*File*, published online August 6, 2009, reviewed *The Monster from Earth's End,* which he found in the 50 cents pile at a used book store. He called it: "The genuine article, the real banana, a taut, suspenseful, exciting and genuinely creepy couple hours packed into 176 pages by a writer who knew how to do it."

The story is set on an island off the coast of Chile, a way-station for supplies and scientists going to and from an Antarctic research station. Briefly, a north-bound plane bringing scientists and specimens from the South Pole lands — empty except for the pilot who blows his brains out.

Members of the staff on the island are then stalked by an unseen creature big enough to devour them and by growing numbers of carnivorous crawling insects. Stumpf praises the development of the characters saying, "the characterization here is ably done indeed; I'd swear I have worked with some of these guys."

In between stories, Will continued to tinker.

> I made a magnificent invention yesterday. Mother gave me an opium pipe — Korean — that she'd bought for Christmas and forgot about. I figured the smoke would be horribly hot. So I remembered about that cigarette ad that says the paper is porous and dilutes the smoke. So I took one of my old pipes that would make a goat sick, and drilled a tiny hole into the smoke passage, arranged to open and close it to the desired degree, and lighted it. I've been smoking it ever since — almost literally. It dilutes the smoke by allowing clear air to leak into the smoke-passage. I can open it wide and the smoke feels cool against my tongue. I've diluted the smoke to mildness. Or, of course one can have it full strength or anything in between. I think I'll try it on cigarette holders and cigar holders. And then what? Damfino.
>
> Letter to Jo-an, January 19, 1963

One of Will's experiments around this time so interested John Campbell, with whom Will discussed most of his ideas, that he contacted the scientist, lecturer and writer Joseph P. Martino, then at the Air Force Office of Scientific Research in Washington, D.C., where he was assigned from 1963 to 1968. Martino later wrote:

> One of the nice features of the assignment was that I was in almost daily contact with colleagues at the research offices of Army, Navy, NASA, National Science Foundation, etc. I knew "everybody who was anybody" in the government agencies funding basic research.
> By then I had published several stories in *Analog*, and knew John W. Campbell fairly well. One day I received a letter from Campbell. He wrote that Murray Leinster had done something that he thought had national security implications. Campbell asked me to get in touch with Leinster, which I did. Leinster sent me a document describing something he had devised. It was a method for electrochemically separating isotopes of the same element. At that time there was considerable interest in signing arms control treaties with the Soviet Union. Leinster was concerned that the U.S. might sign a treaty that banned known methods of separating U235 from U238, but miss the one he had

developed. This might give the Soviets a loophole in any treaty we might sign with them.

The method consisted of a long glass tube filled with a thick sugar solution, and with a high voltage applied between the ends of the tube. The idea was that lighter isotopes would pass through the sugar solution more rapidly than heavier ones, and eventually the two would be separated sufficiently that they could be extracted efficiently. The question was, how did he know he was actually separating isotopes? He had an ingenious scheme. He mixed oxides of several "rare earth" elements whose isotopes, in naturally-occurring material, were "interleaved" in atomic mass. That is, element A had some isotopes that were heavier, and some that were lighter, than an isotope of element B. The hydroxides of the elements had different colors in the sugar solution. After passing through the tube, the isotopes formed colored bands whose order was that expected, given the known atomic masses of the isotopes. It was a really neat proof that he could separate isotopes electrochemically. Moreover, it was something that was simple enough that it could be done for a science fair project.

I copied the material he sent me (on the then-new Xerox machine) and sent the copy to a colleague at the then–Atomic Energy Commission. I expected a long delay for a response. But within a week I received back a stack of Xeroxed articles from scientific journals that proved the method could not be scaled up for practical applications. I passed that on to Leinster, and got back a nice letter thanking me for relieving his concerns.

A few years later, after being re-assigned elsewhere, I read an article in a technical journal describing an electrochemical isotope separation method being used in industry. I realized then that I'd been had. The AEC kept a stack of those "disproving" articles handy. Any time anyone invented an electrochemical method for separating isotopes, they fired off copies to discourage the inventor from pursuing the matter further. Science being what it is, however, discoveries can't be suppressed indefinitely. Someone had re-invented a technique equivalent to Leinster's, and hadn't bothered to ask the AEC about it. They had simply gone ahead and commercialized it.

That was my only contact with Leinster. I had been a fan of his stories, ever since reading *The Murder of the U.S.A.* when I was in high school, and *First Contact* when I was in college. In his correspondence with me, he mentioned *Heart of the Serpent*, the Soviet "reply" to *First Contact*. I wish I'd had the opportunity to meet him personally.

When not tinkering, Will loved to entertain. One of his letters, typical of his sense of humor, was written in September 1964 to his nephew George Cox and his wife, Martha, regarding their daughter Bonnie's wedding. George was the son of Will's brother-in-law, the Rev. G. W. Cox, a Baptist minister.

> A Presbyterian preacher? Evidently, George, you didn't tell her the facts of a preacher's wife's life! Remember those wise and truthful old saws? "If the Lord will keep him humble, then the church will keep him poor." ... I shall hope, in my Papist way, that Bonnie Ann's husband rules his congregation with an iron hand, and his wife in a much gentler fashion....
> Love to the kids, even if they think they're too old.

He lived to see one grandson-in-law become a Presbyterian minister but did not know a great-grandson would also be ordained in the Presbyterian Church.

Billee's girls were growing up and still loving their visits to Clay Bank. With their usual hospitality, Will and Mary even allowed Pam to bring a high school boyfriend down. After she graduated from high school in 1965 and left for Tusculum College in Tennessee, this became a halfway stop on the way to school.

Will's novel *Killer Ship* was published in three parts in *Amazing* beginning with the October 1965 issue, which also included stories by Ray Bradbury, John Wyndham and Jack Williamson. Murray Leinster rated the cover. *Amazing* had just been bought by Sol Cohen and his Universal Publishing Company. Joseph Ross was managing editor, and his editorial in this October issue began, "What does it take to be the dean of science fiction?"

It continues with:

> Well, if you're Murray Leinster, you start out by writing "The Runaway Skyscraper," a different story which immediately wins you the enthusiastic loyalty of Argosy readers back in 1919. Then you follow with "The Red Planet" and its sequel "The Red Dust," classic insect stories that will eventually become "The Forgotten Planet," one of your best books. From then you keep turning out more stories like "Sidewise in Time," "First Contact" and "Exploration Team" (which wins a Hugo in 1956.) And all the while you adapt smoothly to changing styles and the astonishing advances of modern science. Then, as if that wasn't enough, in 1965 you come up with *Killer Ship* and Trent of the Yarrow, one of your most memorable characters. That's what it takes to be the "dean of science fiction," and that's why Murray Leinster holds the title.

Killer Ship was published in book form in 1966 by Ace under the title *Space Captain*.

New Year's Eve in 1966 was like old times. Billee and her family were at the Clay Bank house, and Betty, Billy and Beth, the Allens and many of their long time friends joined the celebrations. There was the usual spread of finger food, plenty of whiskey, but, as usual, no one drank too much. Mary had made cassoulet. She was an excellent cook and loved trying new recipes. She was excited about making this French stew for the first time. There were the usual noisemakers and shouts of "Happy New Year" at midnight and the conga line that had become a tradition. Mary and Will were at the lead, and everyone conga-ed from the living room through the dining room and kitchen and into the sunporch and out the door, in spite of the weather, and back through the front door. It was like all the old time parties and New Year's Eves at Clay Bank through the years. Mary and Will were making plans for their 50th wedding anniversary celebration. No one dreamed that this would be their last party.

Tragedy struck shortly after Mary's 70th birthday. She died suddenly on April 24, 1967. Although they knew she had a heart condition, she refused to slow down and always enjoyed life to the fullest. They were staying at the apartment in New York when she became ill, and she was taken immediately to nearby Booth Memorial Hospital, but nothing could be done.

Mary was buried in the historic Ware Church Cemetery in Gloucester, near the grave of a grandchild, Betty's second daughter, who was stillborn.

• TEN •

After Mary's Death

Will and Mary had been married for almost 46 years in a uniquely close relationship. As he had always worked at home, they were in each other's company constantly, and he would boast, with satisfaction, that they had almost never spent a night apart. Will loved and protected her. Mary organized his life, fixed the meals he liked and laid out his clothes every morning. He read his stories to her as he worked on them, and she listened and commented, carefully correcting typos before the final copies were sent off in the mail. As one of Will's long time friends Edward Chism once said, "Will has the perfect life. He does whatever he wants, and Mary helps him."

After Mary died, Will said he "had the stuffing knocked out of him." He never again slept in their bedroom, instead creating a new, single bed on the sun porch, so, as he said, "I would know the minute I woke up that things were different." Still, as Jo-an experienced, he would wake in the morning and call immediately, "Mary," forgetting for a moment that there would be no reply.

Mary and Will in a happy moment at Clay Bank.

And a year later, in a letter to Jo-an dated April 8, 1968, he told her, "I still forget that I'm alone and every so often I discover I've called Mother to ask her what time it is or something."

He found it hard to concentrate and missed his most helpful audience. Mary had listened and commented on bits of stories as he read them to her. He found it difficult to continue writing as he used to, and his thirty-six year record of contributing to *Astounding Stories, Astounding Science-Fiction* and *Analog* ended in November 1966 with the publication of "Quarantine World."

Also due to his bereavement, he felt, as he told Billee, "No one is going to visit anymore now that your Mother's gone."

Of course, they did. Betty, Bill and Beth lived close by in Gloucester Court House. Billee's daughter Pam and her husband, Cliff Hayes, moved from Tennessee to Clay Bank, while he finished his last year of college at William and Mary in Williamsburg before going on to Louisville Presbyterian Seminary. They rented a house just a short distance upriver from Will's. Subsequently, Billee and her husband purchased that same house, kept it rented, and came down for vacations at Ardudwy just as they always had. Gail was at Westhampton College in Richmond and visited as often as she could. Mary Jr. came down from New Hampshire, where she now lived. And, although Jo-an moved to London in 1968, she came for visits and, after her marriage in 1973, was able to bring her husband, Adrian Evans, to Clay Bank before Will died. Other family members and friends continued to visit, so it went on being the family gathering place that Will had always wanted.

Surprisingly, for a man fascinated by gadgets, Will was never comfortable making long distance phone calls. There was a family joke that he would buy Mary anything she wanted except time talking long distance. If she made a call, he would stand at her shoulder saying, "Mary, this is long distance. Don't forget, this is long distance." He would write to Jo-an, working in New York, asking her to make phone calls to editors for him, rather than call himself. In a letter dated September 10, 1964, he asked: "Did you call Miss Wood at Avon about that book synopsis? If not, please do."

Later, when Jo-an was living in London and telephoned, he could barely talk, saying repeatedly, "Gosh, this is costing you a lot of money."

Billee telephoned regularly, so he rarely wrote to her but passed on the news she told him in letters to Jo-an in London to whom he wrote frequently. This was unexpectedly fortunate, because a record of these last years remains in his letters.

On February 12, 1968, a few days after Jo-an left New York to work in London, he wrote:

I was looking at a map of London last night and finding out where you lived. I was astounded to see how many places I feel like I know — with the damndest associations! Kensington Gardens isn't so much Peter Pan as the place where one of the smallest bridges in the world exists, and is memorable because Chesterton was more frightened there than anywhere else in his lifetime. The British Museum says, "Karl Marx wrote here," though I want to see the Egyptology section.

A few weeks later on February 28, he told her, "I think I understand the way you feel about homesickness. It's very bad. But as you accumulate even trivial things, it will help. And for time — this is my experience — you'll get so that you forget now and then that there's been a change. Things will seem quite normal so long as you don't notice that they aren't. Then it's not so good when you're reminded, but you can carry on."

He kept her up to date on his work, and on March 15, 1968, wrote, "*The Land of the Giants* thing went over. A sequel is already bespoken. I'm trying to get started again. That was the first piece of fiction I've been able to write since last April. [Mary died April 24.] I've covered reams of paper, but none of it would get started, or get ended, or something."

The Land of the Giants was published by Pyramid in 1968, and was followed by *The Hot Spot* (Pyramid, 1969) and *Unknown Danger* (Pyramid, 1969). All were novelizations of the TV series.

His most creative years were behind him but he was not forgotten. Barry N. Malzberg called him

a remarkable, irreplaceable figure. Take him out of the history and as with Campbell that history might collapse ... a remarkable career with many good stories and in my opinion a rare double: He wrote two stories which in essence founded subgenres. I don't think any other science writer can claim that. "Sidewise in Time" in 1934 was the origination of the parallel world story and of course "First Contact" in 1945 about first contact with an alien civilization was the first major investigation of the theme and its implications. Both were endlessly imitated and imitated. To write two stories of such lasting importance is a staggering accomplishment. I think he is one of those few writers who, if he did not exist, would have left the field entirely different today.

In April 1968, Syracuse University collected Will's manuscripts and other papers to preserve in its library. They now fill 71 boxes in the university's archival division and include manuscripts of published stories, story ideas and synopses, and correspondence with publishers, agents and other writers.

At the last minute, he decided to keep many of his earliest writings, and the whole experience unnerved him. Above all, he was disappointed that his papers were not to remain in Virginia. As he told Jo-an in a letter dated April 26, 1968, "William and Mary called me on the phone. They'd heard about Syracuse University announcing the gift of my Mss. They wanted to know wouldn't I rather have them preserved in Virginia. Of course I would. I'd stalled Syracuse for nearly three years."

However, during those three years, Will never contacted any of the Virginia institutions that might have been interested in retaining his papers in their libraries. Not realizing that Syracuse contacted him because they were actively building a science fiction collection, he thought that, if others were interested, they would have gotten in touch with him as well. A friend, a William and Mary alumnus, alerted William and Mary of Syracuse's plans, and, having had it brought to their attention, William and Mary was immediately interested, but by then it was too late.

In the same letter to Jo-an, Will reported an exchange with his granddaughter Pam when she was still in college in Tennessee:

> Pam sent me a book by this Chardin guy — avant garde theology — with the observation that he made her MAD, and that I might like to get mad too. I couldn't stomach the stuff, so I wrote her four pages single space denouncing all pseudo-intellectuals with page and paragraph included. She reported gratefully that she had to turn in two papers at school and she filled them both out of my letter. I had only meant to exercise a grandfather's privilege of being oratorical.

Billee wrote to Jo-an on June 3, 1968, as follows:

> Another letter so soon. I wanted to fill you in on our plans. Pam will be married August 31.... Dad will be up Monday night to stay for Gail's graduation the 13th and his birthday and Fathers Day. Talked to him and Betty Friday night and told them all the news. So they are set to come up and Dad was trying to decide whether to come to England for two weeks in August or September.

He did go to England in September as planned but came to Haddonfield for the wedding first. He was delighted that George Cox, his half-sister Lula's son, and George's wife, Martha, were able to attend and Mary and Betty and Beth were there. Beth was a junior bridesmaid.

During that summer, August of 1968, Will wrote on his favorite subject, gadgets, to his granddaughter Gail:

> What you're talking about is a mobius strip, named after the German mathematician who described its remarkable properties. It might be respectful to call it a Mobius strip.
> You know how to make one. You take a strip of paper and make it into a loop, having turned one end a half turn before pasting it. But were you ever crazy enough to make the pencil line that proves it has only one surface, and then cut along that pencil line as if to cut it in two? You'll be surprised. Making a complete turn before pasting produces something else. Splitting some of these secondary loops is crazy, too.
> In this connotation there is also a thing called a Klein Bottle, which instead of being a two-dimensional object with a single surface, is a three dimensional

object with only one surface. I probably have a picture of it somewhere, but heaven forbid that I try to draw it from memory!

In the autumn of 1968, Will made his first and only trip out of the U.S. to visit Jo-an in London, arriving on a TWA flight on the morning of September 6, 1968, to stay with her at 4a Markham Square in Chelsea.

Although he wrote on July 29 that he planned to work while he was there and also spend time with his British agent, John Carnell, who wanted to arrange a number of meetings with science fiction fans and publishers, he focused on seeing landmarks for what he understood of his British ancestry, based on the family tree handed down in his family.

> I wish you wouldn't make long and elaborate plans for me to do sightseeing. I am going to have to finish this book.... I have just one slightly insane place I would like to see. Your ninth great-grandfather spent most of Cromwell's regime in the Tower. He was officially declared the most stubborn man in England. I'd like to see his cell — maybe even get a picture of it. Also there is his son, Sir Leoline Jenkins whose picture hangs in Jesus College Oxford, who is buried under the altar of that church, who founded scholarships for poor Welsh boys, and got his start as Charles II's secretary, his special qualification being that he knew more dirty stories than any man in England but the King.
>
> I'm mildly curious about these things.... Old Judge David Jenkins must have been a character.

Will loved this story and repeated it many times. Fortunately, he did not live to see it disproved. More accessible records now show that there is no direct male line coming down from the judge or that he and Sir Leoline were related.

In London, Will wrote copious notes in a specially bought notebook, chuckling at road signs — "Heavy Plant Crossing" and "Do not enter box until exit is clear" — that struck him as worthy of a *New Yorker* cartoon. The Egyptology section at the British Museum absorbed him completely, and he happily compared the Museum of Natural History with the one he knew so well in New York. A performance of Oscar Wilde's *The Importance of Being Earnest* particularly pleased him when he discovered he could remember the dialogue almost word for word. He saw Oxford and Cambridge and the changing of the guard at Buckingham Palace, which, he said, was more or less the same as in the A. A. Milne poem he had so often recited to his children.

On his return, he enjoyed telling stories about what he had seen. On October 21 he wrote to Jo-an, "I appear to have passed a new ten pence piece off to someone as a quarter. I know I tried a sixpence in a telephone, thought it was a dime, and it was indignantly returned."

On July 12, 1969, Will gave fatherly advice when Jo-an wrote of trying to plan an American meal for English guests: "You spoke of a party. I believe one can get canned corn on the cob. Very, very American. Can you get cornmeal? Spoon-bread would be a novelty."

On September 9, 1969, he responded to a postcard from St. Tropez: "Stuck in my head somewhere is the statement that the Upper Corniche road to Menton is one of the three most beautiful drives in the world, the others being the road to Clovelly in Devon (where the clotted cream comes from) and El Camino Real in California."

In 1969, Will was awarded the First Fandom Hall of Fame award at the Hugo Awards Ceremony at the 27th World Science Fiction Convention held in St. Louis, Missouri, August 28 to September 1. He decided not to attend, and when the award was delivered to him in September, he described it in a letter to Jo-an, dated September 16, 1969, as follows, "It is two feet high with a very, very golden plate containing fulsome praise of me. Then more gold ... and up on top a sphere with two gold fins on it and a golden space ship on top.... The intention was admirable and I am properly appreciative, I hope."

For the first time there was livestock at Clay Bank. Mary had won a pony in a raffle a few years before, and it was given to their granddaughter Beth. She promptly named him Sandy Joe. As he grew older, a second pony joined him. After Mary died, it was decided that stabling them at Clay Bank might be a welcome diversion, and Will enjoyed them.

He wrote Jo-an on November 16, 1969, "I feed the animals every morning and night. They can spot me from the cliff ... and look at me indignantly because I'm late. Their expressions say: 'where the hell is our breakfast?'"

He reported on Beth's pets later in 1972, in a letter to his granddaughter Gail.

> There is little or no news from these parts. The ponies are well and I've been trying to get Brandy [his dog] to a more girlish figure. She's been at least matronly, and I may be kidding myself that she's lost a few ounces, but I cling to the belief.
> Beth has a kid an eight-months-old lady goat who is actually learning to do tricks. This adds to tropical fish, a gerbal (Spelling?) [sic] a cat, dog, the ponies aforementioned and a recently released robin who throve only on earthworms, so there was usually somebody gathering worms for him or her or it.

In the same letter, he tells Gail that he and Billy DeHardit, Beth's father, have found a discarded piano in a ditch, and he has salvaged some ivory from the keys. He'd cleaned it up with Brillo and Clorox and was sending it on, because she mentioned an interest in trying to carve scrimshaw. She still has the ivory.

As Murray Leinster, Will was featured guest at Disclave 70, held by the Washington Science Fiction Association at the Skyline Inn in Washington,

D.C., in May 1970. He started his speech, "Recollections from My Past," in character saying, "When the idea of my coming to D.C. to talk to the members of the Washington club was first mentioned, I asked what on earth I should talk about. I was at a loss to think of a good start. Then somebody said that he couldn't speak for everyone, but it seemed to him that a good dirty story was always a way to get people's attention."

And he swung into a very mildly dirty story (briefly, Mrs. O'Sullivan has triplets. Her neighbor Mrs. Casey visits her and is astounded when Mrs. O'Sullivan tells her that the doctor has said it only happens once in every two hundred thousand times. "Merciful heavens!" cries Mrs. Casey. "How did you ever find time to do your housework?")

When it finished, he went on, "So I asked if that was all right for a start and was assured it was. Then somebody else spoke up: 'But this is a highly intellectual group, this Disclave thing. We're culture. We're highbrow. Maybe you'd better say something about your literary career.'

"My literary career? You mean what General Lee got me into?"

And he continued with his favorite story about his childhood (with which this biography begins.)

He always appreciated recognition and was not always sure he deserved it. He wrote to Jo-an on October 5, 1971, "I just got a copy of *Analog*. There is a sort of Gallup Poll of the best science fiction stories before 1940. I'm listed with The Mad Planet series and The Runaway Skyscraper (!) In fact, I rate number four with H. G. Wells as number one. Not too bad, considering."

On March 25, 1971, Will became a great-grandfather for the first time. Pam gave birth to Eric Christopher "Chris" Hayes, the first of Cliff's and her four children, in Louisville, Kentucky, where Cliff was completing his studies at the seminary there. She and Cliff were able to bring him to Clay Bank to show him off when he was three. Will reported to Jo-an, "Pam with Cliff and Chris — aged three years of continuous conversation — were down last week and Cliff insists that I have improved his sermons (heaven knows how)."

Cliff, who had studied philosophy in college and Louisville Seminary, said Will was the only person he knew who had read Emmanuel Kant in full, not once, but twice.

Will enjoyed visits by young fans. Michael Swanwick shared a memory with Billee about a visit he made, one that undoubtedly pleased Will very much.

> In 1972, when I was an undergrad at the College of William and Mary, my friend Paul Fuchs and I had the privilege of accompanying my favorite English teacher, Dr. David Clay Jenkins [no relation], on a visit to Ardudwy to see your father. I was overawed by his intelligence, by his kindness, by the enormous piles

of books in his living room, by the experimental apparatus he had set up on the dining room table for an invention he was trying to find a practical use for, indeed by everything about him. He was quite a raconteur. Clustered on a corner of his kitchen table were trophies for several science fiction awards, and he had a funny anecdote for each one, save the last. "And that's my Hugo," he said in a way that indicated he would have valued it more if only it had given him a story to tell about it.

On that same visit, I asked Will Jenkins one of those questions that only a naïve young man can ask: Whether he was optimistic or pessimistic about the future. With a little smile, a distinct twinkle in his eye, and a whimsical touch of an Irish lilt to his voice, he quoted the Virginian ironic fantasist James Branch Cabell, saying, "I contemplate the spectacle with appropriate emotions."

Also in 1971, Will went again to a science fiction convention, an unusual occurrence for him. But it was in Norfolk, his birthplace and just down the road from his Clay Bank home. Bud Webster remembers it in an article in *Jim Baen's Universe*, February 2010. The convention was a small event called Dixieland Fancom, and science fiction writer, editor and publisher Donald Wollheim, comic book writer Wally Wood and science fiction artist Kelly Freas were all there.

Webster remembers Wood as "mostly absent," and Wollheim as "imperious and frighteningly knowledgeable." Since Webster had been primarily a comic fan, attending a science fiction convention was a first for him. But he knew Will's works well, primarily because Will was so frequently reprinted. Groff Conklin, a prolific anthologist, had included Leinster stories in many of them. He had been keeping score in an unofficial competition between Leinster and Sturgeon appearances and noted in *Science Fiction Adventures in Mutations* (Vanguard, 1955) that the race was a draw. Both had appeared in all but one of his sixteen anthologies. Later, Sturgeon won with twenty-three, as opposed to Will's nineteen.

Webster wrote further, "I was barely even a fan back then.... The idea of meeting and speaking with one of my heroes, therefore, was more than a little alien to me. Will, on the other hand was an old pro at this. He knew how not to embarrass or discourage a fanboy, a skill I was later to discover was common in most pros, but appallingly lacking in others."

Later he added, "He was a dyed-in-the-wool Southern Gentleman, generous with his time and advice to younger authors."

Webster's summary of Will's work is insightful: "If there was a market he could figure out a yarn for, he wrote it and sold it. This strikes me as a handy thing for a professional writer to be able to do."

In response to what author, editor and critic Damon Knight has called "Leinster's carefully pedestrian prose," Webster says, "Leinster never fails to entertain, never ceases to amaze. His body of work isn't just long and broad, it's got depth. It isn't self-consciously literary, and he eschewed pretentiousness."

He continued, "Fine dining is fine dining. On the other hand, sometimes you just want a plateful of chili, or a steak and baked, and that's where you will find Leinster, complete with barbeque tongs and 'Kiss the Cook!' apron. You know, comfort food, but without the preprocessed cheese."

In spite of his earlier comment, Knight said in his introduction to "The Eternal Now" in *The Shape of Things* (Popular Library, Inc., 1965) "Murray Leinster, it is safe to suppose, has been responsible for more reader hours of entertainment than any other living science fiction writer."

This is not surprising, for Gary K. Wolfe refers to "Leinster's astonishing publication record — averaging something like a story every two weeks and a novel every nine months for better than a half-century" ("Twentieth-Century American Science-Fiction Writers," David Coward and Thomas L. Wymer, eds. *Dictionary of Literary Biography*, vol. 8 (Detroit: Gale Research, 1981).

Foreign sales continued. In 1972, Will comments to Jo-an in a letter, "The Italian and Japanese governments seem to be competing to see which can ask the more ridiculous amount of income-tax from me. I just got a cheque from Japan, remittance one hundred and sixty-six dollars. Income-tax, twenty-seven thousand yen. A little while back I got a notice of (I think it was) a payment of a little more than thirty thousand lira income-tax from Italy."

About the same time, Ahrvid Engholm, a fan in Sweden, was becoming very active in the Swedish science fiction community. He edited the magazine *Nova Science Fiction*, published science fiction newsletters, organized science fiction conventions, and wrote short stories. He had been reading Murray Leinster since 1954 and shared this memory.

> Murray Leinster died before I became active in science fiction, but as a young sf fan I remember reading him in the newsstand paperback series of sf and horror that existed in Sweden then, and that he was among the best authors in the often rather terrible selection these cheap book series had. I also discovered him in the 1954–1966 Swedish sf magazine Häpna!, e.g. "Proxima Centauri" which made the cover of one issue.
> So I began reading him more and more, and when I began writing science fiction myself I was probably influenced somewhat by his idea-driven, elegant, clear-cut style of writing (because that's at least the way I want to write).
> I have also talked about Murray Leinster on a sf convention, in a program item about old, somewhat forgotten favourites.
> We should especially remember the story "A Logic Named Joe," which is a truly remarkable piece of sf-as-prediction, about personal computers, Internet, multimedia written-in the 1940s. No other early computer story comes close to

this accomplishment by the writer I only later learned was named William F. Jenkins.

Will continued to write, but he told Jo-an on June 7, 1973, how he was reluctant to travel:

> I should go to New York and talk to some editors but I never did like New York. I feel particularly infirm when I think of Leo Margulies' experience. He had offices for his magazines between Fifth and Sixth Avenues. His wife was mugged on that block at 3:00 in the afternoon, and he's moved his business to the Pacific Coast ... I don't think I'll go.

Shortly after that, a letter to Jo-an shows he was still tinkering, "Quite without premeditation, just puttering around, I found I'd made a transparency which is positive if lighted from one side, and a negative if lighted from the other. I'm trying to imagine what could possibly make use of it."

When Jo-an planned to marry in 1973, he wrote to her on January 1:

> In marriage, simple good faith is incredibly important. People who are not passionately romantic about each other can get along reasonably well if they both practice simple good faith. And people who get along reasonably well because they have confidence in each other's good faith — are very likely to be pretty damned romantic about each other.
>
> This, you observe, is not advice. It is a statement of what I think is fact. And I think this is a good place to stop.

In the spring of 1974, Jo-an and her husband, Adrian Evans, visited from London. Will's presence was still felt in Gloucester. Adrian liked to drive fast and was picked up by the local police for speeding. Preparing to use his British accent as an excuse for ignorance of the law, his plans were foiled when the officer immediately recognized Will sitting in the back seat, and said, "Hello, Mr. Jenkins." Adrian got the ticket.

Early in 1975, his health failing, Will entered a nursing home. When Billee talked to him, just after he went in, he was, of course, very unhappy. Betty, Bill and Beth lived close by, and Billee and Gail were able to visit. Jo-an, now expecting her first child, came over from England to see him for the last time. He did not live to see her son Benedict, who was born in September.

That spring, Billee attended a workshop in New Jersey, where Isaac Asimov was the main speaker. They had a nice visit with many reminiscences, and she told him Will was in a nursing home in Gloucester. She had brought along a photograph taken at Discon 1, in 1963 at the Statler Hilton in Washington, where Will was guest of honor, and Isaac was master of ceremonies. Will and Mary are with Isaac at the head table. She asked him to sign it for Will, and he wrote, "To Will, the great dean of them all."

Will and Mary when he was guest of honor at Discon 1, Statler Hotel, Washington D.C. Isaac Asimov is master of ceremonies.

Will died on June 8, 1975, in Gloucester, Virginia, eight days before his 79th birthday. He was buried, as planned, next to Mary in Ware Church cemetery in Gloucester.

In a letter to Will's daughters, his old friends Chick and Toni Fexas wrote the following:

> We'll remember him for his wit, his philosophical discussions into the night, his inventions, his anecdotes, including his "kitchen stories;" we'll remember him on joyous occasions on the boat, at innumerable house parties, on holidays and graduations and during the saddest time of his life; we'll remember him especially in his beloved "Ardudwy" where we saw him last.

After Will's death:

- In the 1979 Italian film *Starcrash* the spaceship in the opening sequences is called the *Murray Leinster*.
- The Sidewise in Time Award for Alternate History was established in 1995—named for the Murray Leinster story "Sidewise in Time."
- The Retro Hugo, 1996, was awarded to Will for "First Contact."
- June 27, 2009, was declared "Will F. Jenkins Day" in the State of Virginia.

Murray Leinster was not only a very good writer, he was a pioneer. He invented the field of parallel-universe stories with his "Sidewise in Time," and his 'First Contact' set the pattern for all the stories that followed of—well—of first contact with alien civilizations. The wondrous thing about his work is that those great, trend-setting stories read as fresh and timely today as they did all those years ago.

— Frederik Pohl in a credit on the cover of *Planets of Adventure*, edited by Eric Flint and Guy Gordon and published by Baen in 2003

Will Jenkins did not die, nor will he as long as his work and mine are in print. I have and always will acknowledge my debt to John Campbell, who taught me so very much about science fiction, but it is to Will that I owe the very bones and sinews of my writing.

— Theodore Sturgeon, *Locus*, June 24, 1975

• ELEVEN •

On Writing

Will loved words. He loved the way they sounded, the way they felt in his mouth, the way you can use them to amuse or confound. He collected exceptional words and phrases in many languages. In addition to the Spanish phrases he used, he taught his daughters antidisestablishmentarianism, an English political term, as soon as they could pronounce it, explaining that they now knew the longest word in the English language. A favorite, frequently repeated Latin phrase was "de gustibus non es disputandum" meaning "there is no accounting for tastes." He wrote to Joan on September 9, 1969:

> Years ago I marveled at hearing the word "dichotomy" used twice in conversation by people I knew. Later it became commonplace among persons in the advertising business. Sunday someone used the word "univocal" (accent on the second syllable) for the first time I've heard it in conversation.... Once I wrote a long letter to get an excuse to use the word "tonsilectotomic." A mild and unimportant but cherished triumph.

Purely for his own amusement, in 1939 he wrote a two thousand-word essay on "The

Will in the mid–1940s.

Speech Habits of Joan Patricia," his year-old baby daughter. In it, he said:

> However, the phonetics of less eccentric utterances are probably of greater importance, scientifically. It is remarkable that she confuses so few of the labial sounds. Words in which labials are necessary she utters with apparent correctness. "May-be," "Da-da," "Mum-mum" are examples of not only accuracy but also distinguished elegance in diction. Palatal sounds, combined with labials, are also correctly used. "Pi-tee" — very, very frequently used, to indicate not only "pretty" but charm in objects as diverse as a cud-chewing cow and a dish of apple sauce — is an example. The R-sound still eludes her, but with that elision allowed for, "Pi-tee" (perhaps "pih-tee" would give the pronunciation more exactly) is an admirable example of correct and stately diction.

He loved nonsense verse. Lewis E. Carroll's "Jabberwocky" was a favorite, and Will would often recite it to his children, wagging his finger in rhythm. So imbedded did it become in at least one daughter's mind that she could recite it from memory to this day.

When granddaughter Gail was in fourth grade and interested in trying to write some poetry, he shared a couple of pieces he had jotted down just for the children's entertainment. He insisted they were not poetry.

"I do not write poetry" he told her, "I write verse."

RELATIVITY
Glsctr, VA by Will Jenkins

It is confusing when I think
My left hand is your right,
And when it's morning here to me
Somewhere it's late at night.

It's also strange night doesn't break,
Although I've seen it fall,
While day can break and break and break
Without a fall at all.

If you are big, a mile is short,
If you are little, long.
I think that everything that's right
Sometimes, some place is wrong.

PHOOEY TO THE AGE OF PERICLES!
by W. F. Jenkins NY

No ancient Greek, not even Plato
Could see a Jet, or watch a JATO
But we can see these things, and soon
Perhaps a rocket to the moon.

The Age of Pericles possessed
Appreciation, Art and Zest,

But did the time which owned Aspasia
Have Dali, Proust or euthanasia?
Did the dim race which built the Stoa
Have Constellations to Samoa?
And what Greek sage, wise and aloof
Had TV aerials on his roof?

(Not even Thebes' Epaminandas
Possessed a platypus or pandas:
No ancient Greek, not even Milo
Could contour farm or build a silo!)
We may not have Praxiteleses
But we've found out what causes sneezes.
Perhaps we have no fair Agora
But we can hybridize our flora,
And we may lack peripatetics
But we've industrialized synthetics.
And who would trade the panorama
Of Hollywood, for Attic drama?

No Greek in all the classic ages
Paid group insurances from his wages.
No bold Hellene, it is quite certain
Could make a simple Iron Curtain

So what? So what indeed indeed
  So what!
The Greeks had Art and Culture
But
Our Nuclear-mass-Neurosis-Money-
Civilization is a honey
  Too!

In his own writing, Will loved to set himself challenges and delighted when one of his self assigned writing experiments worked.

> In "Time Tunnel" I'm vain about the first page and a half of it. It's a description of Paris in 1804, and there's not a word of description of what was there. A page and a half of chapter seven of "Time Tunnel" is a technical trick. Instead of describing what Paris was like in 1804, I list all the things that weren't there—and it makes a nice picture.
>
> *Letter to Jo-an, November 27, 1974*

He loved also to help others with their writing. In "A Personal Note" honoring Will in the program book for Discon 1, the 21st World Science Fiction Convention, held in 1963 at the Statler Hilton in Washington, Theodore Sturgeon said:

> Will taught me, for example, to plot a story from character. Plenty of writing courses will tell you that, but I have never heard it described the way Will described it to me one day in 1945. Create a character, he said, preferably some-

one you know well, who *is* something to the marrow of his bones: a cobbler, say, or a prude, or a Catholic or a railroad man; it almost doesn't matter what. Then put him in a situation where he isn't permitted to be this one special thing. A gross example would be to put a man (who is, to the core, an oxygen breather) out into a vacuum. The plot, then, consists of his working his way out of his predicament *by being what he is.*

Aside from the breathtaking simplicity of this idea, I applaud the aim; for in this day and age, when so many people get paid off in one way or another for being hypocrites, there's something rather wonderful about a man who repeatedly inoculates the public with the idea that it just might pay off to be yourself.

Theodore Sturgeon

To his daughter Jo-an in college he wrote:

Your story outline sounds ok. If you once get the first two paragraphs down, the rest will run out like water out of a tap. I've been tearing my hair out about that Gold story [Horace L. Gold, first editor of *Galaxy Magazine*]. All of a sudden it's running smoothly. They do sometimes.

Letter to Jo-an, March 1957

Later, he told her:

To me, as you know, grammar and syntax are simply the means by which one says something so clearly that one's meaning cannot be mistaken. It is the trick involved in complete lucidness. (And there I said "lucidness" because it is more lucid than "lucidity") I think that, just as old Bill Shakespeare contributed more idioms to the English language than any man before or since, that completely lucid phrasing ought to be as effective now as then. Bill's contribution to English idiom was simply that he said certain things so clearly that nobody could ever comfortably say the same things less clearly after him. If writing has clarity, it has everything.

Letter to Jo-an, January 9, 1963

In another letter to Jo-an that year, Will talked about writing in depth:

A story begins when the reader knows that something is going to happen; when a situation is pictured which cannot stay unchanged; when the state of things stated or implied at the beginning of a story is unstable.

Example: There's a man looking at a wide expanse of smoke, filling more than half the horizon. Flames leap up. He says: "The wind's changed. It's coming this way."

Example: A woman opens a letter. It begins "Dearest Eddie." She's surprised and looks at the envelope. It's addressed to her husband. She opened it by mistake.

Example: A girl says defiantly, "It's wonderful to be able to trust somebody nobody else can trust! And I can trust Joe."

A story is never unemotional. It is always about something important to the protagonist. (The protagonist is almost always the person the reader follows around and watches and listens to — who is the person who has the experience which is the story.) Nothing is important to anybody unless it produces an emotional reaction, because we get emotional about everything that is important. So we arrive at:

A story begins when something important to (almost invariably) the first person mentioned in it. This is a convention very nearly as definite as the convention that we will write the story from left to right. When somebody is mentioned in the first paragraph, it is assumed that this is the person that we are going to follow around and sympathize with.

Here comes another item; it is *possible* to write a story about somebody so unpleasant that we read on hoping for him to get his. It is much easier to write a story about a person we feel kindly toward; about whom we can feel solicitude; with whom in some sense we "identify."

Everybody tells themselves stories. When we have had an experience (or imagined one) that we like to go over and over in our minds, we rearrange our memories of the experience so that they are in the most satisfying order to us. This is not necessarily chronological order. The rearrangement (I am speaking of a perfectly normal, universal practice which is a perfectly natural operation of the mind) changes the emphasis upon incidents, changes the order in which we recall them, and brings out the things — perhaps barely noticed at the time — which were actually important, so that at the end of this rearrangement we have discovered the pattern, the organization, the meaning of the total experience. We like to recall it because it is meaningful.

It is notorious that very many people write one damned good story, and sell it, and can never write another. The reason is that they concocted the one story for their own satisfaction, went over and over it in pleasurable recollection, and then wrote it down the way they liked to remember it. But when it got printed and they got paid for it, they didn't repeat the process for fun, but for cash, fame, kudos, or status. Some people can write for cash, fame, kudos, or status. I still have to kid myself that my stuff is worth writing. The chances are, though, that the way to start writing is to invent or recall a story you like to tell yourself and tell it to yourself until you practically don't change it any more. Then you'll want to write it, to share it. But writing is a fine way to engage in reverie.

The fact that a science fiction story is simply a synthetic memory; that in a reverie we have the same kind of experience (aesthetic experience) that we have when reading a story. This gives an infinite amount of information about stories. For example, in memories of events we do not narrate them to ourselves in words. We remember sensory impressions; how things looked, felt, tasted or sounded.

We recall facts (that so-and-so came from Cincinnati, for example) but a story is conveyed in terms of sensory and emotional experiences with only such declaratory stated facts as are needed to make those sensory and emotional experiences understandable. You can say that a story is never narrated but portrayed. (I've sold straight narratives, but it ain't easy.) You can narrate facts, but you have to portray experiences to convey them to your reader.

Since the aesthetic experience of reading a story and engaging in a reverie are (to my mind) identical, it follows that:

(a) the viewpoint one has toward the events of a story is the viewpoint one would have toward the events in a reverie.

(b) that no two people who've been through the identical experiences would write them — or reverie them — in just the same way. They'd have different viewpoints and ultimately different emotional reactions. So (and this is the important part here) the "tone of voice" of the stories they'd write would differ just as the "tone of voice" of the reveries they'd engage in would be different.

Letter to Jo-an, November 4, 1963

He gave similar advice on writing to his granddaughters as in the following letter to Billee's daughter Gail Stallings when she was in high school.

"Ardudwy," Gloucester, VA.
Feb. 26, 1966
Dear Gail,

Some great man once observed that it is the privilege of grandfathers to be oratorical, but not many have as good an excuse as you've given me. You're assigned to do the job of writing a short-story. You invite advice. I do not think that advice — certainly in the sense of detailed instruction — does anybody's writing any good. But your invitation to be oratorical can be stretched into an invitation to be oracular, and I accept it in that meaning.

(a) A story is an entirely different thing from a report. When in school you are told to write a "composition"— which is another name for a report — the school authorities have asked you to tackle one of the most difficult kinds of writing. It's usually considered the *most* difficult. An "essay" is notoriously hard to write well. Think of the great fiction-writers and compare their number with adequate essayists, and you'll see that. So.... To write a story you throw away all you've learned about writing compositions or essays or reports. Compositions and reports and essays are supposed to tell you about something. To inform you. To give you facts. A fiction story is something else entirely.

(b) In writing a fiction story you are *not* being informative. You are *not* being factual. You are *not* telling anybody about a subject like railroads, space-travel or how to make onion soup. They are subjects to write a reports or compositions or essays about. In a fiction story you're doing something else with them. Suppose you tell about a railroad. People will know more — we hope — for having read and assimilated the information, if it is an essay. But think of a story about a railroad. Somebody once wrote a story about a farmer's wife somewhere in the middle west, miles from a town or even a neighbor. Everything about her life was drab and deadly. But there was a railroad track that ran beside the farm. Every evening, at dusk, she went down to watch the 20th Century Limited go by. It was ultra-modern, stainless steel. The cars were brightly lighted. She saw well-dressed people talking. Presently the dining-car came along. She could glimpse in the windows the white table-cloths and shining silver and the people dining. It was like fairyland to her. And this night she went down to the fence, and it went by. It had never looked so brilliant, so splendid, so glamorous. She yearned over it as never before. It went on. And she went back to the farmhouse wringing her hands. Because the railroad had made a new line, cutting off miles of distance to be run. And this was the last time the 20th Century Limited would run past the farm. From now on, until they tore up the track, the rails would be empty.

(c) A story is not about a subject. It is about an experience. The imaginary composition about a railroad would be to some extent about all railroads. It is about all the things that fit into the class of railroad information, though you may limit it to steam railroads, electric railroads, or even the wind-driven railroads which on one or two of the guano islands have the empty cars pushed to where they're loaded with fertilizer and then have sails hoisted and the wind propels them to where they're to be unloaded. You can, as I said, limit the subject-matter of a report. But the subject-matter of an experience is inherently limited to the person or people, the place, the time, and the event involved. The woman in that railroad story had an experience. The writer of that story made you see, smell, feel, touch, and taste the experience. But much more than that, he made you see what the experience, meant to the person who had it.

(d) To share an experience, you write quite differently from the way you write a report. A story is actually a sort of artificial memory, with the happenings in it arranged sometimes out of chronological order because they are more satisfying to remember them that way, but it is also like a memory in that it calls up an experience. Nobody remembers a party or a swim or a cook-out as a set of words. One remembers sights, sounds, smells, feelings, touches and tastes. To use words to call up sights, sounds, smells, etc. to reproduce those sensations or experiences is the important thing, if the story is to seem like a remembered experience. One of the especially good tricks for doing this, by the way, is to assume everything you mention is alive. Suppose you saw a crooked tree at the edge of a cliff. There was a crooked tree at the end of a cliff. But the impression you'd get and I really shouldn't have to tell you this (because you do it so often in your poetry) would be that there was a gnarled and crooked tree *clinging* to the edge of a cliff. A golf-ball isn't alive when somebody drives through the air. But it is when it goes whistling through the air. And so on and so on and so on.

(e) An experience is inevitably a happening of some sort, even if it's as limited as the farm-woman going down to watch the luxury-train go by for the last time, and if the action is limited to the wringing of her hands. Therefore, a story begins when the reader knows that something has to happen; that the state of things in being at the opening is unstable; that it can't keep on that way; that something is bound to take place. Look at printed stories and you'll find that this is true. A story begins when something is going to happen so that somebody will have an experience. And it follows that

(f) A story ends when something can go on indefinitely; when it's stable; when nothing more is bound to happen. You don't have to tell the story and then go on like the Arabian Nights to say; "And they lived on until they were separated by the Terminator of Delights and Separator of Companions." When the thing that has happened has wound itself up,— the story is ended no matter how much you write after it.

(g) I could go on indefinitely. I would like to be oracular and oratorical about the tail-end of a story always being a summing-up of what the experience just told of meant to the person or persons who had it. In my personal writing I always try to have the last lines amount to that. But I do *not* "report" what it meant to them. I do not, as the author, analyze the significance of what has happened. I try to show the reader what it meant. There's a high-school book, "Learning Life from Literature" which has one of my stories in it. It's about a boy on a whaling ship, and four things that happened to him in it. He wanted to be grown up and a man like the rest of the crew. But they treated him like a boy. (Which he was.) They called him "Tommy." The last of the four events made him think like a man, though he didn't realize it. But when the other sailors called him "Tom" he knew he was a man,—and how he'd gotten to be a man. Other men recognized the fact, too.

The last item stems from that. Never tell, in a story, anything you can show, except when you are trying to get by some facts that have to be known before some experience can be experienced. Never say that somebody was a mean person. Show him doing something mean. You can do it simply by saying, "as usual, he twisted the meaning of what Sam had told him, so Sam would get into trouble." And so on and so on and so on.

If you want more of this, say so. But I suspect this is too much. Anyhow I've been oratorical and oracular, and I conclude by being,

Tuyo affmo abuelo, Granddaddy

Because she was studying Spanish at the time and because of his love of playing with language, he tried his hand at signing it in Spanish. Later, when she was studying French, he sent her a foreign language copy of *Invaders of Space* (*L'Astronef Pirate*) inscribed in French:

A Gail, Ce n'est pas convenable à dire (Ma petit chou) mais c'est convenable à dire (Ma petite fille,—que charmante!) Mais, tiens, Il y a beaucoup de raison!
Grandpère "Murray Leinster" (Will F. Jenkins)

Will was generous with his advice and tips on writing and did not limit it to family and friends. Strangers wrote to him or visited, often bringing stories for critique. He was frustrated with those he felt did not try to understand the market and were rigid about what they wanted to write and how they wanted to write it. Yet they wanted "to hit the big magazines, make a lot of money and be famous." Will always said he was a professional, like any other professional, and to be a professional you had to sell. He always knew the market, which gave people what they wanted to read, and that was what kept him writing and selling for over 50 years.

In a July 1953 essay on writing for *The Writer* magazine called "What's in a Pro," Will explained:

The professional touch is unmistakable. One cannot miss it in a published story. The amateur touch is also unmistakable. One can only fail to see it in a story of one's own.

The difference between "professional" and "amateur" is that of perspective, viewpoint, attitude towards the story itself.... An amateur tends to think of a story as a series of incidents which will add up to a narrative, while a professional thinks of a story as a whole—a sum—which can be broken down into incidents for writing. The amateur thinks that if he puts down enough interesting things they will add up to a sum. The professional thinks of a sum and then finds out what parts will add up to it. An amateur writes as he reads someone else's work, zestfully following his own charming take to find out what is coming next. Most professionals read other people's work as they write their own; fitting pieces together, as readers, to arrive at a whole.

This was followed by an exercise in which he invited the aspiring writer to edit a professional, published story.

> You are going to edit this story so that it will contain only what the narrator or the protagonist would have known at the moment each incident happened. For example, you might take Conrad's "Youth." The story is about the narrator's youth, but told where he is much older. You would edit it down to the narrative the boy might have written in the boat before he stepped ashore in the Far East.
>
> Take the first paragraph of your chosen story and cross out every word, every statement, every thought, every implication that would not have been written with no more knowledge than the reader had at the beginning of the tale. Assume that you are in the exact time and place of the beginning. Cross out everything that you would not put down under exactly those circumstances. Then go through the story doing the same thing.
>
> You won't blue-pencil many paragraphs before you see what's happening to the yarn. It's losing all organization. It's ceasing to become a story. It's becoming a mere sequence of events which don't seem to be heading somewhere or having any point. Actually you are making the story much more amateurish.... You'll cut out the difference between amateur and professional writing to such a degree that it will seem nobody could write so badly.
>
> The process goes further. Take the blue-penciled yarn and put it back together again. Restore the blue-penciled parts. But play fair. Restore the stuff you have cut out only when, as, and if you see why it's there. If you don't see why it was put there in the first place, leave it out.
>
> I give you a test so you can catch yourself cheating. If you feel inclined to put back everything the original author wrote, you are probably cheating; if you don't want to put in something the author left out, you are probably cheating. No two persons, writing honestly, will ever make exactly the same set of incidents say the same thing.
>
> Nobody likes to work. Amateur writers like it less than anybody else, as I should know. But by taking out of a story everything but the narrative (which many amateurs think is the whole story) and then restoring, one discovers what else a good yarn contains — call it hindsight or perspective or point of view or whatever you please. Put two or three or 10 stories through the mill I have described and you are bound to glimpse the professional attitude, the professional touch.

Ned Brooks, editor of the fanzine "It Goes on the Shelf," lived near Will in Virginia for a while, and was one of the many young fans who visited Clay Bank. Brooks remembers receiving writing advice from Will during one visit that was similar to the blue-penciling of a favorite story discussed above.

"He described a process that he claimed always worked — you would copy out in longhand six times a story by a good writer of the sort you wanted to write, then try to write your story. I have never heard if anyone tried it, or how well it worked."

It has been estimated that only 5 percent to 10 ten percent of Will's work was science fiction, despite his importance in that genre, and, as he often said, he wrote it because he loved to read it and to write it.

As he said in an essay on "Writing Science Fiction Today" in the May 1968 issue of *The Writer*:

> There was a time when one had only to write about fantastic places and incredible events and it was called science fiction.... [Now] it has improved out of all recognition. So far as attracting and holding an audience is concerned, it is incomparable. There are countless science fiction fan clubs, with regular meetings, annual conventions (up to a thousand people attending), awards, orations and other forms of to-do about the stories which unite science fiction readers into an enthusiastic babbling fellowship.... I have copies of no fewer than fifty strictly amateur magazines put out by science fiction addicts at more or less regular intervals. And I myself have a "Hugo," rating among science fictioneers with the movie Oscars and the TV Emmy awards. If somebody wants a loyal following, let him write science fiction. A single outstanding story can make his reputation.
>
> But writing of fantastic places and incredible events is no longer the way to break into print. One has only to read the science fiction fans gloat over to notice it. There is still trash, of course, there always will be. But modern science fiction trends to be very solid reading matter.
>
> I think of a fictional "article" by Isaac Asimov, which was called "Pate de Foie Gras." In this piece, he gravely made a scientific report on the nuclear physics setup which caused an imaginary goose to lay golden eggs. The science was magnificent. It instantly inspired actual nuclear physicists to write the magazine suggesting means — highly technical and beautifully plausible — by which the theoretically sterile golden-egg-laying good could be developed into a breed. For science fiction fans, it was very good fun....
>
> Just before Sputnik crossed our skies, there were more than twenty science fiction magazines on the newsstands. Only a few months later there were three. (There are more now.) It is one guess that a lot of people were reading those magazines as fantasy only, and they got scared. Another guess is that real science fiction fans felt they had been sold out. They had been reading stories in which artificial satellites were being examined as imaginary, and then they were confronted with them as facts. Satellites had been a matter for speculation, and suddenly they were subjects of newspaper feature articles, which spoiled the fun.
>
> I think Sputnik changed all science fiction. Nowadays a science fiction story very rarely deals with a remarkable gadget whipped up with a pink of this and a dab of that to meet some emergency. A new convention has developed. Just as a detective story writer has to give his readers all the clues he uses to solve his mystery ... so a science fiction writer has to give his readers all the "science" they want to think about the story....
>
> And the science has to be more than fantasy. It has to be possible. It has to be thinkaboutable. If one writes a story and assumes that at some time and place space travel will be possible, that's all right. It probably — anyhow conceivably — will be. But if a story mentions somebody making a four-sided triangle, it is not acceptable because it simply can't happen.
>
> Again, one can write about a monster. But to be believable there must be an environment in which the monster wouldn't be monstrous, but normal. In the

same way, we can have gadgets which are impossible now, but not forever. I think of a story called *The Brick Moon* by Edward Everett Hale, author of *A Man Without a Country*.

The Brick Moon was written in the 1850s. (My copy used to belong to Jefferson Davis.) It's about an artificial satellite. At the time it was impossible technically but not inherently. It was science fiction in the modern manner except it could have been better.

Today, science fiction is as distinct a genre as satire or comedy or farce. You can say that in comedy one takes the possible and stretches it, while in farce one takes the impossible and stretches it. Science fiction does not deal with the impossible. It deals with the only temporarily impossible, which is another thing entirely. And it examines the temporarily impossible and how it will affect people who live when and where it ceases to be impossible. I am saying that it takes situations and relationships and circumstances and examines them as satire or comedy does (but never farce). It often ends with conclusions of a precision and accuracy no literal-minded approach could possibly develop.

Also, science fiction often makes a prediction of a scientific invention or discovery that later comes true. At least six devices used in World War II were not only like science fiction inventions, but were deliberately modeled on things first described in science fiction stories. Yet the function of science fiction is not only to make predictions; it may also look backward. I once wrote a story called "The Power" set in the thirteenth century which required me to do elaborate historical research. It has been included in several anthologies and translated into various languages. And there is a classic story — "Don't Look Now" — by Henry Kuttner — which is told as happening in the corner saloon, either yesterday or tomorrow or perhaps an hour from now.

I've been trying to clarify what science fiction is, because I take great pleasure in writing it and perhaps even more in reading it.... But I do say one thing firmly. It applies to all kinds of writing and especially to science fiction.

Don't try writing science fiction unless you honestly like to read it! If you don't enjoy writing it for the sake of getting it down on paper, if you write for any other reason but wanting to, it's extremely likely that a reader will share your indifference!

Appendix A.
"A Logic Named Joe"

"A Logic Named Joe" was published in the March 1946 issue of *Astounding Science-Fiction*. There was a Murray Leinster story, "The Adapter," in the same issue so it was bylined under his own name, Will F. Jenkins. The story was immediately popular with the readers, and they rated it the number one for that month.

"A Logic Named Joe" has been credited as being the first to predict the home computer and the internet. Interest has not only endured over the years but increased as we became more and more a wired world.

It is worth repeating what Joe Rico, editor of several anthologies and a Fellow of the New England Science Fiction Association (NESFA), wrote: "At a time in which the world had about 10 electronic computers, he wrote a story about a future in which every household has a personal computer and is connected to an internet-like system. If this story had been written in 1956, 1966 or 1976 it would have been known as the most predicative story in the genre, but it was written in 1946!"

A Logic Named Joe
by Will F. Jenkins

It was on the third day of August that Joe come off the assembly line, and on the fifth Laurine come into town, an' that afternoon I saved civilization. That's what I figure, anyhow. Laurine is a blonde that I was crazy about once — and crazy is the word — and Joe is a logic that I have stored away down in the cellar right now. I had to pay for him because I said I busted him, and sometimes I think about turning him on and sometimes I think about taking an ax to him. Sooner or later I'm gonna do one or the other. I kinda hope it's the ax. I could use a coupla million dollars — sure! — an' Joe'd tell me how to get or make 'em. He can do plenty! But so far I've been scared to take a chance. After all, I figure I really saved civilization by turnin' him off.

The way Laurine fits in is that she makes cold shivers run up an' down my spine when I think about her. You see, I've got a wife which I acquired after I had parted from Laurine with much romantic despair. She is a reasonable good wife, and I have some kids which are hell-cats but I value 'em. If I have sense enough to leave well enough alone, sooner or later I will retire on a pension an' Social Security an' spend the rest of my life fishin' contented an' lyin' about what a great guy I used to be. But there's Joe. I'm worried about Joe.

I'm a maintenance man for the Logics Company. My job is servicing logics, and I admit modestly that I am pretty good. I was servicing televisions before that guy Carson invented his trick circuit that will select any of 'steenteen million other circuits — in theory there ain't no limit — and before the Logics Company hooked it into the tank-and-integrator set-up they were usin' 'em as business-machine service. They added a vision screen for speed — an' they found out they'd made logics. They were surprised an' pleased. They're still findin' out what logics will do, but everybody's got 'em.

I got Joe, after Laurine nearly got me. You know the logics setup. You got a logic in your house. It looks like a vision receiver used to, only it's got keys instead of dials and you punch the keys for what you wanna get. It's hooked in to the tank, which has the Carson Circuit all fixed up with relays. Say you punch "*Station SNAFU*" on your logic. Relays in the tank take over an' whatever vision-program SNAFU is telecastin' comes on your logic's screen. Or you punch "*Sally Hancock's Phone*" an' the screen blinks an' sputters an' you're hooked up with the logic in her house an' if somebody answers you got a vision-phone connection. But besides that, if you punch for the weather forecast or who won today's race at Hialeah or who was mistress of the White House durin' Garfield's administration or what is PDQ and R sellin' for today, that comes on the screen too. The relays in the tank do it. The tank is a big buildin' full of all the facts in creation an' all the recorded telecasts that ever was made — an' it's hooked in with all the other tanks all over the country — an' everything you wanna know or see or hear, you punch for it an' you get it. Very convenient. Also it does math for you, an' keeps books, an' acts as consultin' chemist, physicist, astronomer, an' tea-leaf reader, with a "Advice to the Lovelorn" thrown in. The only thing it won't do is tell you exactly what your wife meant when she said, "Oh, you think so, do you?" in that peculiar kinda voice. Logics don't work good on women. Only on things that make sense.

Logics are all right, though. They changed civilization, the highbrows tell us. All on accounta the Carson Circuit. And Joe shoulda been a perfectly normal logic, keeping some family or other from wearin' out its brains doin' the kids' homework for 'em. But somethin' went wrong in the assembly line. It was somethin' so small that precision gauges didn't measure it, but it made Joe a individual. Maybe he didn't know it at first. Or maybe, bein' logical, he figured out that if he was to show he was different from other logics they'd scrap him. Which woulda been a brilliant idea. But anyhow, he come off the assembly-line, an' he went through the regular tests without anybody screamin' shrilly on findin' out what he was. And he went right on out an' was duly installed in the home of Mr. Thaddeus Korlanovitch at 119 East Seventh Street, second floor front. So far, everything was serene.

The installation happened late Saturday night. Sunday morning the Korlanovitch kids turned him on an' seen the Kiddie Shows. Around noon their parents peeled 'em away from him an' piled 'em in the car. Then they come back in the house for the lunch they'd forgot an' one of the kids sneaked back an' they found him punchin' keys for the Kiddie Shows of the week before. They dragged him out an' went off. But they left Joe turned on.

That was noon. Nothin' happened until two in the afternoon. It was the calm before the storm. Laurine wasn't in town yet, but she was comin'. I picture Joe sittin' there all by himself, buzzing meditative. Maybe he run Kiddie Shows in the empty apartment for awhile. But I think he went kinda remote-control exploring in the tank. There ain't any fact that can be said to be a fact that ain't on a data plate in some tank somewhere — unless it's one the technicians are diggin' out an' puttin' on a data plate now. Joe had plenty of material to work on. An' he musta started workin' right off the bat.

Joe ain't vicious, you understand. He ain't like one of these ambitious robots you read about that make up their minds the human race is inefficient and has got to be wiped out an' replaced by thinkin' machines. Joe's just got ambition. If you were a machine, you'd wanna work right, wouldn't you? That's Joe. He wants to work right. An' he's a logic. An' logics can do a lotta things that ain't been found out yet. So Joe, discoverin' the fact, begun to feel restless. He selects some things us dumb humans ain't thought of yet, an' begins to arrange so logics will be called on to do 'em.

That's all. That's everything. But, brother, it's enough!

Things are kinda quiet in the Maintenance Department about two in the afternoon. We are playing pinochle. Then one of the guys remembers he has to call up his wife. He goes to one of the bank of logics in Maintenance and punches the keys for his house. The screen sputters. Then a flash comes on the screen.

"Announcing new and improved logics service! Your logic is now equipped to give you not only consultive but directive service. If you want to do something and don't know-how to do it — ask your logic!"

There's a pause. A kinda expectant pause. Then, as if reluctantly, his connection comes through. His wife answers an' gives him hell for somethin' or other. He takes it an' snaps off.

"Whadda you know?" he says when he comes back. He tells us about the flash. "We shoulda been warned about that. There's gonna be a lotta complaints. Suppose a fella asks how to get ridda his wife an' the censor circuits block the question?"

Somebody melds a hundred aces an' says:

"Why not punch for it an' see what happens?"

It's a gag, o' course. But the guy goes over. He punches keys. In theory, a censor block is gonna come on an' the screen will say severely, "Public Policy Forbids This Service." You hafta have censor blocks or the kiddies will be askin' detailed questions about things they're too young to know. And there are other reasons. As you will see.

This fella punches, "How can I get rid of my wife?" Just for the fun of it. The screen is blank for half a second. Then comes a flash. "Service question: Is she blonde or brunette?" He hollers to us an' we come look. He punches, "Blonde." There's another brief pause. Then the screen says, "Hexymetacryloaminoacetine is a constituent of green shoe polish. Take home a frozen meal including dried-pea soup. Color the soup with green shoe polish. It will appear to be green-pea soup. Hexymetacryloaminoacetine is a selective poison which is fatal to blond females but not to brunettes or males of any coloring. This fact has not been brought out by human experiment, but is a product of logics service. You cannot be convicted of murder. It is improbable that you will be suspected."

The screen goes blank, and we stare at each other. It's bound to be right. A logic workin' the Carson Circuit can no more make a mistake than any other kinda computin' machine. I call the tank in a hurry.

"Hey, you guys!" I yell. "Somethin's happened! Logics are givin' detailed instructions for wife-murder! Check your censor-circuits — but quick!"

That was close, I think. But little do I know. At that precise instant, over on Monroe Avenue, a drunk starts to punch for somethin' on a logic. The screen says, "Announcing new and improved logics service! If you want to do something and don't know how to do it — ask your logic!" And the drunk says, owlish, "I'll do it!" So he cancels his first punching and fumbles around and says: "How can I keep my wife from finding out I've been drinking?" And the screen says, prompt: "Buy a bottle of Franine hair shampoo. It is harmless but contains a detergent which will neutralize ethyl alcohol immediately. Take one teaspoonful for each jigger of hundred-proof you have consumed."

This guy was plenty plastered — just plastered enough to stagger next door and obey instructions. An' five minutes later he was cold sober and writing down the information so he couldn't forget it. It was new, and it was big! He got rich offa that memo! He patented "*SOBUH, The Drink That Makes Happy Homes!*" You can top off any souse with a slug or two of it an' go home sober as a judge. The guy's cussin' income taxes right now!

You can't kick on stuff like that. But a ambitious young fourteen-year-old wanted to buy some kid stuff and his pop wouldn't fork over. He called up a friend to tell his troubles. And his logic says: "If you want to do something and don't know how to do it — ask your logic!" So this kid punches: "How can I make a lotta money, fast?"

His logic comes through with the simplest, neatest, and the most efficient counterfeitin' device yet known to science. You see, all the data was in the tank. The logic — since Joe had closed some relays here an' there in the tank — simply integrated the facts. That's all. The kid got caught up with three days later, havin' already spent two thousand credits an' havin' plenty more on hand. They hadda time tellin' his counterfeits from the real stuff, an' the only way they done it was that he changed his printer, kid fashion, not bein' able to let somethin' that was workin' right alone.

Those are what you might call samples. Nobody knows all that Joe done. But there was the bank president who got humorous when his logic flashed that "Ask your logic" spiel on him, and jestingly asked how to rob his own bank. An' the logic told him, brief and explicit but good! The bank president hit the ceiling, hollering for cops. There musta been plenty of that sorta thing. There was fifty-four more robberies than usual in the next twenty-four hours, all of them planned astute an' perfect. Some of 'em they never did figure out how they'd been done. Joe, he'd gone exploring in the tank and closed some relays like a logic is supposed to do — but only when required — and blocked all censor-circuits an' fixed up this logics service which planned perfect crimes, nourishing an' attractive meals, counterfeitin' machines, an' new industries with a fine impartiality. He musta been plenty happy, Joe must. He was functionin' swell, buzzin' along to himself while the Korlanovitch kids were off ridin' with their ma an' pa.

They come back at seven o'clock, the kids all happily wore out with their afternoon of fightin' each other in the car. Their folks put 'em to bed and sat down to rest. They saw Joe's screen flickerin' meditative from one subject to another an' old man Korlanovitch had had enough excitement for one day. He turned Joe off.

An' at that instant the pattern of relays that Joe had turned on snapped off, all the offers of directive service stopped flashin' on logic screens everywhere, an' peace descended on the earth.

For everybody else. But for me — Laurine come to town. I have often thanked Gawd fervent that she didn't marry me when I thought I wanted her to. In the intervenin' years she had progressed. She was blonde an' fatal to begin with. She had got blonder and fataler an' had had four husbands and one acquittal for homicide an' had acquired a air of enthusiasm and self-confidence. That's just a sketch of the background. Laurine was not the kinda former girlfriend you like to have turning up in the same town with your wife. But she came to town, an' Monday morning she tuned right into the middle of Joe's second spasm of activity.

The Korlanovitch kids had turned him on again. I got these details later and kinda pieced 'em together. An' every logic in town was dutifully flashin' a notice, "If you want to do something and don't know how to do it — ask your logic!" every time they was turned on for use. More'n that, when people punched for the morning news, they got a full account of the previous afternoon's doin's. Which put 'em in a frame of mind to share in the party. One bright fella demands, "How can I make a perpetual motion machine?" And his logic sputters a while an' then comes up with a set-up usin' the Brownian movement to turn little wheels. If the wheels ain't bigger'n a eighth of an inch they'll turn, all right, an' practically it's perpetual motion. Another one asks for the secret of transmutin' metals. The logic rakes back in the data plates an' integrates a strictly practical answer. It does take so much power that you can't make no profit except on radium, but that pays off good. An' from the fact that for a coupla years to come the police were turnin' up new and improved jimmies, knob-claws for gettin' at safe-innards, and all-purpose keys that'd open any known lock — why — there must have been other inquirers with a strictly practical viewpoint. Joe done a lot for technical progress!

But he done more in other lines. Educational, say. None of my kids are old enough to be int'rested, but Joe bypassed all censor-circuits because they hampered the service he figured logics should give humanity. So the kids an' teenagers who wanted to know what comes after the bees an' flowers found out. And there is certain facts which men hope their wives won't do more'n suspect, an' those facts are just what their wives are really curious about. So when a woman dials: "How can I tell if Oswald is true to me?" and her logic tells her — you can figure out how many rows got started that night when the men come home!

All this while Joe goes on buzzin' happy to himself, showin' the Korlanovitch kids the animated funnies with one circuit while with the others he remote-controls the tank so that all the other logics can give people what they ask for and thereby raise merry hell.

An' then Laurine gets onto the new service. She turns on the logic in her hotel room, prob'ly to see the week's style-forecast. But the logic says, dutiful: "If you want to do something and don't know how to do it — ask your logic!" So Laurine prob'ly looks enthusiastic — she would! — and tries to figure out something to ask. She already knows all about everything she cares about — ain't she had four husbands and shot one? — so I occur to her. She knows this is the town I live in. So she punches, "How can I find Ducky?"

O.K., guy! But that is what she used to call me. She gets a service question. "Is Ducky known by any other name?" So she gives my regular name. And the logic can't find me. Because my logic ain't listed under my name on account of I am in Maintenance and don't want to be pestered when I'm home, and there ain't any data plates on code-listed logics, because the codes get changed so often — like a guy gets plastered an' tells a redhead to call him up, an' on gettin' sober hurriedly has the code changed before she reaches his wife on the screen.

Well! Joe is stumped. That's prob'ly the first question logics service hasn't been able to answer. "How can I find Ducky?" Quite a problem! So Joe broods over it while showin' the Korlanovitch kids the animated comic about the cute little boy who carries sticks of dynamite in his hip pocket an' plays practical jokes on everybody. Then he gets the trick. Laurine's screen suddenly flashes:

"Logics special service will work upon your question. Please punch your logic designation and leave it turned on. You will be called back."

Laurine is merely mildly interested, but she punches her hotel-room number and has a drink and takes a nap. Joe sets to work. He has been given a idea.

My wife calls me at Maintenance and hollers. She is fit to be tied. She says I got to do something. She was gonna make a call to the butcher shop. Instead of the butcher or even the "If you want to do something" flash, she got a new one. The screen says, "Service question: What is your name?" She is kinda puzzled, but she punches it. The screen sputters an' then says: "Secretarial Service Demonstration! You — " It reels off her name, address, age, sex, coloring, the amounts of all her charge accounts in all the stores, my name as her husband, how much I get a week, the fact that I've been pinched three times — twice was traffic stuff, and once for a argument I got in with a guy — and the interestin' item that once when she was mad with me she left me for three weeks an' had her address changed to her folks' home. Then it says, brisk: "Logics Service will hereafter keep your personal accounts, take messages, and locate persons you may wish to get in touch with. This demonstration is to introduce the service." Then it connects her with the butcher.

But she don't want meat, then. She wants blood. She calls me.

"If it'll tell me all about myself," she says, fairly boilin', "it'll tell anybody else who punches my name! You've got to stop it!"

"Now, now, honey!" I says. "I didn't know about all this! It's new! But they musta fixed the tank so it won't give out information except to the logic where a person lives!"

"Nothing of the kind!" she tells me, furious. "I tried! And you know that Blossom woman who lives next door! She's been married three times and she's forty-two years old and she says she's only thirty! And Mrs. Hudson's had her husband arrested four times for nonsupport and once for beating her up. And —"

"Hey!" I says. "You mean the logic told you this?"

"Yes!" she wails. "It will tell anybody anything! You've got to stop it! How long will it take?"

"I'll call up the tank," I says. "It can't take long."

"Hurry!" she says, desperate, "before somebody punches my name! I'm going to see what it says about that hussy across the street."

She snaps off to gather what she can before it's stopped. So I punch for the tank and I get this new "What is your name?" flash. I got a morbid curiosity and I punch my name, and the screen says: "Were you ever called Ducky?" I blink. I ain't got no suspicions. I say, "Sure!" And the screen says, "There is a call for you."

Bingo! There's the inside of a hotel room and Laurine is reclinin' asleep on the bed. She'd been told to leave her logic turned on an' she done it. It is a hot day and she is trying to be cool. I would say that she oughta not suffer from the heat. Me, being human, I do not stay as cool as she looks. But there ain't no need to go into that. After I get my breath I say, "For Heaven's sake!" and she opens her eyes.

At first she looks puzzled, like she was thinking is she getting absent-minded and is this guy somebody she married lately. Then she grabs a sheet and drapes it around herself and beams at me.

"Ducky!" she says. "How marvelous!"

I say something like "Ugmph!" I am sweating.

She says: "I put in a call for you, Ducky, and here you are! Isn't it romantic? Where are you really, Ducky? And when can you come up? You've no idea how often I've thought of you!"

I am probably the only guy she ever knew real well that she has not been married to at some time or another.

I say "Ugmph!" again, and swallow.

"Can you come up instantly?" asks Laurine brightly.

"I'm ... workin'," I say. "I'll ... uh ... call you back."

"I'm terribly lonesome," says Laurine. "Please make it quick, Ducky! I'll have a drink waiting for you. Have you ever thought of me?"

"Yeah," I say, feeble. "Plenty!"

"You darling!" says Laurine. "Here's a kiss to go on with until you get here! Hurry, Ducky!"

Then I sweat! I still don't know nothing about Joe, understand. I cuss out the guys at the tank because I blame them for this. If Laurine was just another blonde — well — when it comes to ordinary blondes I can leave 'em alone or leave 'em alone, either one. A married man gets that way or else. But Laurine has a look of unquenched enthusiasm that gives a man very strange weak sensations at the back of his knees. And she'd had four husbands and shot one and got acquitted.

So I punch the keys for the tank technical room, fumbling. And the screen says: "What is your name?" but I don't want any more. I punch the name of the old guy who's stock clerk in Maintenance. And the screen gives me some pretty interestin' dope — I never woulda thought the old fella had ever had that much pep — and winds up by mentionin' a unclaimed deposit now amountin' to two hundred eighty credits in the First National Bank, which he should look into. Then it spiels about the new secretarial service and gives me the tank at last.

I start to swear at the guy who looks at me. But he says, tired:

"Snap it off, fella. We got troubles an' you're just another. What are the logics doin' now?"

I tell him, and he laughs a hollow laugh.

"A light matter, fella," he says. "A very light matter! We just managed to clamp off all the data plates that give information on high explosives. The demand for instructions in counterfeiting is increasing minute by minute. We are also trying to shut off, by main force, the relays that hook in to data plates that just barely might give advice on the fine points of murder. So if people will only keep busy getting the goods on each other for a while, maybe we'll get a chance to stop the circuits that are shifting credit-balances from bank to bank before everybody's bankrupt except the guys who thought of askin' how to get big bank accounts in a hurry."

"Then," I says hoarse, "shut down the tank! Do somethin'!"

"Shut down the tank?" he says, mirthless. "Does it occur to you, fella, that the tank has been doin' all the computin' for every business office for years? It's been handlin' the distribution of ninety-four per cent of all telecast programs, has given out all information on weather, plane schedules, special sales, employment opportunities and news; has handled all person-to-person contacts over wires and recorded every business conversation and agreement — Listen, fella! Logics changed civilization. Logics *are* civilization! If we shut off logics, we go back to a kind of civilization we have forgotten how to run! I'm getting hysterical myself and that's why I'm talkin' like this! If my wife finds out my paycheck is thirty credits a week more than I told her and starts hunting for that redhead —"

He smiles a haggard smile at me and snaps off. And I sit down and put my head in my hands. It's true. If something had happened back in cave days and they'd hadda stop usin' fire — If they'd hadda stop usin' steam in the nineteenth century or electricity in the twentieth — It's like that. We got a very simple civilization. In the nineteen hundreds a man would have to make use of a typewriter, radio, telephone, teletypewriter, newspaper, reference library, encyclopedias, office files, directories, plus messenger service and consulting lawyers, chemists, doctors, dieticians, filing clerks, secretaries — all to put down what he wanted to remember an' to tell him what other people had put down that he wanted to know; to report what he said to somebody else and to report to him what they said back. All we have to have is logics. Anything we want to know or see or hear, or anybody we want to talk to, we punch keys on a logic. Shut off logics and everything goes skiddoo. But Laurine —

Somethin' had happened. I still didn't know what it was. Nobody else knows, even yet. What had happened was Joe. What was the matter with him was that he wanted to work good. All this fuss he was raisin' was, actual, nothin' but stuff we shoulda thought of ourselves. Directive advice, tellin' us what we wanted to know to solve a problem, wasn't but a slight extension of logical-integrator service. Figurin' out a good way to poison a fella's wife was only different in degree from figurin' out a cube root or a guy's bank balance. It was gettin' the answer to a question. But things was goin' to pot because there was too many answers being given to too many questions.

One of the logics in Maintenance lights up. I go over, weary, to answer it. I punch the answer key. Laurine says:

"Ducky!"

It's the same hotel room. There's two glasses on the table with drinks in them. One is for me. Laurine's got on some kinda frothy hangin'-around-the-house-with-the-boy-friend outfit that automatic makes you strain your eyes to see if you actual see what you think. Laurine looks at me enthusiastic.

"Ducky!" says Laurine. "I'm lonesome! Why haven't you come up?"

"I ... been busy," I say, strangling slightly.

"Pooh!" says Laurine. "Listen, Ducky! Do you remember how much in love we used to be?"

I gulp.

"Are you doin' anything this evening?" says Laurine.

I gulp again, because she is smiling at me in a way that a single man would maybe get dizzy, but it gives a old married man like me cold chills. When a dame looks at you possessive —

"Ducky!" says Laurine, impulsive. "I was so mean to you! Let's get married!"

Desperation gives me a voice.

"I ... got married," I tell her, hoarse.

Laurine blinks. Then she says, courageous:

"Poor boy! But we'll get you outta that! Only it would be nice if we could be married today. Now we can only be engaged!"

"I ... can't —"

"I'll call up your wife," says Laurine, happy, "and have a talk with her. You must have a code signal for your logic, darling. I tried to ring your house and noth —"

Click! That's my logic turned off. I turned it off. And I feel faint all over. I got nervous prostration. I got combat fatigue. I got anything you like. I got cold feet.

I beat it outta Maintenance, yellin' to somebody I got a emergency call. I'm gonna get out in a Maintenance car an' cruise around until it's plausible to go home. Then I'm gonna take the wife an' kids an' beat it for somewheres that Laurine won't ever find me. I don't wanna be' fifth in Laurine's series of husbands and maybe the second one she shoots in a moment of boredom. I got experience of blondes. I got experience of Laurine! And I'm scared to death!

I beat it out into traffic in the Maintenance car. There was a disconnected logic in the back, ready to substitute for one that hadda burned-out coil or something that it was easier to switch and fix back in the Maintenance shop. I drove crazy but automatic. It was kinda ironic, if you think of it. I was goin' hoopla over a strictly personal problem, while civilization was crackin' up all around me because other people were havin' their personal problems solved as fast as they could state 'em. It is a matter of record that part of the Mid-Western Electric research guys had been workin' on cold electron-emission for thirty years, to make vacuum tubes that wouldn't need a power source to heat the filament. And one of those fellas was intrigued by the "Ask your logic" flash. He asked how to get cold emission of electrons. And the logic integrates a few squintillion facts on the physics data plates and tells him. Just as casual as it told somebody over in the Fourth Ward how to serve left-over soup in a new attractive way, and somebody else on Mason Street how to dispose of a torso that somebody had left careless in his cellar after ceasing to use same.

Laurine wouldn't never have found me if it hadn't been for this new logics service. But now that it was started — Zowie! She'd shot one husband and got acquitted. Suppose she got impatient because I was still married an' asked logics service how to get me free an' in a spot where I'd have to marry her by 8:30 P.M.?

It woulda told her! Just like it told that woman out in the suburbs how to make sure her husband wouldn't run around no more. *Br-r-r-r!* An' like it told that kid how to find some buried treasure. Remember? He was happy totin' home the gold reserve of the Hanoverian Bank and Trust Company when they caught on to it. The logic had told him how to make some kinda machine that nobody has been able to figure how it works even yet, only they guess it dodges around a couple extra dimensions. If Laurine was to start askin' questions with a technical aspect to them, that would be logics' service meat! And fella, I was scared! If you think a he-man oughtn't to be scared of just one blonde — you ain't met Laurine!

I'm drivin' blind when a social-conscious guy asks how to bring about his own particular system of social organization at once. He don't ask if it's best or if it'll work. He just wants to get it started. And the logic — or Joe — tells him! Simultaneous, there's a retired preacher asks how can the human race be cured of concupiscence. Bein' seventy, he's pretty safe himself, but he wants to remove the peril to the spiritual welfare of the rest of us. He finds out. It involves constructin' a sort of broadcastin' station to emit a certain wave-pattern an' turnin' it on. Just that. Nothing more. It's found out afterward, when he is solicitin' funds to construct it. Fortunate, he didn't think to ask logics how to finance it, or it woulda told him that, too, an' we woulda all been cured of the impulses we maybe regret afterward but never at the time. And there's another group of serious thinkers who are sure the human race would be a lot better off if everybody went back to nature an' lived in the woods with the ants an' poison ivy. They start askin' questions about how to cause humanity to abandon cities and artificial conditions of living. They practically got the answer in logics service!

Maybe it didn't strike you serious at the time, but while I was drivin' aimless, sweatin' blood over Laurine bein' after me, the fate of civilization hung in the balance. I ain't kiddin'. For instance, the Superior Man gang that sneers at the rest of us was quietly asking questions on what kinda weapons could be made by which Superior Men could take over and run things...

But I drove here an' there, sweatin' an' talkin' to myself.

"What I oughta do is ask this wacky logics service how to get outa this mess," I says. "But it'd just tell me a intricate and' foolproof way to bump Laurine off. I wanna have peace! I wanna grow comfortably old and brag to other old guys about what a hellion I used to be, without havin' to go through it an' lose my chance of livin' to be a elderly liar."

I turn a corner at random, there in the Maintenance car.

"It was a nice kinda world once," I says, bitter. "I could go home peaceful and not have belly-cramps wonderin' if a blonde has called up my wife to announce my engagement to her. I could punch keys on a logic without gazing into somebody's bedroom while she is giving her epidermis a air bath and being led to think things I gotta take out in thinkin'. I could —"

Then I groan, rememberin' that my wife, naturally, is gonna blame me for the fact that our private life ain't private any more if anybody has tried to peek into it.

"It was a swell world," I says, homesick for the dear dead days-before-yesterday. "We was playin' happy with our toys like little innocent children until somethin' happened. Like a guy named Joe come in and squashed all our mud pies."

Then it hit me. I got the whole thing in one flash. There ain't nothing in the tank set-up to start relays closin'. Relays are closed exclusive by logics, to get the information the keys are punched for. Nothin' but a logic coulda cooked up the relay patterns that constituted logics service. Humans wouldn't ha' been able to figure it out! Only a logic could integrate all the stuff that woulda made all the other logics work like this...

There was one answer. I drove into a restaurant and went over to a pay-logic an' dropped in a coin.

"Can a logic be modified," I spell out, "to cooperate in long-term planning which human brains are too limited in scope to do?"

The screen sputters. Then it says:

"Definitely yes."

"How great will the modifications be?" I punch.

"Microscopically slight. Changes in dimensions," says the screen. "Even modern precision gauges are not exact enough to check them, however. They can only come about under present manufacturing methods by an extremely improbable accident, which has only happened once."

"How can one get hold of that one accident which can do this highly necessary work?" I punch.

The screen sputters. Sweat broke out on me. I ain't got it figured out close, yet, but what I'm scared of is that whatever is Joe will be suspicious. But what I'm askin' is strictly logical. And logics can't lie. They gotta be accurate. They can't help it.

"A complete logic capable of the work required," says the screen, "is now in ordinary family use in —"

And it gives me the Korlanovitch address and do I go over there! Do I go over there fast! I pull up the Maintenance car in front of the place, and I take the extra logic outta the back, and I stagger up the Korlanovitch flat and I ring the bell. A kid answers the door.

"I'm from Logics Maintenance," I tell the kid. "An inspection record has shown that your logic is apt to break down any minute. I come to put in a new one before it does."

The kid says "O.K.!" real bright and runs back to the livin'-room where Joe — I got the habit of callin' him Joe later, through just meditatin' about him — is runnin' somethin' the kids wanna look at. I hook in the other logic an' turn it on, conscientious making sure it works. Then I say:

"Now kiddies, you punch this one for what you want. I'm gonna take the old one away before it breaks down."

And I glance at the screen. The kiddies have apparently said they wanna look at some real cannibals. So the screen is presenting a anthropological expedition scientific record film of the fertility dance of the Huba-Jouba tribe of West Africa. It is supposed to be restricted to anthropological professors an' post-graduate medical students. But there ain't any censor blocks workin' any more and it's on. The kids are much interested. Me, bein' a old married man, I blush.

I disconnect Joe. Careful. I turn to the other logic and punch keys for Maintenance. I do not get a services flash. I get Maintenance. I feel very good. I report that I am goin' home because I fell down a flight of steps an' hurt my leg. I add, inspired:

"An' say, I was carryin' the logic I replaced an' it's all busted. I left it for the dustman to pick up."

"If you don't turn 'em in," says Stock, "you gotta pay for 'em."

"Cheap at the price," I say.

I go home. Laurine ain't called. I put Joe down in the cellar, careful. If I turned him in, he'd be inspected an' his parts salvaged even if I busted somethin' on him. Whatever part was off-normal might be used again and everything start all over. I can't risk it. I pay for him and leave him be.

That's what happened. You might say I saved civilization an' not be far wrong. I know I ain't goin' to take a chance on havin' Joe in action again. Not while Laurine is livin'. An' there are other reasons. With all the nuts who wanna change the world to their own line o' thinkin', an' the ones that wanna bump people off, an' generally solve their problems — Yeah! Problems are bad, but I figure I better let sleepin' problems lie.

But on the other hand, if Joe could be tamed, somehow, and got to work just reasonable — He could make me a coupla million dollars, easy. But even if I got sense enough not to get rich, an' if I get retired and just loaf around fishin' an' lyin' to other old duffers about what a great guy I used to be — Maybe I'll like it, but maybe I won't. And after all, if I get fed up with bein' old and confined strictly to thinking — why I could hook Joe in long enough to ask: "How can a old guy not stay old?" Joe'll be able to find out. An' he'll tell me.

That couldn't be allowed out general, of course. You gotta make room for kids to grow up. But it's a pretty good world, now Joe's turned off. Maybe I'll turn him on long enough to learn how to stay in it. But on the other hand, maybe —

Appendix B.
"To Build a Robot Brain"

"To Build a Robot Brain" was published in *Astounding Science-Fiction* in April 1954. In this essay, Will plays with the idea of how far scientists can go in developing computers that could function as well as human brains. It was selected for this biography because, as an essay, it shows how Will's mind worked, how he developed an idea and tried to explain it to his audience, as in conversation. The last sentence also gives a glimpse of his inner self and his core beliefs.

To Build a Robot Brain
by Murray Leinster

The technician will use the tools, and assemble the parts. Before that, the physicist-engineer will design the parts. But even before that, the philosopher has to design the concept.

Not too long ago a man I'll call Casey got scared nearly to death by a thinking machine. This is not fiction, you understand. This is honest-to-Hannah fact. You'd recognize the name of the machine if I told you. It's one of those big computers with an all-capital-name like a government agency in Washington. It is a honey of a device, with some thousands of vacuum tubes, relays, special devices to prepare tape for it to read, and an electric typewriter to type out its answers. It handles letters as well as numbers, and you can feed it lists of names, for example, and it will sort them out alphabetically and make its answer-typewriter write them out in proper sequence. Also it calculates ballistic data and how to make wings for jet planes, and tabulates percentages on presidential elections, and little things like that.

But it nearly scared Casey to death.

It was two o'clock in the morning and the machine was running silently as usual. The whole building in which it was set up was empty of people. Maybe a watchman or two on other floors, but nobody but Casey right here on the job. Light bulbs glowed at one spot and another, with plenty of darkness in between.

The thinking machine didn't even hum. There was no sign of activity anywhere about it, except small indicator-lights on the monitor panel, which turned on and off in a sort of meditative fashion. The spool of metal tape feeding to the computer was turning slowly. Now and again it paused in its movement. That was when the memory banks were being consulted for instructions on memory-data. At such moments the machine was doing exactly what a man does when he scratches his head.

Casey — and I repeat that this is history, not fiction — leaned back in his comfortable chair. There was a two-spool problem being run through. Somebody else had prepared the tape. Casey was simply there. He hadn't a thing to do. So, on stand-by watch over the most intellectual machine in creation, Casey was reading a comic book.

Suddenly there was uproar. Against all precedent, the electric output typewriter was clicking furiously before the problem was solved. A loudspeaker made a din. The thinking machine was working the typewriter and had turned on the loudspeaker alarm to call Casey on the run. He got to the typewriter in a hurry. Its keys still clicked. They stopped indignantly, as he read: *"Casey, you blank-blanked-son-of a so-and so, you forgot to change the spool to Number Two."*

Casey's hair stood on end, and he wanted to run. He thought for a moment that the machine had come alive on him and was bawling him out.

Two seconds later he was hopping mad, of course. As soon as he thought, he knew what had happened. The man who'd prepared the two spools of tape had known Casey would run the problem through. So, at the end of the first tape, he'd zestfully included instructions for the machine to blast the loudspeaker and type that abuse to Casey, before the normal signal for change-of-spools came on. When those instructions-on-tape took effect, Casey's tranquil ease was shattered.

Far a moment though, it had seemed even to Casey, that the machine had a personality and reactions of its own. It hadn't. But most of us are inclined to think that machines have minds of their own, and practically all of us, expect that presently we will have actually thinking machines. As of now, the people who handle this machine say that it can only do half of the things a human brain can do — remember, recall, associate these instructions with that action, integrate numerals, and so on. Half of what a human brain can do is rather remarkable, but Casey's fellow-workers tend to restrain the use of the word "thinking" to the things an electronic computer cannot do.

Still, what with the progress of science and all, most of us assume that presently we will have robots to do all the heavy labor of the world. Perhaps the most eagerly awaited robots are robot minds to do that especially heavy labor known as thought. But up to now nobody seems to have estimated the problems to be faced in designing a truly thinking machine. Not in print at any rate. The basic principles for the operation of robot minds do not seem to be stated. Here goes.

It looks rather promising at the beginning. A baby starts out with a mind that is blank of information and ideas. It receives sense-perceptions of this and that. After some tens of thousands of days, during which its eyes and ears and fingers and sensory equipment generally feed data to it, the formerly bland mind has a reasonably coherent idea of the universe around it. In fact, a baby starts out as a potentially rational animal, and with nothing but constant information to help, winds up an adult with occasional flashes of reasonableness.

A thinking machine should be able to duplicate that, with greater ease and more efficiency. A machine that is to think about science doesn't need all the data a human needs for living. A machine doesn't need to know what will happen if he drinks boiler-makers, because it won't drink. It needn't know the difference between Republicans or Democrats. It won't vote. A great deal of painfully learned information can be skipped by a machine which has no gender. So a robot's brain can work to splendid advantage with only the education needed for its specialty.

We don't have to duplicate interests to make a useful machine. It has to be able to take in information — the computer just referred to does just that, and so does a human baby — and make use of it. The computer that scared Casey takes its information from dots of magnetism on a metal tape. It would seem that if one feeds specialized information to a thinking machine — a robot brain — with specialized interests, it should reason merrily away. A computer is "interested" only in numerals and letters. Make a brain to handle other thoughts, and it should reason with a speed and precision no man could duplicate. Given a process for thinking instead of computation, it seems that we should be able to make a high-speed, high-precision brilliant brain.

The process for thinking looks practical enough. With symbolic logic one can reduce any problem to graphic statement and the processes of logic are beautifully adaptable to robot operations.

Take a routine logical operation. "James is a man. A man is a rational animal. Therefore James is a rational animal."

Put symbolically, it reads:

$$J)M$$
$$\underline{M)RA}$$

That's the problem only: "The idea of 'James' implies or includes the idea of 'Man.' The idea 'Man' implies or includes the idea 'Rational Animal.'" Such a problem can be fed to a perfectly practical machine-brain. It will cancel the identical terms, and come up with:

$$J)M$$
$$\underline{M)RA}$$
$$J)RA$$

"The idea of 'James' implies or includes the idea 'Rational Animal.'" In short, 'James' is a rational animal. Nothing could be clearer, and Aristotle himself couldn't do better. It is certainly within the capacity of a machine to do so. We could use numbers instead of letters, to stand for our terms, like a short of algebra used hind-and-foremost. So:

Let 5 — James
6 — Man
7 — Rational Animal

We get:

$$5)6$$
$$\underline{6)7}$$
$$5)7$$

Here numerals — familiarly used in machines — are used in a mechanical duplication of thought. It works. Obviously, a machine can be made to perform logical operations — which is to say is to think.

You might contemplate this lovely set-up for a while. If you care to gloat over it, go ahead. Have your fun. But there is s slight objection that can be raised, which ultimately produces a small chilly sensation in the midsection of one's enthusiasm. This is a thinking process that a machine can perform. But it does not necessarily give a right answer under normal operating conditions with a man working the machine.

Mr. Will Durant exemplifies the catch in his book, "The Story of Philosophy." His raising of the point will do as well as any. Using the same logical process, only with the name "Socrates" instead of "James," he arrives at the same result: "Socrates is a rational animal." But then he triumphantly points out that this particular Socrates might be insane, in which case no logic would make him rational.

The objection is not quite right, of course. When we say that James or Socrates is a man, and that man is a rational animal, we use the term "man" with the same value in both statements. We reassert the equality of meaning when we let the two cancel mathematically or logically or otherwise. Mr. Durant didn't think of that. His argument would be expressed by somebody using the numerical expression above, with 5s and 6s and 7s, and then crying gleefully "April Fool!" One of those sixes wasn't a six, but only five and seven-eighths! So your system of thinking doesn't work!" It is a way of saying that a method is wrong if it isn't proof against cheating. I think one can drop the objection—*qua* objection—in the wastebasket.

But one cannot dismiss the objection that if a robot brain has to depend on the honesty or the reasonableness of the human who gives it information, then the answers are going to depend on the man and not the machine. This is true of mathematical computers, but people do not have opinions about numbers. They are neither dishonest nor unreasonable when they ask for the result of the integration of numerals. But they do cheat when they ask questions about matters of general interest—which is exactly why we want a thinking machine, a robot brain, to be able to answer.

A thinking machine has a highly special requirement for utility. It has to have sense. It has to be presented with the problem, not merely with symbols plus instructions to do such-and-such with them. That is where a computer falls short of being a thinking machine. It does not do anything better or more brilliantly than a human brain. It simply and exclusively does it faster. But a real robot brain will need to be smarter than mere men, or there is no point in making one.

To dodge the difficulty of depending on a man to tell it what to do and what with, a true thinking machine needs to understand a problem presented to it, so that it can tell whether it has adequate data for a solution. Make a machine that can tell you when it needs information, and what kind, and that means you have, at least, a rudimentary thinker right away.

But if it depends on men to provide it with information, it will be slow! And also it will accept any data given it. It can hardly tell that a man *says* six when it really is five and seven-eighths. So such a machine will be slow and no more accurate in its answers than the man-provided information. For accuracy alone—not to mention speed—a useful robot brain will need to hunt up the information to solve any problem presented to it. The only useful kind of robot brain will accept a problem, devise its own method of solution, seek out the data needed for the solution, and then produce the answer.

And in theory, at this point, that looks possible. A robot brain could use photocells for eyes, microphones for ears, and all sorts of artificial sensory organs to gather information. As a matter of fact, our most accurate information comes from artificial sensory devices. Microscopes are sharper than eyes and microphones than ears. Spectroscopes can gather information our senses balk at, calipers make measurements we can't approach, and in case of need, a robot brain might use an electron microscope to get accurate information otherwise unobtainable.

A robot brain could, then, have information of a much higher degree of accuracy than we human brains can attain. Its information would not be slanted by prejudice, distorted by personal errors of observation, or tied in knots by emotional associations. A robot brain that gathers its own information should be vastly better informed than any man could possibly be. It should think with strictly accurate logical processes. It should think sounder, faster, more sanely. A robot brain like this is exactly what we want — and do we need it!

But I suggest a slight pause here for deflation announcement.

The process outlined here for a robot mind is exactly the way a human mind works — as far as it goes. But something new has been subtracted. It just happens to be the fact that one can know the shape of a thing, and how big it is, and what it's made of, and its color and the way its atoms are linked together — and still not have the ghost of a notion what it happens to be or do. One can know everything about an object that the most imaginable senses can tell us, and know no more about it than a baby. Which is the point. After the first few months a baby's eyes are pretty good. It sees things clearly, but it doesn't know what they are. Its eyes don't tell that. Its mind has to do the job.

Well... We're working on a mind.

I went to an auction some years ago to bid on some books because there was a copy of Parson Weems' *Life of George Washington* in one lot. (I got the book and it's ghastly. I do not believe the cherry-tree story.) The auctioneer put up a small, varnished box and pulled a brass object out of it. I bought it out of curiosity for a quarter. Nobody knew what it was. It was brass and it was made to do something, but it was completely cryptic, and the printed instructions were printed in some completely unknown language. Now, the thing had no telescope or plumb-bob or degree-circle or anything resembling any of those things. And I'd never heard of such an instrument, but I made up my mind that it was a sort of eccentric, patented, impractical level for running levels for ditches. Eventually I found someone who could read the directions. They were Swedish and I'd guessed right. I'm very vain of that achievement though I haven't the slightest use for the gadget.

Now how the devil would a thinking machine work out a problem like that?

How do we work out such problems? We do, and by a very simple system. We know that a hammer is made to hit, a saw to saw, a knife to cut, a boat to sail, a gun to shoot, and so on. When a new object comes to our attention, we look for its purpose, its function, its use — what a philosopher would call its "act." We don't know what a thing is until we know what it does. When we can build that conscious ignorance into a robot mind, it will look for the same things a baby's mind looks for, and accomplish probably more.

It's worth thinking over. It's quite a simple problem, after all. We can make a machine that will inspect something and learn and record that it is a one-inch-in-diameter thing, an iron thing, a flat thing, and a pierced thing — that it has a hole in it. It's a round, flat, pierced, one-inch object. The machine can discover and apply all those adjectives to it. But it can't discover a verb or a noun so it can make a really intelligent statement about it.

A human being, looking at that object will discover that it can go under the nut of a bolt to spread the pressure when the nut is tightened. That's the verb. The noun follows. It's a washer.

The key to a robot's mind's construction would seem to be simply the discovery and/or recording of the equivalent of verbs and nouns so the robot can know what a thing is by what it does — or, of course, the other way about. If we make a machine do that very simple little trick, performed by human babies the first time they grab for a bottle, we can add as much to the effective intelligence at our disposal, as computers have added to our ability to do sums.

Such a trivial thing! But if you want to acquire a really fine case of pure intellectual frustration, just work on it for a while. Just try to invent a way to key a machine so it will recognize what a thing is, and never miss what it is, and never mistake it for something else. Accomplish that very minor feat, and all generations henceforth will revere you. You will have cracked the problem whose solution will give us thinking machines. A machine, which can do that, will think straighter than a man — and if it can't do that it can't think. But it seems that it ought to be so easy!

The difficulty is as idiotically simple as the thing to be done. Think, say, of a boat. When you do, a picture comes in your mind. Maybe your picture is of a Star Class racer. (Mine is.) But an outboard motorboat is a boat too, and so is a sea-sled and a canoe and a wind-up toy and a ship with a mast and a note-paper sailboat and the liner *United States* and a destroyer and a catamaran and a pirogue. Upon Lake Titicaca in the Andes they make boats out of bundles of straw. They are all boats. But there is not one single thing abut them — as objects, aside from what they do — which is applicable to describe all of them and which a mechanical device can detect or record.

One more. You know what a timepiece is. A clock is a timepiece. So is a wristwatch and a grandfather's clock and a time-clock in a factory. But also a sundial is a timepiece, and an hourglass and a clepsydra — water clock — and a chronograph and the ammonia clocks that have no moving mechanical parts and are the most accurate clocks we possess. Even the Carbon 14 in organic matter makes any organic matter a timepiece of sorts!

Name a means by which any possible device, examining a Nuremburg egg, would identify it as a pocket watch and therefore in a class of time pieces along with alarm clocks, sundials, sextants — which in one use determines local time — and a wax taper of King Alfred's time with hours and quarter hours marked on it to tell the time by its rate of burning.

Looked at that way, it appears that thinking is simply impossible, not only for a robot mind, but for a human one. But we do think. We can identify things with ideas. The process, even, is perfectly clear. It's simply one that nobody has been able to duplicate. If you work on it, you may hit the jackpot.

It works like this: When I think "timepiece" a picture comes in my mind. It's rather fuzzy, but in my individual case it does have a clock face. It is not the idea of a timepiece, however, but simply a sort of filing-envelope to contain the idea of a timepiece for use. When I want to think about timepieces I drag that out and use the idea — not that picture — in my thinking. In the same way, when I think of "water," I usually think of water as contained in a glass. I use "glass-of-water," as a file clue, as an index-symbol, as a container for the idea of water, without pretending for a moment that it is actually what I think water is. In the same way I'm apt to think of a bluebird when I think of happiness, because it's a good symbolic container for an idea. It suffices to hold the idea for use. But I know a clock-face is not essential to a timepiece, or a glass to water, and since I live in the country, any day all summer I can go outdoors and see bluebirds fighting like hell on the lawn. (But, of course, that may be their idea of happiness.)

I'm trying to establish that the idea of a thing — the notion of what something really is; the thingumbob that we use in thinking about things and that a robot mind needs to be able to handle — is not itself a picture. We can store ideas in pictures for convenience, but we know that the containers aren't the things. And that's the trouble. A robot mind or a thinking machine is going to have to handle knowledge of what things are, if only because it has to take account of what they do. At its baldest, simplest, barest statement — how could you write down the idea of anything at all? How could you note down the idea "food" so a machine could identify a substance as food? How, again, would you arrange for them to be hunted for in the robot's brain? (Don't ask me how we associate ideas! Or find them! But just for simplicity's sake...) If we knew that ideas range through this variation in size or shape or weight or volume, or if we could detect something about two ideas that a mechanical or electronic device so it could distinguish between them ... well ... we might get started. Maybe you can work something out. But as of now nobody seems able to detect anything about ideas at all. There is definite evidence that they exist, of course, We know them and live with them and dream them and think with them every second we're alive. But what kind of gizmo is an idea, anyway.

There are some very definite details — mostly of what they aren't and do not contain or possess. For one thing, an idea does not contain anything that — as a matter of perception or by our senses — we have seen or heard or tasted or smelled. But ideas are contained in things we see and notice — even such unsubstantial things as magnetic fields. And ideas do not contain specifications of material, but they may be contained in specific material. A ball is an idea, and we can find that idea in round objects of any imaginable solid or liquid, and even some stars are said to be made of mere balls of gas. An idea does not contain a design, though it can be obtained in designs. The idea of a house or a cabin cruiser doesn't include the idea of a blueprint, to most of us, but anybody can see the idea of a house or a cruiser in a blueprint. Perhaps the most baffling of all facts about ideas considered as things is that they do not even seem to have any parts. Each idea is simply itself. Which is an item you can check with your inner consciousness.

With these rather depressing details to go on, it's clear why we have trouble imagining a robot mind — a mechanical or electronic device — to deal with ideas. We can imagine the robot mind, all right, but all imagining is simply a shuffling and reshuffling of things we have in some fashion perceived. If we haven't perceived something with our senses, in one way or another, we can't imagine it. Thus, a blind man who has never seen light can't imagine it. He can think about it, but not have a picture of it. In the same way we can think about ideas, but we can't picture them. So when we try to think about a robot brain to handle ideas, we are trying to imagine something we *can* imagine, dealing with things we *can't* imagine.

Naturally, we have some trouble with the details. But it is certainly possible in theory that somebody might concoct some gadget to perform with ideas what can't be done with numbers.

After all, ideas are realities. They have effects, and unreal things do not produce effects. Ideas not only produce passes at girls who wear glasses, but cities, wars, and streptomycin packaged ready for use. Nations exist because of them, statues are carved because of ideas. This magazine, as a matter of fact, is printed for the express purpose of giving you perceptions from which you can abstract ideas. And while it is true that ideas are fundamentally in the universe around us, ideas are formally and specifically in our minds. They exist in a certain place — my ideas are in my skull, and your ideas are in your skull — and they have effects, but they haven't any dimensions or any inside or outside, and they are utterly different from each other. To cut down the discovery need to make a robot brain possible, you can say quite truthfully that the basic need for a thinking machine is simply some way by which it can tell one idea from another.

We do it all the time. It must be quite simple, if only one can get the right approach.

All through this article I have been tackling the problems of a robot mind by comparing the needed process with the observed operation of a human mind. The system does not work so well when one gets this far. But it could be changed a bit and tried further. Maybe the approach to understanding how a machine could be made to think would be possible if one understood how an animal which could not think became capable of it. I suggest that a machine, right now, can do just about everything an animal's brain can do. We can make machines to perceive, to recall, and even to scramble recollections and arrive at imagination akin to dreaming — and no more packed with sense. We can make mechanical devices which actually learn by experience and acquire rudimentary conditioned response.

We humans are animals, in a sense. Only we can think, which is all the difference anybody needs. It might be that one could get a clue to building a robot mind if he worked out the process by which — to be respectable one has to say by evolution — an animal's brain became capable of ideas, as it has done in our case. It is a singularly isolated phenomenon. There are hundreds of thousands of other species of creatures on Earth, but we are the only one capable of thinking in terms of ideas. If there were another creature capable of it, we'd have some keen competition.

The difference between our brains and those of other higher creatures is more of function than of structure. If you can work out the difference in operation, you may make robot minds immediately possible and deserve well of your fellow-citizens.

If the direct approach, of seeking to understand how we happen to be human, does not yield results, you might try still more. You might try to figure out why we are human.

There is only one theory that I know of. It does not offer a solution to the technical problem of making a robot brain, but it is pretty plausible.

You learned it in Sunday School.

Bibliography

In addition to writing as Murray Leinster, Will F. Jenkins often used his real name and, occasionally, the pseudonyms William Fitzgerald, Louisa Carter Lee, and Florinda Martel. Entries are chronological.

Books

SCIENCE FICTION

Jenkins, Will F. *The Murder of the U.S.A.* New York: Crown, 1946. (Also known as *Destroy the U.S.A.*)
_____. *Destroy the U.S.A.* Toronto, Canada: New Stand Library Pocket Edition, 1950. (Also known as *The Murder of the U.S.A.*)
Leinster, Murray. *Fight for Life.* New York: Crestwood, 1949.
_____. *Space Platform.* New York: Pocket Books, 1953.
_____. *Space Tug.* Chicago: Shasta, 1953.
_____. *The Black Galaxy.* New York: Galaxy Novels, 1954.
_____. *The Brain-Stealers.* New York: Ace Books, 1954. (Ace Double D-79. Also known as "The Man in the Iron Cap," published in *Startling Stories*, November 1947.)
_____. *The Forgotten Planet.* New York: Gnome Press, 1954.
_____. *Gateway to Elsewhere.* New York: Ace Books, 1954. (Ace Double D-53. Part 1 published as "Journey to Barkut" in *Fantasy Book* 2, no. 1, 1950, complete story in *Startling Stories*, January 1950.)
_____. *Operation: Outer Space.* New York: Fantasy Press, 1954.
_____. *The Other Side of Here.* New York: Ace Books, 1955. (Also known as "The Incredible Invasion." Published in five parts in *Astounding Stories,* August–December 1936.)
_____. *City on the Moon.* New York: Avalon Books, 1957.
_____. *War with the Gizmos.* New York: Fawcett, 1958. (Also known as "Long Ago and Far Away." Published in *Amazing Stories*, September 1959.)
_____. *The Duplicators.* New York: Ace Books, 1959. (Ace Double D-403. Also known as "The Lost Race." Published in *Thrilling Wonder Stories*, April 1949.)
_____. *The Monster from Earth's End.* New York: Fawcett, 1959.
_____. *The Mutant Weapon.* New York: Ace Books, 1959. (Ace Double D-403, backed with Murray Leinster's *The Pirates of Zan*. Also known as "Med Service." Published in *Astounding Science-Fiction,* August 1957.)
_____. *The Pirates of Zan.* New York: Ace Books, 1959. (Ace Double D-403, backed with Murray Leinster's *The Mutant Weapon.*) (Also known as "The Pirates of Erzatz." Published in three parts in *Astounding Science-Fiction,* February–April 1959.)

_____. *Men into Space*. New York: Berkley, 1960.
_____. *The Wailing Asteroid*. New York: Avon Books, 1960.
_____. *Creatures of the Abyss*. New York: Berkley, 1961. (Also known as *The Listeners*.)
_____. *Operation Terror*. New York: Berkley, 1962.
_____. *Talents Incorporated*. New York: Avon Books, 1962.
_____. *The Greks Bring Gifts*. New York: Macfadden, 1964.
_____. *Invaders of Space*. New York: Berkley, 1964.
_____. *The Other Side of Nowhere*. New York: Berkley, 1964. (Also known as "Spaceman." Published in two parts in *Analog*, March–April 1964.)
_____. *Time Tunnel*. New York: Pyramid Books, 1964.
_____. *Checkpoint Lambda*. New York: Berkley, 1966.
_____. *Space Captain*. New York: Ace Books, 1966. (Ace Double M-135. Also known as "Killer Ship." Published in three parts in *Amazing Stories*, October–December 1965.)
_____. *Tunnel Through Time*. Philadelphia: Westminster Press, 1966.
_____. *Miners in the Sky*. New York: Avon Books, 1967.
_____. *Space Gypsies*. New York: Avon Books, 1967.
_____. *Time Tunnel*. New York: Pyramid Books, 1967. (Novelization of TV series.)
_____. *Timeslip!* New York: Pyramid Books, 1967. (Novelization of TV series.)
_____. *The Listeners*. London, UK: Sidgwick & Jackson, 1969. (Also known as *Creatures of the Abyss*.)

WESTERN AND ADVENTURE

Jenkins, Will F. *The Gamblin' Kid*. New York: King, 1933.
_____. *Mexican Trail*. New York: King, 1933. (Also known as "Dead Man's Shoes." First published in three parts in *West*, March 4, 18, and April 1, 1931.)
_____. *Fighting Horse Valley*. New York: King, 1934.
_____. *Outlaw Sheriff*. New York: King, 1934. (Also known as *Rustlin' Sheriff*.)
_____. *Rustlin' Sheriff*. London, UK: Eldon Press, 1934. (Also known as *Outlaw Sheriff*.)
_____. *Kid Deputy*. New York: King, 1935. (Published in three parts in *Triple X Western*, February–April 1928.)
_____. *Black Sheep*. London, UK: Wright & Brown, 1936. (Published in *Adventure*, January 1, 1928.)
_____. *Dallas*. New York: Fawcett, 1950. (Novelization of screenplay by John Twist.)
_____. *Son of the Flying Y*. New York: Fawcett, 1951.
_____. *Cattle Rustlers*. London, UK: Ward Lock, 1952.
Leinster, Murray. *Guns for Achin*. London, UK: Wright & Brown, 1936. (See **Collections**, below.)
_____. *Two Gun Showdown*. New York: Astro Distributors, West in Action, 1948. (Also known as *The Gamblin' Kid*.)
_____. *Texas Gun-Law*. New York: Quarter Books, 1949. (Abridgment of *Black Sheep*.)
_____. *Texas Gun Slinger*. New York: Star Books, 1949. (Abridgment of *Fighting Horse Valley*.)
_____. *Wanted Dead or Alive!* New York: Quarter Books, 1949.
_____. *Outlaw Deputy*. New York: Star Guidance, 1950.
_____. *Outlaw Guns*. New York: Star Books, 1950.

MYSTERY

Jenkins, Will F. *The Man Who Feared*. New York: Gateway Books, 1942. (First published in four parts in *Detective Fiction Weekly*, August 9–30, 1930.)
Leinster, Murray. *Scalps*. New York: Brewer & Warren, 1930. (Also known as *Wings of Chance*.)
_____. *Murder Madness*. New York: Brewer & Warren, 1931. (First published in four parts in *Astounding Stories*, May–August 1930.)

Bibliography

_____. *Murder Will Out*. London, UK: John Hamilton, 1932.
_____. *Sword of Kings*. London, UK: Long, 1933.
_____. *Murder in the Family*. London, UK: John Hamilton, 1935.
_____. *No Clues*. London, UK: Wright & Brown, 1935.
_____. *Wings of Chance*. London, UK: John Hamilton, 1935. (Also known as *Scalps*.)

ROMANCE

Lee, Louisa Carter. *Her Desert Lover*. New York: Chelsea House, 1925.
_____. *Love and Better: A Love Story*. New York: Chelsea House, 1931.

Stories

SCIENCE FICTION

Fitzgerald, William. "The Gregory Circle." *Thrilling Wonder Stories*, April 1947.
_____. "The Nameless Something." *Thrilling Wonder Stories*, June 1947.
_____. "The Deadly Dust." *Thrilling Wonder Stories*, August 1947.
_____. "The Seven Temporary Moons." *Thrilling Wonder Stories*, February 1948.
_____. "The Devil of East Lupton, Vermont." *Thrilling Wonder Stories*, August 1948.
_____. "Cure for a Ylith." *Startling Stories*, November 1949.
Jenkins, Will F. "Uneasy Home-coming." *Weird Tales*, April 1935.
_____. "The Man Who Blew Up a War." *Blue Book*, May 1939.
_____. "Escape." *Argosy*, May 1944.
_____. "The Web." *Good Housekeeping*, September 1944.
_____. "Preview of Tomorrow." *Coronet*, October 1944.
_____. "A Logic Named Joe." *Astounding Science-Fiction*, March 1946.
_____. "From Beyond the Stars." *Thrilling Wonder Stories*, June 1947.
_____. "Symbiosis." *Collier's*, June 14, 1947.
_____. "Wall of Fear." *Suspense*, Fall 1951.
_____. "Devil's Henchman." *Argosy*, May 1952.
_____. "The Soldado Ant." *American Science Fiction*, August 1952. (Also known as "Doomsday Deferred.")
_____. "The Little Terror." *The Saturday Evening Post*, August 22, 1953.
_____. "Last Day on Earth." *Adventure*, July 1956.
Leinster, Murray. "The Runaway Skyscraper." *The Argosy*, February 22, 1919.
_____. "A Thousand Degrees Below Zero." *Thrill Book*, July 15, 1919.
_____. "The Silver Menace." *Thrill Book*, September 1 and 15, 1919. (Two-part serial.)
_____. "Juju." *Thrill Book*, October 15, 1919.
_____. "Oh, Aladdin." *All Story Weekly*, November 1919.
_____. "The Mad Planet." *The Argosy*, June 12, 1920.
_____. "The Red Dust." *Argosy All-Story Weekly*, April 2, 1921.
_____. "The Oldest Story in the World." *Weird Tales*, August 1925.
_____. "The Strange People." *Weird Tales* (March–May 1928). (Three-part serial.)
_____. "The Darkness on Fifth Avenue." *Argosy*, November 1929.
_____. "The City of the Blind." *Argosy*, December 1929.
_____. "The Murderers." *Weird Tales*, January 1930.
_____. "Tanks." *Astounding Stories*, January 1930.
_____. "The Storm That Had to Be Stopped." *Argosy*, March 1930.
_____. "The Man Who Put Out the Sun." *Argosy*, June 1930.
_____. "The Fifth-Dimension Catapult." *Astounding Stories*, January 1931.
_____. "The Power Planet." *Amazing Stories*, June 1931.
_____. "Morale." *Astounding Stories*, December 1931.
_____. "The Sleep Gas." *Argosy*, January 13, 1932.

———. "The Racketeer Ray." *Amazing Stories*, February 1932.
———. "Nemesis." *Argosy*, March 12, 1932.
———. "Politics." *Amazing Stories*, June 1932.
———. "The Fifth Dimension Tube." *Astounding Stories*, January 1933.
———. "The Monsters." *Weird Tales*, January 1933.
———. "Borneo Devils." *Amazing Stories*, February 1933.
———. "Invasion." *Astounding Stories*, March 1933.
———. "The Earth Shaker." *Argosy*, April 15–May 6, 1933. (Four-part serial.)
———. "Beyond the Sphinxes' Cave." *Astounding Stories*, November 1933.
———. "War of the Purple Gas." *Argosy* (February 24, March 3, 1934. (Two-part serial.)
———. "Sidewise in Time." *Astounding Stories*, June 1934.
———. "The Mole Pirate." *Astounding Stories*, November 1934.
———. "The Rollers." *Argosy*, December 29, 1934.
———. "Conquest of the Stars." *Astounding Stories*, March 1935.
———. "Proxima Centauri." *Astounding Stories*, March 1935.
———. "The Morrison Monument." *Argosy*, August 19, 1935.
———. "The Challenge from Beyond." *Fantasy Magazine*, September 1935.
———. "Crime on Tristan." *Argosy*, November 1935.
———. "The Extra Intelligence." *Argosy*, November 30, 1935.
———. "The Fourth-Dimensional Demonstrator." *Astounding Stories*, December 1935.
———. "The Incredible Invasion." *Astounding Stories* (August–December 1936. Five-part serial. Also known as *The Other Side of Here*, published by Ace Books, 1955).
———. "The Board Fence." *Argosy*, July 23, 1938.
———. "Swords and Mongols." *Golden Fleece*, April 1939.
———. "Plague Ship." *Argosy*, July 15, 1939.
———. "The Wabbler." *Astounding Science-Fiction*, October 1942.
———. "Four Little Ships." *Astounding Science-Fiction*, November 1942.
———. "If You Can Get It." *Astounding Science-Fiction*, November 1943.
———. "Plague." *Astounding Science-Fiction*, February 1944.
———. "Trog." *Astounding Science-Fiction*, June 1944.
———. "The Eternal Now." *Thrilling Wonder Stories*, Fall 1944.
———. "First Contact." *Astounding Science-Fiction*, May 1945.
———. "The Ethical Equations." *Astounding Science-Fiction*, June 1945.
———. "Tight Place." *Astounding Science-Fiction*, July 1945.
———. "Pipeline to Pluto." *Astounding Science-Fiction*, August 1945.
———. "Things Pass By." *Thrilling Wonder Stories*, Summer 1945.
———. "Incident on Calypso." *Startling Stories*, Fall 1945.
———. "The Power." *Astounding Science-Fiction*, September 1945.
———. "Interference." *Astounding Science-Fiction*, October 1945.
———. "De Profundis." *Thrilling Wonder Stories*, Winter 1945.
———. "The Plants." *Astounding Science-Fiction*, January 1946.
———. "Adapter." *Astounding Science-Fiction*, March 1946.
———. "Like Dups." *Thrilling Wonder Stories*, Spring 1946.
———. "Malignant Marauder." *Thrilling Wonder Stories*, Summer 1946. (Also known as "Dead City.")
———. "Atoms Over America." *Argosy*, June–July 1946. (Two-part serial.)
———. "Pocket Universes." *Thrilling Wonder Stories*, Fall 1946.
———. "The Castaway." *Argosy*, September 1946.
———. "The End." *Thrilling Wonder Stories*, December 1946.
———. "The Disciplinary Circuit." *Thrilling Wonder Stories*, Winter 1946.
———. "Friends." *Startling Stories*, January 1947.
———. "Time to Die." *Astounding Science-Fiction*, January 1947.

Bibliography

_____. "The Manless Worlds." *Thrilling Wonder Stories*, February 1947.
_____. "The Laws of Chance." *Startling Stories*, March 1947.
_____. "The Skit-Tree Planet." *Thrilling Wonder Stories*, April 1947.
_____. "The Boomerang Circuit." *Thrilling Wonder Stories*, June 1947.
_____. "Propagandist." *Astounding Science-Fiction*, August 1947.
_____. "The Day of the Deepies." *Famous Fantastic Mysteries*, October 1947.
_____. "The Man in the Iron Cap." *Startling Stories,* November 1947. (Also known as *The Brain-Stealers*, published by Ace Books, 1954.)
_____. "Planet of Sand." *Famous Fantastic Mysteries*, February 1948.
_____. "West Wind." *Astounding Science-Fiction*, March 1948.
_____. "The Strange Case of John Kingman." *Astounding Science-Fiction*, May 1948.
_____. "Space Can." *Thrilling Wonder Stories*, June 1948.
_____. "The Night Before the End of the World." *Famous Fantastic Mysteries*, August 1948.
_____. "Regulations." *Thrilling Wonder Stories*, August 1948.
_____. "The Ghost Planet." *Thrilling Wonder Stories*, December 1948.
_____. "The Story of Rod Cantrell." *Startling Stories*, January 1949.
_____. "Assignment on Pasik." *Thrilling Wonder Stories*, February 1949. (Published by Galaxy Novels, 1964.)
_____. "The Lost Race." *Thrilling Wonder Stories*, April 1949. (Also known as *The Duplicators*, published by Ace Books, 1964.)
_____. "The Life-Work of Professor Muntz." *Thrilling Wonder Stories*, June 1949.
_____. "Fury from Lilliput." *Thrilling Wonder Stories*, August 1949.
_____. "Doomsday Deferred." *The Saturday Evening Post*, September 24, 1949. (Also known as "The Soldado Ant.")
_____. "The Queen's Astrologer." *Thrilling Wonder Stories*, October 1949.
_____. "The Other World." *Startling Stories*, November 1949.
_____. "This Star Shall Be Free." *Super Science Stories*, November 1949.
_____. "The Lonely Planet." *Thrilling Wonder Stories*, December 1949.
_____. "The Fear Planet." *Super Science Stories*, January 1950.
_____. "Planet of Small Men." *Thrilling Wonder Stories*, April 1950.
_____. "Nobody Saw the Ship." *Future Combined with Science Fiction Stories*, May–June 1950.
_____. "Be Young Again." *Future Combined with Science Fiction Stories*, July–August 1950.
_____. "Journey to Barkut." Parts I and II printed in *Fantasy Book*, October 1950 and January 1951. The complete version appeared in *Startling Stories* in January 1952 and in book form as *Gateway to Elsewhere*, Ace Books, 1954. (Ace Double D-53.)
_____. "Historical Note." *Astounding Science-Fiction*, February 1951.
_____. "The Other Now." *Galaxy*, March 1951.
_____. "Slag with the Queer Head." *Marvel Science Fiction*, August 1951.
_____. "If You Was a Moklin." *Galaxy*, September 1951.
_____. "Keyhole." *Thrilling Wonder Stories,* December, 1951.
_____. "The Gadget Had a Ghost." *Thrilling Wonder Stories*, June 1952.
_____. "Nightmare Planet." *Argosy*, June 12, 1952.
_____. "The Middle of the Week After Next." *Thrilling Wonder Stories*, August 1952.
_____. "The Barrier." *Space Science Fiction*, September 1952.
_____. "Overdrive." *Startling Stories,* January 1953.
_____. "The Sentimentalists." *Galaxy*, April 1953.
_____. "The Invaders." *Amazing Stories*, April–May 1953.
_____. "Dear Charles." *Fantastic Story Magazine*, May 1953.
_____. "Nightmare Planet." *Science Fiction +*, June 1953.
_____. "The Ship Was a Robot." *Thrilling Wonder Stories*, June 1953.
_____. "The Jezebel." *Startling Stories*, October 1953.

———. "The Trans-Human." *Science Fiction +*, December 1953.
———. "Fugitive from Space." *Amazing Stories*, May 1954.
———. "The Amateur Alchemist." *Thrilling Wonder Stories*, Fall 1954.
———. "Second Landing." *Thrilling Wonder Stories*, Winter 1954.
———. "The Psionic Mousetrap." *Amazing Stories*, March 1955.
———. "Sam, This Is You." *Galaxy*, May 1955.
———. "Honeymoon on Dlecka." *Fantastic Universe*, July 1955.
———. "White Spot." *Startling Stories*, Summer 1955.
———. "Scrimshaw." *Astounding Science-Fiction*, September 1955.
———. "Sand Doom." *Astounding Science-Fiction*, December 1955.
———. "Exploration Team." *Astounding Science-Fiction*, March 1956.
———. "Critical Difference." *Astounding Science-Fiction*, July 1956.
———. "The Swamp Was Upside Down." *Astounding Science-Fiction*, September 1956.
———. "Women's Work." *Original Science Fiction Stories*, November 1956.
———. "Anthropological Note." *Fantasy and Science Fiction*, April 1957.
———. "Ribbon in the Sky." *Astounding Science-Fiction*, June 1957.
———. "Med Service." *Astounding Science-Fiction*, August 1957. (Also known as *The Mutant Weapon*, Ace Books, 1959.)
———. "The Grandfather's War." *Astounding Science-Fiction*, October 1957.
———. "The Machine That Saved the World." *Amazing Stories*, December 1957.
———. "Short History of World War Three." *Astounding Science-Fiction*, January 1958.
———. "The Strange Invasion." *Satellite Science Fiction*, April 1958.
———. "Pirates of Ersatz." *Astounding Science-Fiction* (three-part serial February–April 1959). (Also known as *The Pirates of Zan*, Ace Books, 1959.)
———. "The Aliens." *Astounding Science-Fiction*, August 1959.
———. "Long Ago and Far Away." *Amazing Stories*, September 1959. (Also known as *Four from Planet 5*, Fawcett, 1959.)
———. "A Matter of Importance." *Astounding Science-Fiction*, September 1959.
———. "Attention Saint Patrick." *Astounding Science-Fiction*, January 1960.
———. "The Leader." *Astounding Science-Fiction*, February 1960.
———. "Tyrants Need to be Loved." *Fantastic*, February 1960.
———. "The Ambulance Made Two Trips." *Astounding Science-Fiction*, April 1960.
———. "The Corianis Disaster." *Science Fiction Stories*, May 1960.
———. "The Covenant, Part IV." *Fantastic*, July 1960. (Parts I, II, III, and V by other authors.)
———. "Doctor." *Galaxy*, February 1961.
———. "Pariah Planet." *Amazing Stories*, July 1961. (Also known as *This World Is Taboo*, Ace Books, 1961.)
———. "The Case of the Homicidal Robots." *Fantasy and Science Fiction*, August 1961.
———. "Planet of Dread." *Fantastic*, May 1962.
———. "Imbalance." *Fantastic*, December 1962.
———. "Third Planet." *Worlds of Tomorrow*, April 1963.
———. "The Hate Disease." *Analog*, August 1963. (Also known as "Tallien Three.")
———. "Manners and Customs of the Thrid." *Worlds of If*, September 1963.
———. "Med Ship Man." *Galaxy*, October 1963.
———. "Lords of the Uffts." *Worlds of Tomorrow Science Fiction*, February 1964. (Also known as *The Duplicators*, Ace Books, 1964.)
———. "Spaceman." *Analog*, March–April 1964. (Two-part serial. Also known as *The Other Side of Nowhere*, Berkley, 1964.)
———. "Plague of Cryder II." *Analog*, December 1964.
———. "Killer Ship." *Amazing Stories*, October–December 1965. (Three-part serial. Also known as *Space Captain*, Ace Books, 1966.)

———. "A Planet Like Heaven." *Worlds of If,* January 1966.
———. "Stopover in Space." *Amazing Stories,* June–August 1966. (Three-part serial. Also known as *Checkpoint Lambda,* Berkley, 1966.)

Westerns and Adventure

Jenkins, Will F. "The Man Who Went Black." *Ace-High Magazine,* October 1922.
———. "Grist." *Short Stories,* July 10, 1924.
———. "The Poisoned Glass." *Fighting Romances from the West and East,* January 1926.
———. "Texas Gun Law." *Adventure,* January 1, 1928.
———. "The Kid Deputy." *Triple X Magazine,* February–April 1928. (Three-part serial. Published in book form by King, 1935.)
———. "The Emerald Buddha." *Short Stories,* February 10, 1930.
———. "The Black Stone of Agharti." *Short Stories,* September 10, 1930.
———. "Guns Over Hell's Sink." *Complete Western Book Magazine,* October 1936.
———. "The Maintop." *Blue Book,* November 1936.
———. "The Sheriff Writes a Letter." *Smashing Western,* January 1937.
———. "The Gamblin' Kid." *Western Action Novels,* March 1937. (Published in book form by King, 1933.)
———. "The Ending of El Jefe." *Real Western,* April 1937.
———. "Rustlin' Spooks." *Smashing Western,* April 1937.
———. "The Second Avenue Kid." *Double-Action Gang Magazine,* April 1937.
———. "In Spring Thaws." *Complete Northwest Novels,* July 1937.
———. "Malay Guns." *Adventure Novels,* July 1937.
———. "Hell for a Gringo." *Famous Western,* December 1937.
———. "The Law of the Six-Gun." *Smashing Western,* January 1938.
———. "The Trail to Mexico Runs Red, *Double Action Western,* June 1938.
———. "Border Renegade." *Cowboy Short Stories,* October 1938.
———. "Man Against Sea." *Argosy* (UK), November 1938.
———. "A Loan of Dynamite." *Blue Book,* March 1939.
———. "Sauvetage." *Rie et Rac,* March 29, 1939.
———. "New Heads for the Devil-Devil Doctor." *Adventure Novels and Short Stories,* April 1939.
———. "The Man Who Blew Up a War." *Blue Book,* May 1939.
———. "The Law Wants Slim Galway." *Double Action Western,* June 1939.
———. "The Kid Dies Again." *The Star Weekly,* April 27, 1940.
———. "The Lion-Mane Collar." *Illustrated,* January 11, 1941.
———. "The Fourth Moment." *This Week Magazine,* April 27, 1941.
———. "The Island That Looked Like Paradise." *Blue Book,* November 1941.
———. "Mauki." *Argosy* (UK), July 1942.
———. "From Dusk to Dawn." *Argosy* (UK), November 1942.
———. "Proposal." *Argosy* (UK), April 1943.
———. "Artist." *Argosy* (UK), October 1943.
———. "Escape." *Argosy,* May 1944.
———. "One Traitor Among Us." *Life Story Magazine,* August 1944.
———. "The Secret of Room 917." *Life Story Magazine,* March 1945.
———. "Under Suspicion." *Life Story Magazine,* April 1945.
———. "The Dream." *Life Story Magazine,* June 1945.
———. "Captain Morgan Was a Gentleman." *Short Stories,* July 25, 1945.
———. "For Services Rendered." *Argosy,* August 1945.
———. "The Devil on Apuru." *Adventure,* October 1947.
———. "The Falling Trapeze." *Star Weekly,* May 1, 1948.
———. "Forbidden Sanctuary." *Argosy,* November 1948.

_____. "Mr. Waddy." *Argosy* (UK), January 1950.
_____. "Love Letter." *Argosy* (UK), August 1950.
_____. "The Sheriff Deals in Facts." *Esquire,* November 1952.
_____. "Something for Steve." *Grit,* April 5, 1954.
_____. "The Second Mrs. Frayne." *The Star Weekly*, December 31, 1955.
_____. "Last Day on Earth." *Adventure,* July 1956.
_____. "Shootout." *Ranch Romances,* September 6, 1957.
Leinster, Murray. "Atmosphere." *The Argosy,* January 26, 1918.
_____. "You Can't Get Away with It." *All-Story Weekly,* February 2, 1918.
_____. "A Cabin in the Wilderness." *All-Story Weekly,* April 6, 1918.
_____. "In Cold Blood." *The Argosy,* May 4, 1918.
_____. "The Hour After Supper." *The Argosy,* July 13, 1918.
_____. "Jiggy Jazz." *The Argosy,* September 21, 1918.
_____. "Honesty." *The Argosy*, September 28, 1918.
_____. "Grooves." *All-Story Weekly,* October 13, 1918.
_____. "Izzy." *The Argosy*, November 16, 1918.
_____. "Food of Eagles." *All-Story Weekly,* December 14, 1918.
_____. "No-Man's Reef." *Young's Magazine,* June 1919.
_____. "Footprints in the Snow." *All-Story Weekly,* June 7, 1919.
_____. "Evidence." *All-Story Weekly,* July 12, 1919.
_____. "W.S.S." *All-Story Weekly,* August 2, 1919.
_____. "JuJu." *Thrill Book,* October 15, 1919.
_____. "High Jinks in Denver." *Western Story Magazine*, April 30, 1921.
_____. "Nerves." *Argosy All-Story Weekly,* June 4, 1921.
_____. "Baldy Rides a Hunch." *Argosy All-Story Weekly,* July 30, 1921.
_____. "The $500.00 Reward." *Action Stories,* September 1921.
_____. "Lynch Law." *Ace-High Magazine,* September 1921.
_____. "Run, Race-Haws!" *Argosy All-Story Weekly,* October 29, 1921.
_____. "When the Death Bird Sings." *Ace-High Magazine,* November 1921.
_____. "Leon the Magnificent." *Ace-High Magazine,* March 1922.
_____. "Bull's-eye." *People's Story Magazine,* May 1922.
_____. "Business Is Pleasure." *Argosy All-Story Weekly,* June 17, 1922.
_____. "The Street of Magnificent Dreams." *Argosy All-Story Weekly*, August 5, 1922.
_____. "Thief." *People's Story Magazine,* August 10, 1922.
_____. "The End of the Trail." *Ace-High Magazine,* October 1922.
_____. "Dust and Nuggets and Furs." *Ace-High Magazine,* November 1922.
_____. "Blind Eyes of the Sea." *Ace-High Magazine,* December 2, 1922.
_____. "Romanced to Freedom." *Western Story Magazine,* January 27, 1923.
_____. "No Sentiment." *People's Magazine,* February 1, 1923.
_____. "Signal Weird." *Top-Notch Magazine,* February 1, 1923.
_____. "The Man Who Was Fired." *Argosy All-Story Weekly,* March 3, 1923.
_____. "Heroes." *People's Magazine,* May 1, 1923.
_____. "The Sheriff Writes a Letter." *People's Magazine,* May 15, 1923.
_____. "The Man Who Carried the Sky Line." *Sea Stories,* July 20, 1923.
_____. "The Off-Shore Breeze." *Argosy All-Story Weekly,* July 21, 1923.
_____. "The Juice Hog's Battle." *Top-Notch Magazine,* August 15, 1923.
_____. "Wormwood and General Detecting." *Argosy All-Story Weekly,* August 25, 1923.
_____. "In Account with Destiny." *Short Stories,* September 10, 1923.
_____. "A Wireless for the Fangless One." *Short Stories,* January 25, 1924.
_____. "The Captain of the Quiberon." *Short Stories,* April 10, 1924.
_____. "The Duplex Cross." *People's Magazine,* May 1, 1924.
_____. "Rose O'Sharon." *Triple-X,* June 1924.

Bibliography 203

_____. "The Lunatic Railroad." *Triple-X*, August 1924.
_____. "Fog." *Short Stories*, September 10, 1924.
_____. "Sagebrush Slings the Bull." *Short Stories*, September 25, 1924.
_____. "The Curse of Golden Hill." *Triple-X*, December 1924.
_____. "Ample Water." *Sunset*, January 1925.
_____. "All Rescuers Will Be Prosecuted." *Ace-High Magazine*, January 18, 1925.
_____. "The Eyes of the Eagle." *Flynn's*, April 4, 1925.
_____. "The Killer." *Ranch Romances*, June 1925.
_____. "His Bid for Fame." *Top-Notch Magazine*. July 1, 1925.
_____. "Merritt Takes a Chance." *Fighting Romances from the East and West*, November 1925.
_____. "Racing with Death." *Fighting Romances from the East and West*, December 1925.
_____. "Aztec Gold." *Fighting Romances from the East and West,* January 1926.
_____. "Howdy!" *West*, January 20, 1926.
_____. "Sonny." *West*, February 5, 1926.
_____. "Island Honor." *Short Stories*, February 10, 1926.
_____. "The Red Stone." *Short Stories*, February 25, 1926.
_____. "Fool's Gold." *Fighting Romances from the East and West,* March 1926.
_____. "The Seventh Bullet." *The Danger Trail*, March, 1926.
_____. "Sharks." *The Danger Trail*, April 1926.
_____. "The Owner of the Aztec." *Western Magazine*, May 5, 1926.
_____. "The Man Who Didn't Shoot." *The Danger Trail*, June 1926.
_____. "The Trail of Blood." *The Danger Trail*, September 1926.
_____. "Tuilagi." *The Danger Trail*, April 1927.
_____. "The Wreck of the Israel Holman." *Sea Stories*, May 1927.
_____. "Jungle Stream." *The Danger Trail*, June 1927.
_____. "The Boys in the Bunkhouse." *Golden West Magazine* (UK), July 1927.
_____. "Sword of Kings." *Frontier Stories*, July 1927. (Published in book form by Long, 1933.)
_____. "According to the Directory." *The Danger Trail*, August 1927.
_____. "Lady Luck's Stepchild." *West*, August 27, 1927.
_____. "The God Who Carried a Cane." *The Danger Trail*, October 1927.
_____. "Wells of Pilduri." *Frontier Stories*, October 1927.
_____. "Kuantan." *Adventure*, February 15, 1928.
_____. "Village of the Devil-Devil Drums." *The Danger Trail*, June 1928.
_____. "Gun Cargo." *Everybody's*, July 1928.
_____. "Payung." *Everybody's*, September 1928.
_____. "Six Guns Across the Border." *West*, September 15, 1928.
_____. "Death Lagoon." *Three Star Magazine*, December 2, 1928.
_____. "The Skipper Knows Best." *Short Stories*, December 10, 1928.
_____. "Maeho." *Adventure Trails*, February 1929.
_____. "Wanted — Dead or Alive." *Triple-X Magazine,* February–May 1929. (Four-part serial. Published by Quarter Books, 1949.)
_____. "Khilit." *Everybody's,* March 1929.
_____. "The Deep Sea Trail." *Adventure*, June 1, 1929.
_____. "Sons of the Eagle." *West*, August 1929.
_____. "The Trap." *Munsey's*, August 1929.
_____. "Boots." *Adventure*, August 15, 1929.
_____. "Bosom Friends." *Everybody's Combined with Romance*, January 1930.
_____. "The Driving Force." *Complete Northwest Magazine*, January 1930.
_____. "The Eye of Black A'Wang." *Short Stories*, January 10, 1930.
_____. "The Mystery of the Scalping Blade." *Triple-X Magazine*, January–May 1930. (Five-part serial.)

———. "White-Man-Devil." *Wide World Adventures,* June 1930.
———. "The Law of the Forty-Five." *West,* June 25, 1930.
———. "The Hand of God." *Short Stories,* July 25, 1930.
———. "The Hippopotamus Bullet." *Star Novels Magazine,* November 1930.
———. "Flying Fish Milk." *Star Magazine,* December 1930.
———. "Storm Wings." *Air Trails,* March 1931.
———. "Dead Man's Shoes." *West,* March 4–April 15, 1931. (Four-part serial. Also known as *Mexican Trail* as by Will F. Jenkins, King, 1933, and filmed as *Border Devils,* Supreme Features, Inc., 1932.)
———. "The Great Joke of Lope Da Gama." *Far East Adventure Stories,* April 1931.
———. "The Radio Pilot." *Street & Smith Air Trails,* June 1931.
———. "The Affair at Ensenada." *Two Gun Stories,* July 1931.
———. "The Two Gun Kid." *Triple X Western,* July–October 1931. (Four-part serial.)
———. "Checkmate." *Star Novels Magazine,* September 1931.
———. "The Killing." *Western Romances,* October 1931.
———. "The Boast of Mat Drus." *Popular Fiction Magazine,* November 1931.
———. "Pete Blades Pulls a Gun." *Western Romances,* November 1931.
———. "The Sheriff Was a Runt." *West,* April 27, 1932.
———. "A Buckaroo Rides." *Triple-X Magazine,* June 1932.
———. "The Mystery of Renegade Range." *Triple-X Magazine,* August 1932.
———. "A Dead Man Started It." *Triple-X Magazine,* October 1932.
———. "The Spook Rustler." *Five-Novels Monthly,* October 1932.
———. "Death Rides with the Kid." *All Western,* May 1933.
———. "Destiny Is Respectable." *Argosy,* May 20, 1933.
———. "The Private God, Conflict." *Tales of Fighting Adventures,* Fall 1933.
———. "Ten Grand." *Short Stories,* September 10, 1933.
———. "Pete Rides His Luck." *Cowboy Stories,* November 1933.
———. "The Lost Niggerhead." *Short Stories,* July 10, 1934.
———. "One Tough Hombre." *Western Round-Up,* August 1934.
———. "The Only Honest Deck." *Short Stories,* September 10, 1934.
———. "The Battle of the Bunkhouse." *Thrilling Western,* November 1934.
———. "Trouble on the Bar-Q." *Danger Trail,* November 1934.
———. "The Rollers." *Argosy,* December 29, 1934.
———. "One Solitary Virtue." *Cowboy Stories,* January 1935.
———. "Murder on Ruari." *Street & Smith's Complete Stories,* March 8, 1935.
———. "The Private and the Lady." *Street & Smith's Complete Stories,* April 1, 1935.
———. "After Two Cigarettes." *Short Stories,* July 25, 1935.
———. "The Calidad Holdup." *Cowboy Stories,* September 1935.
———. "The Boy." *Argosy,* September 28, 1935.
———. "Charley's Partner." *Short Stories,* December 10, 1935.
———. "The Devil-Devil Stone." *Adventure,* February 1936.
———. "The Friend of Capt. Dick." *Short Stories,* March 25, 1936.
———. "Trouble on the Voyage." *Short Stories,* April 25, 1936.
———. "Jungle Loot." *All Aces Magazine,* May–June, 1936.
———. "The Mob Knows Best." *Argosy,* July 4, 1936.
———. "Death on Cow Creek." *Complete Western Book Magazine,* August 1936.
———. "Tradition." *Street & Smith's Complete Stories,* November 1936.
———. "The Outlaw." *Argosy,* November 7, 1936.
———. "Battle Piece." *Argosy,* April 3, 1937.
———. "Quest of the Golden Lie." *Argosy,* June 12, 1937.
———. "The Chromatic Cat." *Adventure Novels and Short Stories,* July 1937
———. "And See the World." *Argosy,* July 24, 1937.

_____. "The Greatest Scoundrel Unhung." *Argosy,* September 11, 1937.
_____. "Gunfighter." *All American Fiction,* January 1938.
_____. "Illusion." *All American Fiction,* February 1938.
_____. "Bad Man." *Short Stories,* February 25, 1938.
_____. "The First Mate of the Bulgora." *Adventure Yarns,* August 1938.
_____. "The King of Halstead Street." *Argosy,* November 5, 1938.
_____. "The Captain of the Carnatic." *Adventure Yarns,* December 1938.
_____. "Smart Bird, Hugin." *Short Stories,* January 10, 1939.
_____. "Young Men and Prideful." *Argosy,* February 18, 1939.
_____. "The Pebble of Justice." *Argosy,* April 1, 1939.
_____. "Buck Comes Home." *Short Stories,* April 25, 1939.
_____. "An Old Persian Customer." *Argosy,* May 6, 1939.
_____. "The Black Rattlesnake." *Adventure,* June 1939.
_____. "The Kidder." *Argosy,* June 24, 1939.
_____. "Dames." *Short Stories,* August 10, 1939.
_____. "Maxie." *Short Stories,* April 10, 1940.
_____. "No More Battles." *Argosy,* May 11, 1940.
_____. "The Young Signor." *Short Stories,* August 25, 1940.
_____. "Friends." *Short Stories,* December 25, 1940.
_____. "Ham Flier." *Short Stories,* April 10, 1941.
_____. "The Vixen." *The Star Weekly,* July 26, 1942.
_____. "The War Goes On." *Sky Fighters,* November 1942.
_____. "Half-Wolf." *Thrilling Adventures,* February 1943.
_____. "Deputy." *Thrilling Western,* September 1943.
_____. "King's Pirate." *Adventure,* October 1944.
_____. "Trapped." *True Experience,* November 1947.
_____. "By the Guns Forgot." *Fifteen Western Tales.* December 1947.
_____. "Argument." *True Experience,* January 1948.
_____. "Vengeance." *Short Stories,* March 10, 1948.
_____. "Panhandle." *Movie Magazine,* May 1948.
_____. "Wanted." *Movie Magazine,* June 1948.
_____. "The Night Has a Thousand Eyes." *Movie Magazine,* November 1948.
_____. "Whiplash." *Movie Magazine,* January 1949.
_____. "Panic." *The Star Weekly,* June 13, 1949.
_____. "East of Java." *Movie Magazine,* December 1949.
_____. "Man-Trap." *Western Story Magazine,* February 1951.
_____. "Hell-Roarin's Range." *Real Western Stories,* October 1951.
_____. "A Killer for Tombstone." *Western Tales Magazine* (British), September 1953.
_____. "Poor Devils." *Short Stories,* April 1958.
_____. "The Last Grubstake." *Fifteen Western Tales,* May 1958.
_____. "Death in the Jungle." *The Saint Detective Magazine,* June 1958.
_____. "Youth." *Short Stories,* December 1958.

Mysteries

Jenkins, Will F. "The Square Guy." *Detective Fiction Weekly,* June 8, 1929.
_____. "The Man Who Feared." *Detective Fiction Weekly,* August 9, 16, 23 and 30, 1930. (Four-part serial. Published by Gateway Books, 1942.)
_____. "The Trouble on the Dude Ranch." *Black Bat Detective Mysteries,* November 1933.
_____. "In the Fog." *Thrilling Detective,* September 1942.
_____. "Possessed." *Manhunt,* February 1957.
_____. "Killing in Chanco Lane." *The Saint Detective Magazine,* September 1958.
_____. "Innocent Victims." *Mike Shayne's Mystery Magazine,* May 1964.

_____, with Helen Jenkins. "Lethion." *Complete Detective Novel Magazine*, April 1933.
Leinster, Murray. "The Purple Hieroglyph. " *Snappy Stories*, March 1, 1920.
_____. "The Day of the Dead, Chapter 6." *Black Mask*, July 1921 (with other writers).
_____. "One Small Smudge of Soot." *Black Mask*, March 1922.
_____. "Pink Ears." *Black Mask*. April 1922.
_____. "The Frankenstein Twins." *Black Mask*, June 1922.
_____. "The Vault." *Black Mask*, August 1922.
_____. "The Wallet That Weighed Too Much." *Black Mask*, October 1922.
_____. "Nerved with Black." *Detective Story Magazine*, March 31, 1923.
_____. "Third Man's It." *Black Mask*. May 1924.
_____. "The Cleverness of Baron DeCittabola." *Mystery Stories*, November 1927.
_____. "The Grand Canal Street Robbery." *Mystery Stories*, April 1928.
_____. "The Killer at Thunder Mountain." *Mystery Stories*, May 1928.
_____. "The Cow Creek Murder." *Mystery Stories*, December 1928.
_____. "The Man Wolves." *Mystery Stories*, February–March 1929. (Two-part serial.)
_____. "Brains." *Mystery Stories*, May 1929.
_____. "The Murdered Wax Figure." *Detective Fiction Weekly*, August 3, 1929.
_____. "The Man Who Wouldn't Squeal." *Detective Fiction Weekly*, August 17, 1929.
_____. "Murder at the Sty." *Prize Detective Magazine*, November 1929.
_____. "A Flyer of Old Masters." *Complete Detective Novel Magazine*, January 1930.
_____. "Murder Island." *Detective Fiction Weekly*, March 29, 1930.
_____. "Murder Madness." *Astounding Stories*, May–August 1930. (Four-part serial. Published in book form by Brewer and Warren, 1931.)
_____. "The Purple Warning." *Illustrated Detective Magazine*, October 1930.
_____. "Dead Man's Isle." *All-Star Detective*, March 1931.
_____. "Gang War." *Clues*, August 1931.
_____. "Murphy Makes a Pitch." *Detective Fiction Weekly*, December 19, 1931.
_____. "Gat." *Clues*, February 1932.
_____. "Something New in Crime." *Detective Fiction Weekly*, June 18, 1932.
_____. "Beats Big Shot's Finger." *Detective Fiction Weekly*, October 15, 1932.
_____. "Hot and Cold." *Detective Fiction Weekly*, February 4, 1933.
_____. "The Big Mob." *International Detective Magazine*, July 1933.
_____. "Cops Think Crooks Are Fools." *Detective Fiction Weekly*, August 5, 1933.
_____. "The Body in the Taxi." *Black Bat Detective Mysteries*, October 1933.
_____. "The Coney Island Murders." *Black Bat Detective Mysteries*, November 1933.
_____. "The Hollywood Murders." *Black Bat Detective Mysteries*, December 1933.
_____. "Murder at the First Night." *Black Bat Detective Mysteries*, January 1934.
_____. "The Maniac Murders." *Black Bat Detective Mysteries*, February 1934.
_____. "Murder in the Family." *Complete Detective Novel Magazine*, April 1934. (Published in book form by John Hamilton as by Will F. Jenkins, 1935.)
_____. "The Warehouse Murders." *Black Bat Detective Mysteries*, April 1934.
_____. "North of Sixty-Three." *Detective Fiction Weekly*, May 26, 1934.
_____. "Village of Plenty Fella Hell." *Detective Fiction Weekly*, January 12, 1935.
_____. "M'Fella Boy Fir." *Detective Fiction Weekly*, March 16, 1935.
_____. "One-Fella Memena's Sting." *Detective Fiction Weekly*, March 16, 1935.
_____. "Last of the Big Shots." *Detective Tales*, September 1942.
_____. "The Smart Guy." *Detective Tales*, October 1942.
_____. "Double for Murder." *Strange Detective Mysteries* (Canada), November 1942.
_____. "Indiscretion." *Thrilling Detective*, October 1943.
_____. "New Father." *Thrilling Detective*, November 1943.
_____. "Chuckles." *Popular Detective*, December 1943.
_____. "The Barber Shaves Himself." *Thrilling Detective*, January 1944.

———. "Transfusion." *Popular Detective,* February 1944.
———. "Payday." *Thrilling Detective,* April 1944.
———. "Crime Wave." *Phantom Detective,* October 1944.
———. "Bargain for an Enemy." *Popular Detective,* December 1944.
———. "People Are Funny." *Phantom Detective,* December 1944.
———. "One Corpse, Guaranteed." *Famous Detective Stories,* August 1950.
———. "Homicide's Sweetheart." *Smashing Detective Stories,* March 1952.
———. "Crazy." *Black Mask,* Winter 1953.
———. "Murderer's Encore." *Dime Detective,* February 1953.
———. "The Mousy Man." *Mike Shayne's Mystery Magazine,* April 1962.
———. "Party Line." *Mike Shayne's Mystery Magazine,* May 1962.
———. "Mr. Thomas." *Thrilling Detective,* June 1963.
———. "The Man with the Floppy Ears." *Mike Shayne's Mystery Magazine,* July 1964.

OTHERS

Jenkins, Will F. "Love." *The Parisienne,* August 1915 (poem).
———. "My Neighbor." *The Smart Set,* February 1916 (sketch).
———. "On the Country Club Verandah." *The Parisienne,* February 1916 (playlet).
———. "The Foreigner." *The Smart Set,* May 1916 (sketch).
———. "Tell Me of Your Love." *The Smart Set,* June 1916 (sketch).
———. "The Anti-Climax." *The Smart Set,* July 1916.
———. "The Saint." *The Smart Set,* October 1916 (sketch).
———. "My Neighbor's Wife." *The Smart Set,* November 1916 (sketch).
———. "They Do Not Understand It." *The Smart Set,* November 1916 (sketch).
———. "We Were in the Smoking-Room." *The Smart Set,* December 1916.
———. "The Syncopated Marriage." *The Smart Set,* March 1917.
———. "Finis." *The Smart Set,* August 1917.
———. "I Have a Neighbor." *The Smart Set,* August 1917 (sketch).
———. "The Beast." *The Parisienne,* October 1917.
———. "Lie to Me, Millicent." *The Smart Set,* November 1917 (sketch).
———. "Semiramis." *The Smart Set,* November 1917.
———. "The Kitchen Strain." *The Parisienne,* December 1917.
———. "Music." *The Smart Set,* January 1918 (sketch).
———. "We Were Middle-Aged and Fat." *The Smart Set,* January 1918 (sketch).
———. "The First Sweetheart." *The Smart Set,* March 1918.
———. "The Ass." *Pleiades Club Yearbook,* New York, 1918–1919.
———. "Philosophie Ephemerale." *The Parisienne,* February 1919.
———. "Betty." *The Parisienne,* May 1919.
———. "For Legal Expenses." *The Parisienne,* July 1919.
———. "The Haunted Sausage." *The Parisienne,* August 1919.
———. "The Clothes Fakers." *The Parisienne,* September 1919.
———. "The Crag in the Pyrenee." *The Parisienne,* October 1919.
———. "The Bronze Buddha." *The Parisienne,* November 1919.
———. "The House of the Apaches." *The Parisienne,* November 1919.
———. "The Ghost of Elderd Boone." *Saucy Stories,* January 1920.
———. "The Man Who Could Not Smile." *The Parisienne,* June 1920.
———. "Portrait of a Nude." *The Parisienne,* November 1920.
———. "The Kid." *Liberty Magazine,* September 26, 1925.
———. "The Lucky Guy." *Sunset,* August 1926.
———. "Just a Kiss or Two." *Sweetheart Stories,* March 13, 1928.
———. "Politeness Always Pays." *The Passing Show,* October 1, 1928.
———. "The Trap." *Munsey's,* August 1929.

———. "Little Miss Holcomb." *Liberty Magazine*, November 9, 1929.
———. "Wild Waters." *Collier's*, January 4, 1936.
———. "Two in a Boat." *Collier's*, March 7, 1936.
———. "Between Moves." *Collier's*, May 23, 1936
———. "Beautiful Widow." *Collier's*, July 11, 1936.
———. "The Bad Samaritan." *Collier's*, September 5, 1936.
———. "Lucky Break." *Collier's*, September 26, 1936.
———. "Trailing Trouble." *Collier's*, October 24, 1936.
———. "For a Lady." *Collier's*, December 5, 1936.
———. "A Very Nice Family." *Liberty Magazine*, January 2, 1937.
———. "White Man's Burden." *Collier's*, March 6, 1937.
———. "No More Walls." *Collier's*, June 26, 1937. (Also known as "Wall of Fear.")
———. "Side Bet." *Collier's*, July 31, 1937.
———. "Tik-Lui, the God." *Country Gentleman*, August 1937.
———. "Broken Engagement." *Collier's*, October 30, 1937.
———. "Enemy of the State." *Collier's*, November 20, 1937.
———. "Message from the Countess." *Collier's*, February 12, 1938.
———. "Hit and Run." *MacLean's*, February 15, 1938.
———. "River Pride." *Collier's*, February 26, 1938.
———. "Manhunt." *Liberty Magazine*, March 5, 1938.
———. "Portrait of an Artist." *The American Magazine*, April 1938.
———. "Mr. Wildbeck's Brother-in-Law." *Liberty Magazine*, April 9, 1938.
———. "Shark Meat." *Collier's*, April 16, 1938.
———. "Mike Comes to Lunch." *Collier's*, May 21, 1938.
———. "Front Man." *Collier's*, June 11, 1938.
———. "Vixen." *Collier's*, October 29, 1938.
———. "Shelter Hut." *Collier's*, 1939.
———. "No More Trouble." *Country Gentleman*, April 1939.
———. "The Man Who Lived Alone." *Collier's*, April 22, 1939.
———. "Headline." *Cosmopolitan*, June 1939.
———. "High Justice." *Collier's*, June 3, 1939.
———. "Terror Above." *Collier's*, June 10, 1939.
———. "Pygie Takes a Wife." *Esquire*, July 1939.
———. "He Looked Like Robert Taylor." *Woman's Home Companion*, September 1939.
———. "Old Flame." *Collier's*, October 14, 1939.
———. "Under Chitna's Clouds." *Collier's*, November 11, 1939.
———. "The Lion Mane Collar." *Collier's*, November 25, 1939.
———. "East Face." *The Strand Magazine*, February 1940.
———. "Survival." *Collier's*, May 11, 1940.
———. "Dusk to Daybreak." *Collier's*, July 13, 1940.
———. "Song for Two Hands." *Country Gentleman*, August 1940.
———. "I Give My Life." *American Magazine*, October 1940.
———. "The Hunters." *Collier's*, October 5, 1940.
———. "Once and for All." *Collier's*, November 23, 1940.
———. "High Spot." *Collier's*, December 21, 1940.
———. "The Brief Case." *Cosmopolitan*, February 1941.
———. "Fate Doesn't Care." *Collier's*, March 22, 1941.
———. "The Forth Moment." *This Week Magazine*, April 27, 1941.
———. "Knight on a Bike." *The American Magazine*, August 1941.
———. "Ending, with Honor." *Collier's*, August 16, 1941.
———. "Mrs. Justice Is Whitewashed." *Washington Post*, August 23, 1941.
———. "Exile." *Country Gentleman*, September 1941.

Bibliography

———. "A Tale of the Sea." *Esquire*, September 1941.
———. "Lifeboat." *Country Gentleman*, November 1941.
———. "Captains All." *Collier's*, November 15, 1941.
———. "The Hermit." *Cosmopolitan*, March 1942.
———. "Biography." *Country Gentleman*, October 1942.
———. "Child's Play." *The Strand Magazine*, October 1942.
———. "Man with Bad Smell." *Sir!*, October, 1942.
———. "Good Neighbor." *Sir!*, March 1943.
———. "The Payoff." *Cosmopolitan*, August 1943.
———. "George Is a Noble Guy." *Collier's*, November 20, 1943.
———. "Career." *Liberty Magazine*, May 29, 1944.
———. "The Web." *Good Housekeeping*, September 1944.
———. "The God from the Five-and-Ten." *Esquire*, December 1944.
———. "No Pining for Spike." *Liberty Magazine*, July 7, 1945.
———. "The Mine That Laughed." *Esquire*, April 1946.
———. "Terror." *The American Magazine*, August 1946.
———. "Persian Love Story." *The Saturday Evening Post*, January 18, 1947.
———. "A Bad One for an Enemy." *American Magazine*, March 1947.
———. "Insult to the Family." *The Saturday Evening Post*, May 31, 1947.
———. "RX Marks the Sore Spot." *Esquire*, May 1948.
———. "The General Was an Honest Man." *Collier's*, June 26, 1948.
———. "The Betrothal of Juana." *Woman's Home Companion*, July 1948.
———. "The Marauders." *American Magazine*, September 1949.
———. "Red Wine for Love." *Today's Woman*, January 1950.
———. "Night Drive." *Today's Woman*, March 1950.
———. "By an Unknown Lover." *Woman's Home Companion*, June 1950.
———. "Search in the Mist." *The Saturday Evening Post*, July 1, 1950.
———. "Emergency for Doctor Hamlin." *The Saturday Evening Post*, January 6, 1951.
———. "The Sheriff Deals in Facts." *Esquire*, November 1952.
———. "The Girl with Secret Charm." *The Saturday Evening Post*, February 20, 1954.
———. "I'll Wait for You." *The Saturday Evening Post*, March 10, 1956.
———. "Teletype." *Collier's*, March 16, 1956.
———. "The Men at the Top." *The Saturday Evening Post*, February 18, 1961.
———. "No Road Too Hard." *The Saturday Evening Post*, May 12, 1962.
———. "Night to Survive." *The Saturday Evening Post*, May 19, 1962.
———, and Betty Jenkins. "Fly for Your Life." *The American Magazine*, August 1940.
———, with George B. Jenkins, Jr. "The Beautiful Thing." *The Smart Set*, August 1919 (play).
———, with Cody Marsh. "Porthole." *Romance*, May 1929.
Lee, Louisa Carter. "A Chivalrous Silence, Part I." *Love Story Magazine*, August 18–August 25, 1921. (Two-part serial.)
———. "Cupid MD." *Love Story Magazine*, date unknown, before March 1922.
———. "Mystery of the Magnolias." *Love Story Magazine*, date unknown, before March 1922.
———. "The Unkissed Wife." *Love Story Magazine*, March 25, 1922.
———. "The Hidden Love." *Love Story Magazine*, October 6, 1923.
———. "A Shadow Has Passed." *Love Story Magazine*, May 3, 1924.
———. "Something to Love." *Love Story Magazine*, August 1, 1925.
———. "Shackled Love." *Love Story Magazine*, October 3, 1925.
———. "The Girl Who Was Branded." *Love Story Magazine*, January 2, 1926.
———. "The Lure of Gold." *Love Story Magazine*, February 6, 1926.
———. "A Strange Inheritance." *Love Story Magazine*, March 27, 1926.

_____. "The Gypsy's Prophecy." *Love Story Magazine,* May 29, 1926.
_____. "A Splendid Deception." *Love Story Magazine,* June 5, 1926.
_____. "False Hearts and True." *Love Story Magazine,* June 19, 1926.
_____. "Woman Shy." *Love Story Magazine,* September 11, 1926.
_____. "For Honor." *Love Story Magazine,* September 18, 1926.
_____. "Love — The Most Wanted Thing in the World." *Love Story Magazine,* September 25, 1926.
_____. "Her Charming Sister." *Love Story Magazine,* October 2, 1926.
_____. "Cast Aside." *Love Story Magazine,* October 23, 1926.
_____. "There Is a Romance." *Love Story Magazine,* November 20, 1926.
_____. "Man May Propose." *Love Story Magazine,* November 27, 1926.
_____. "Understanding." *Popular Love,* July 1944.
_____. "A Couple of Nice Kids." *Thrilling Love,* May 1945.
_____. "Flamingoes." *Exciting Love,* July 1945.
_____. "Red Canyon." *Movie Magazine,* May 1949.
Leinster, Murray. "The Third Love of Aileen Duzant." *Saucy Stories,* March 1917.
_____. "You, Woman!" *Snappy Stories,* April 1917.
_____. "Choice." *Saucy Stories,* November 1917.
_____. "Sacrifice." *Breezy Stories,* February 9, 1918.
_____. "The Woman Who Sold Herself." *Breezy Stories,* March 19, 1918.
_____. "The Bell of Virgil." *Snappy Stories,* July 1918.
_____. "The Flat in the Bronx." *Breezy Stories,* August 1918.
_____. "The Seekers." *Snappy Stories,* August 1918.
_____. "Jose of Ticao: Stories of the Hungry Country No. 1." *Snappy Stories,* September 1918.
_____. "Padre Silvestre." *Snappy Stories,* October 1918.
_____. "Flying-Fish Milk." *Snappy Stories,* October 4, 1918.
_____. "The Funeral." *Love Stories,* November 1918.
_____. "Mboka." *Snappy Stories,* November 18, 1918.
_____. "The Great Joke of Lope de Gama." *Snappy Stories,* December 1918.
_____. "Carefulness." *Snappy Stories,* January 4, 1919.
_____. "Casey." *Snappy Stories,* January 8, 1919.
_____. "Cleverness." *Love Stories,* March 1919.
_____. "In the Knickerbocker Lounge." *Snappy Stories,* March 4, 1919.
_____. "The Slipper of Lizette." *Snappy Stories,* April 4, 1919.
_____. "A for Alice." *Saucy Stories,* May 1919.
_____. "It's Very Simple." *Breezy Stories,* May 1919.
_____. "The Curse." *Snappy Stories,* May 18, 1919.
_____. "The Man Who Couldn't Do Wrong." *Saucy Stories,* August 1919.
_____. "My Friend Raoul." *Snappy Stories,* August 1, 1919.
_____. "The Impossible Romance." *Saucy Stories,* September 1919.
_____. "There's No Accounting for Girls." *Snappy Stories,* September 4, 1919.
_____. "The Man Who Paid to be Murdered." *Saucy Stories,* November 1919.
_____. "The Queen's Peacock." *Snappy Stories,* November 4, 1919.
_____. "The Benevolence of Suzanne." *Snappy Stories,* January 18, 1920.
_____. "The Wretchedness of Estafan." *Snappy Stories,* February 4, 1920.
_____. "The Mustache of Achille." *Snappy Stories,* February 18, 1920.
_____. "The Impenetrable Virtue of Elise." *Snappy Stories,* March 1920.
_____. "The Embonpoint of Angelica." *Snappy Stories,* March 4 1920.
_____. "The Touch of Midas." *Breezy Stories,* April 1920.
_____. "Fever." *Snappy Stories,* August 1, 1920.
_____. "Enui." *Snappy Stories,* September 1920.

_____. "Garments of Illusion." *Snappy Stories*, January 1921.
_____. "Virgil and the Angel." *Snappy Stories*, February 25, 1921.
_____. "A Novelty in Ethics." *Telling Tales*, June 1921.
_____. "Magic Bathing Suits." *Breezy Stories*, September 1921.
_____. "Bull's-eye." *People's*, May 10, 1922.
_____. "Damned by Prejudice." *Telling Tales*, June 1922.
_____. "The Obtuse Angle." *Telling Tales*, August 1922.
_____. "As It Turns Out." *Telling Tales*, September 1922.
_____. "The Mistake." *Telling Tales*, November 1922.
_____. "Ellen." *Breezy Stories*, February 1923.
_____. "No Sentiment." *People's*, February 1923.
_____. "A Lady of Indiscretion." *Young's Magazine*, March 1923.
_____. "Heroes." *People's*, May 1, 1923.
_____. "The Generosity of the Sidi Joss Piang." *Telling Tales*, April 10, 1924.
_____. "The Duplex Cross." *People's*, May 1, 1924.
_____. "Gone Native." *Telling Tales*, June 10, 1924.
_____. "The Beachcomber." *Telling Tales*, August 10, 1924.
_____. "The Lamboyo." *Telling Tales*, November 25, 1924.
_____. "Black Sheep." *Telling Tales*, September 1925.
_____. "Bosom Friends." *Everybody's Combined With Romance*, January 1930.
_____. "Spooner's Ride." *Complete Love Novel Magazine*, January 1930.
Martel, Florinda. "The Ugly Duckling." *Lover's Lane*, 1923.

Collections

Leinster, Murray. *Guns for Achin*. London, UK: Wright & Brown, 1936. ("Kuantan, Khlit," "The Eye of Black A'Wang," "The Emerald Buddha," "The Black Stone of Agharti," "Payung," "The Dream of Sungi Gut," "Guns for Achin," "Tuilagi," "The Village of the Devil-Devil Drums.")
_____. *The Last Space Ship*. New York: Fell, 1949. ("The Boomerang Circuit," "The Disciplinary Circuit," "The Manless Worlds.")
_____. *Sidewise in Time*. Chicago: Shasta, 1950. ("Sidewise in Time," "Proxima Centauri," "A Logic Named Joe," "De Profundis," "The Fourth-Dimensional Demonstrator," "The Power.")
_____. *Colonial Survey*. New York: Gnome Press, 1957. (Also known as *The Planet Explorer*. New York: Avon, 1957.) ("Combat Team"—also known as "Exploration Team," "Sand Doom," "Solar Constant"—also known as "Critical Difference," "The Swamp Was Upside Down.")
_____. *Out of This World*. New York: Avalon, 1958. ("The Deadly Dust," "The Gregory Circle," "The Nameless Something.")
_____. *Monsters and Such*. New York: Avon, 1959. ("The Castaway," "De Profundis," "If You Was a Moklin," "The Lonely Planet," "Nobody Saw the Ship," "Proxima Centauri," "The Trans-Human.")
_____. *The Aliens*. New York: Berkley, 1960. ("The Aliens," "Anthropological Note," "Fugitive from Space," "The Skit-Tree Planet," "Thing from the Sky.")
_____. *Twists in Time*. New York: Avon, 1960. ("Dead City," "Dear Charles," "The End," "The Fourth-Dimensional Demonstrator," "The Other Now," "Rogue Star," "Sam, This Is You.")
_____. *Get Off My World*. New York: Belmont, 1966. ("Planet of Sand," "Second Landing," "White Spot.")
_____. *The Best of Murray Leinster*, edited by Brian Davis. London, UK: Corgi, 1976. ("Sidewise in Time," "Proxima Centauri," "The Fourth-Dimensional Demonstrator,"

"First Contact," "The Ethical Equations," "Pipeline to Pluto," "The Power," "A Logic Named Joe," "Symbiosis," "The Strange Case of John Kingman," "The Lonely Planet," "Keyhole," Critical Difference"—also known as "Solar Constant.")

_____. *The Best of Murray Leinster*, edited by John J. Pierce. New York: Del Ray, April 1978. ("Sidewise in Time," "Proxima Centauri," "The Fourth-Dimensional Demonstrator," "First Contact," "The Ethical Equations," "Pipeline to Pluto," "The Power," "A Logic Named Joe," "Symbiosis," "The Strange Case of John Kingman," "The Lonely Planet," "Keyhole," "Critical Difference"—also known as "Solar Constant.")

_____. *First Contacts: The Essential Murray Leinster*, edited by Joe Rico. Framingham, MA: NESFA, 1998. ("A Logic Named Joe," "If You Was a Moklin," "The Ethical Equations," "Keyhole," "Doomsday Deferred," "First Contact," "Nobody Saw the Ship," "Pipeline to Pluto," "The Lonely Planet," "De Profundis," "The Power," "The Castaway," "The Strange Case of John Kingman," "Proxima Centauri," "The Fourth-Dimensional Demonstrator," "Sam, This Is You," "Sidewise in Time," "Scrimshaw," "Symbiosis," "Cure for Ylith," "Plague on Kryder II," "Exploration Team"—also known as "Combat Team," "The Great Catastrophe," "To All Fat Policemen.")

_____. *Med Ship*, edited by Eric Flint and Guy Gordon. Riverdale, NY: Baen, 2002. ("Med Ship Man," "Plague on Kryder II," "The Mutant Weapon"—also known as "Med Service," "Ribbon in the Sky," "Tallien Three"—also known as "The Hate Disease," "Quarantine World," "The Grandfather's War," "Pariah Planet"—also known as "This World Is Taboo.")

_____. *Planets of Adventure*, edited by Eric Flint. Riverdale, NY: Baen, 2003. ("The Forgotten Planet," "Solar Constant"—also known as "Critical Difference," "Sand Doom," "Combat Team"—also known as "Exploration Team," "The Swamp Was Upside Down," "Anthropological Note," "Scrimshaw," "Assignment on Pasik," "Regulations," "The Skit-Tree Planet.")

_____. *A Logic Named Joe*, edited by Eric Flint. Riverdale, NY: Baen, 2005. ("Gateway to Elsewhere," "The Pirates of Zan"—also known as "The Pirates of Erzatz," "The Duplicators"—also known as "Lord of the Uffts," "A Logic Named Joe," "Dear Charles," "The Fourth-Dimensional Demonstrator.")

_____. *The Runaway Skyscraper and Other Tales of the Pulps*. Rockville, MD: Wildside Press, 2007. ("The Runaway Skyscraper," "The Gallery of the Gods," "The Street of Magnificent Dreams," "Nerve," "Stories of the Hungry Country: The Case of the Dona Clothilde," "Morale," "Grooves," "Footprints in the Snow.")

Nonfiction

Fitzgerald, William. "The Story Behind the Story: The Gregory Circle." *Thrilling Wonder Stories*, April 1947.
_____. "The Story Behind the Story: The Nameless Something." *Thrilling Wonder Stories*, June 1947.
Jenkins, Will F. "An Interview with Murray Leinster." *Fantasy Magazine*, October–November 1934.
_____. "Why I Use a Pen Name." *Fantasy Magazine*, October–November, 1934.
_____. "I'm About Fed Up." *Writer's Digest*, January 1935.
_____. "Which Story?" *Writer's Digest*, January 1936.
_____. "What Do You Mean—Success in Writing?" *Writer's Digest*, May 1937.
_____. "Go Poultryman, Thou Writer." *Writer's Digest*, July 1937.
_____. "He's Simply Nuts." *Writer's Digest*, May 1942.
_____. "Your Great Great Great Grandmother and the Atom Bomb." *National Home Monthly*, February 1946.
_____. "Author, Author." *The Fanscient*, Spring 1949.

———. "What's in a Pro?" *Writer's Digest*, July 1953.
———. "The Monumental Mistake." *The Writer*, March 1955.
———. "I Don't Dig Those Beats." *Space Diversions*, #11, 1960.
———. "Will Jenkins Says." *PITFiCS*, August 1961.
———. "Applied Science Fiction." *Analog*, November 1967.
Leinster, Murray. "The Story Behind the Story: The Eternal Now." *Thrilling Wonder Stories*, Fall 1944.
———. "The Friendly Atom." *Today's Woman*, 1945.
———. "The Story Behind the Story: Things Pass By." *Thrilling Wonder Stories*, Summer 1945.
———. "The Story Behind the Story: The End." *Thrilling Wonder Stories*, December 1946.
———. "Meet the Author: Murray Leinster." *Startling Stories*, March 1947.
———. "The Story Behind the Story: The Boomerang Circuit." *Thrilling Wonder Stories* June, 1947.
———. "Science Non-Fiction in Fanzines." *The Grotesque*, January 1948.
———. "Guest Editorial." *Startling Stories*, September 1952.
———. "To Quote: Murray Leinster." *Amazing Stories*, April–May 1953.
———. "Where Are Those Space Ships?" *Startling Stories*, August 1953.
———. "To Build a Robot Brain." *Astounding*, April 1954.
———. "Labor of Love." *Astounding Science Fiction*, January 1956.
———. "Reverie." *Science Fiction Review*, April 27, 1964,
———. "Writing Science Fiction Today." *The Writer*, May 1968.

Films

Jenkins, Will F., and J. Grubb Alexander. *The Purple Cipher*. Vitagraph Company of America, 1920. (Based on Murray Leinster's short story "The Purple Hieroglyph.")
Leinster, Murray. *Murder Will Out*. First National Pictures, 1930. (Based on Murray Leinster's short story "The Purple Hieroglyph.")
———, and Jack Jungmeyer. *Good as Gold*. Fox Films Corp., 1927. (Based on Murray Leinster's short story "The Owner of the Aztec.")
———, and Harry L. Frazier. *Border Devils*. Supreme Features, Inc., 1932. (Based on Murray Leinster's novel "Dead Man's Shoes.")
———, and George Bricker. *Torchy Blane in Chinatown*. Warner Brothers Pictures, Inc., 1939. (Based on Murray Leinster's short story "The Purple Hieroglyph.")
———, and Michael A. Hoey. *The Navy vs. The Night Monsters*. Standard Club of California Productions, 1966. (Based on Murray Leinster's book *The Monster from Earth's End*.)
———, and John Brunner. *The Terrornauts*. Amicus Productions, Ltd., UK, 1967. (Based on Murray Leinster's book *The Wailing Asteroid*.)

Television

Leinster, Murray. "The Strange Case of John Kingman." *Lights Out*, March 6, July 31, 1950.
———. "Biography." *The Web*, starring Brandon de Wilde. Hosted by Jonathan Blake, 1953.
———. "First Contact." *Out There*, produced by John Haggott, 1967.

Radio

Leinster, Murray. "The Lost Race." *Dimension X*, May 20, 1950.
———. "A Logic Named Joe." *Dimension X*, July 1, 1950.

____. "The Castaways." *Dimension X,* August 11, 1950.
____. "First Contact." *Dimension X*, September 8, 1951.
____. "The Other Now." *Tales of Tomorrow*, January 22, 1953.
____. "If You Was a Moklin." *X Minus One*, June 12, 1956.
____. "Sam, This Is You." *X Minus One*, October 30, 1956.
____. "The Mad Planet." *2000X* (NPR series, dates unknown).

Index

Numbers in **_bold italics_** indicate pages with photographs.

Ace Double 66, 119, 133, 195–196
Alfred A. King Publishers 52, 67, 78
All-Story 30, 32, 49, 59, 197, 202
Allen, Adeline *see* Mandola, Adeline
Allen, Lewis E. 53, 67–68, 86, 127, 150
Allen, Little Adeline **_68_**, 86, 89, 127, 150
Amazing Stories 33, 49–51, 66, 103, 150, 195–201, 213
American Astronautical Society 131
American Magazine 79, 83, 86, 90, 208–209
Analog 61, 93, 134, 137, 142, 146, 148, 153, 158, 196, 200, 209, 213
Ardudwy 43, 45, 53, **_55–56_**, 79, 115, 132–133, 146, 153, 158, 162
Argosy 6, 30, 33–36, 46, 49, 50, 52, 59, 109, 121, 150, 197–199, 201–202, 204–205
Asimov, Isaac 62, 65, 83, 91, 93–94, 96, 110, 118–119, 121–122, 137, **_162_**, 173
Astounding Science-Fiction 2, 4–5, 52, 59, 81, 93–96, 153, 187, 195, 197–199, 200
Astounding Stories 2, 4, 61–62, **_63_**, 81, 119, 153, 195–198
Avalon Books 106, 120, 125, 195, 211
Avon Books 118–119, 132–133, 196, 211

Baen Books 118, 123, 145, 159, 163, 212
Barneymule **_44_**
Barrett, William E. 79
Bates, Harry 61
Beebe, Ralph 35
Beechhurst, NY 87–89, 93, 108, 111–112, 115, 125, 129
Berkeley, Bishop George 122
"Beyond the Sphinxes' Cave" 62, **_63_**, 198
Black Bat Detective Mysteries 66–67, 205–206

Black Mask Magazine 42, 59, 67, 206–207
Blassingame, Lurton 67
Blue Book 49, 197, 201
bookplate **_77_**
The Boomerang Circuit 105, 199, 211, 213
Botetourt Hotel 37, 46, 115, 124
Bova, Ben 93, 100
Breezy Stories 28, 30, 59, 210–211
Brewer & Warren 62, 78, 196, 206
The Brick Moon 174
Briggs, Dr. George Washington 14
Briggs, Lucretia 13–14, 16
Briggs, Mary Virginia 13, **_14_**
Briggs, Merit 13–14, 16
Brooks, Ned 172
Brown, Dr. Raymond 79, 137
Buckley, Faith 88–89
Buckley, Floyd 88–89
Buckley, Joy 88–89
Buckley, Julie 88–89
Buckley, Tom 88–89
Bull, Cornelius "Neely" 19, 95

Cabell, James Branch 24
Calvert School 69
Campbell, John 64, 81–83, 91–93, 101–102, 104, 110, 115, 118, 125–126, 144, 148, 154, 163
Cannon, Capt. James 16
Cannon, Mary Elizabeth 16
Carnell, John 156
Carroll, Bill, Sr. 132
Cartmill, Cleve 83, 93 94
Cerutti, Vera 117
Chelsea House 47, 197
Chesterton, G.K. 115, 136, 154
Chism, Edward 152

215

Civil War 14–16
Clarke, Arthur C. 92, 96
Clay Bank, Virginia 42–43, *44*, 55, 72, 79, 87, 111, 115–116, 124, 129, 133–134, 136, 144, 150, 153, 157–158, 172
Clayton, William 46, 61–62
Cleveland, Ohio 20
Clues 46, 49, 67, 206
Clute, John 113, 145
Colbert, Stephen 104–105
College of William and Mary 13, 77, 153–155, 158
Collier's 4, 22, 79, 86, 90, 108–109, 146, 197, 208–209
Collins, Allan *84*, 85–86
Conklin, Groff 121, 159
Conklin, Lucy 121, 159
Cooking Out of This World 116
Cooper, Ben 89
Coronet Magazine 109, 197
Cosmopolitan 79, 208–209
Country Gentleman 79, 86, 90, 208–209
Cowboy Stories 46, 204
Cox, Miss Ada 37
Cox, Miss Emma 37
Cox, George, Jr. 149, 155
Cox, Rev. George William 36–37
Cox, Martha 149, 155
Cox, Ned 37
Crosby, Alanson 53
Crowe, Col. Eugene R. 25
Curtis Brown *84*, 85–86
Curtis Publishing Company 79–81

Daniels, Vahan "Danny" 113
Davis, Grace 16–17, 124, 127, ***128***
Davis, "Jenny" 16–17, 124, 127, ***128***
Day, Don 73–74
Day, Jean 73–74
Day, Reenie 73–74
Day, "Scrapper" 73–74
"De Profundis" 107, 119, 198, 211–212
The Dean of Gloucester, Virginia 118
The Dean of Science Fiction 1, 144–145, 150, 161, *162*
Dearing, Gen. James 15
de Camp, L. Sprague 94
DeHardit, Beth 96, 133, 150, 155, 157, 161
DeHardit, William "Billy" 127, 143–144, 157
Dischinger, Irving 127
"The Disciplinary Circuit" 105, 198
Disclave 1970 12, 47, 157–158
Discon 1, 21st World Science Fiction Convention, 1963 144–145, 161, *162*, 166
Dolmetsch, Carl R. 28
"Doomsday Deferred" 82, 108, 197, 199, 212
DuBlan 57

Engholm, Ahrvid 160
Esquire 79, 202, 208–209
Evans, Adrian 153, 161
Evans, Benedict 161
"Exploration Team" 1, 119, 122–123, 137, 150, 200, 211–212
Explorer Program 130

Fabre, Jean Henri 35
Fairchild, Sherman 142
The Fanscient 109, 212
Farquhar, Franz 133
Faulkner, William 36
Fawcett 51, *84*, 114, 147, 195–196, 200
FBI 5, 83, 93–94
Ferro, David 99–100
Fexas, Achilles "Chick" 111–113, 162
Fexas, Penny 111–113, 162
Fexas, Tom 111–113, 162
Fexas, Toni 111–113, 162
"First Contact" 2, 4, 95–96, 107, 118, 123, 126, 137, 149–150, 154, 162–163, 198, 212–214
First Contacts: The Essential Murray Leinster 52, 65, 118, 212
Flint, Eric 123, 163, 212
Fly: The National Aeronautic Magazine 7, *8*, 9–10, ***11***–12
Friend, Oscar 105
Front Projection 1, 4, 132, 137–138, ***139***, 140–143
Futurians 118–119

Galaxy 96, 117–118, 120, 126, 146, 167, 199–200
Gale, Emma 16
Gale, Enoch 16
Gale, Louisa 16
Gernsback, Hugo 49–51, 66, 105, 122
glider "Condor" 7, 9, ***10***, ***11***, 12
Glo-Quips 129
Gloucester, Virginia 36–37, 42, 46, 58, 69, 86, 115, 127, 161
Gloucester Gazette 53, 67, 127
Gnome Press 35–36, 78, 119, 125, 195, 211
Gold, Horace L. 117–118, 167
Goldin, Stephen 133, 147
Gordon, Guy 163, 212
Greenberg, Martin H. 121
Greenberg, Martin "Marty" 119, 125–126
Gregory, Bud 106
Groh, Alan 44, 75
Groh, Frieda 44, 75
Groh, Louis 44, 75
Groh, Norman 44, 75
Guinn, Robert M. 118
Gunn, James v, 1, 2

Index

Haddonfield, NJ 129, 136, 142, 155
Haggard, Edith **84**, 85
Haggott, John 137–138, 213
Hamilton, Edmund 145
Hapgood, Norman 22
Hardy, Robert T. 42, 50–51
Harned, Bob v
Hayes, Clifford 113, 153
Hayes, Eric Christopher "Chris" 158
The Heart of the Serpent 96, 149
Heinlein, Robert 2, 67, 91, 94, 109–110, 119
Hershey, Harold 34–35
Hertzberg, Max L. 120
Hibbs, Ben 79–80, 86
Hoey, Michael A. 147, 213
Hoover, Cmdr. George W. 131
Hopper, Adm. Grace 101
Hubbard, L. Ron 92, 94
Hume, Ivor Noel 143–144

Isle of Wight County, Virginia 16
"Isn't It Odd" 129

"Jabberwocky" 165
Jenkins, Betty 49, **58**, 69, **70**, **76**, 83, 89–90, 111, ***112***, 124, 127, 129, 133, 144, 153, 155, 209
Jenkins, Billee 54–55, 58, **68**, 69, **76**, 89–90, 113, 123, 129, 137, 142
Jenkins, George Briggs 13, 14–17, **18**, **19**, 20, 44
Jenkins, George Briggs, Jr. 9, 19, **20**, 22, 28, 30–31, 36, 44, 49, 58–60, 209
Jenkins, James Edward 13–16
Jenkins, Jo-an 73, 78, **84**, 89, 111, ***112***, 114–116, 123–124, 127, 129, 133, 152–153, 156, 161
Jenkins, Gov. John 13, 45, 55
Jenkins, Little Mary 42, ***43***, **58**, 68, **70**, **76**, 78, 83, 113, 133
Jenkins, "Lula" Louisa Dryden 16–19, 21, 36–37, 42, 44, 134, 145, 155
Jenkins, "Mamie" Mary Louisa 13, 16, 17, **18**, 19, **20**, 22, **29**, 36, 44, 58–60, 123–125, 127
Jenkins, Mary Mandola 38, **39**, **40**, 42, **45**, **58**, **70**, **76**, ***112***, 151, **152**, **162**
Jenkins, Will F. 1, 8, **10**, **17**, 18, **20**, 25, 26, **27**, 33, 40–42, **43**, **54**, **58**, **61**, **70**, **73**, 96, 108, ***112***, 122–123, **128**, **135**, 137, 150–151, **152**, 157, 159, 162, **162**, **164**, 165, 173,
John Hamilton, Ltd. 78–79, 197, 206

"Keyhole" 121, 199, 212
Killer Ship (Space Captain) 150, 196, 200
King, Adm. Ernest J. 95

King, Hannibal 65
Kipling, Rudyard 110,
Knight, Damon 159–160
Kornbluth, Cyril 118
Ku Klux Klan 53
Kyle, David A. 119

LaCossitt, Henry 86
Lammo lammo 18
The Last Murray Leinster Interview 67
Lawson, Edith 37, 46, 115
Lawson, Gussie 37, 46, 115
Lawson, Hatch 37, 46, 115
Lawson, Hylda 37, 46, 115
Lee, Louisa Carter 3, 46, **47**, **48**, 49, 195, 197, 209
Lee, Robert E. 6–7
Leeper, Evelyn C. 65
Leigh, Ophelia 75, **76**
Ley, Willie 120
Liberty Magazine 79, 90, 207–209
Littauer, Kenneth 79
"The Little Terror" 122, 197
"A Logic Named Joe" 2, 3, 96, **97**, **98**, 99, 101, 108, 118–119, 121, 126, 160, 175–186, 197, 211–213
London, England 123, 153–154, 156, 161
"The Lost Race" 106–107, 195, 199, 213
louse magazines 26
"Love" 26, **27**
Love Story Magazine 46, **47**, 49, 209–210

Macfadden Publishing 66, 133, 146, 196
"The Mad Planet" 2, 35, 50, 158, 197, 214
Maeterlinck, Maurice 35
Magazine of Fantasy and Science Fiction 117, 200
Malzberg, Barry N. 91, 118, 154
The Man Who Feared 66, 78, 196, 205
Mandola, Adeline 38, 43, **44**, 67–68, 86, 127, 150
Mandola, Atillio 38, **58**
Mandola, Carmen 45, 75
Mandola, Jackie 45, 75
Mandola, John 45, 75
Mandola, Julia 38, **58**
Mandola, Marianna 38, **58**
Mandola, Mary *see* Jenkins, Mary Mandola,
Mandola, Rita 45, 75
Mandola, Rose 38, **58**
Mandola, Rudolph 38, **58**
"The Manless Worlds" 105, 199, 211
Mann, Charles Riborg 122
Mann, Col. William D'Alton 22, 24, 26
Margulies, Leo 46, 105, 146, 161
Martino, Joseph P. 148–149

Martyn, Wyndham 26, 31
McDevitt, Jack 107–108
Med Service 146–147, 200, 212
Mencken, H. L. (Henry Louis) 3, 22, 24–26, 28, 42
Meredith, Scott 146
Merwin, Phil 114
Merwin, Sam, Jr. 105
Mike Shayne's Mystery Magazine 146, 205, 207
Mines, Sam 137
Monroe Hotel, Portsmouth, Virginia 124
The Monster from Earth's End 147–148, 195, 213
"Morale" 62, 87, 109, 197, 212
Morgan, Harvey 71, 80, 82
Morgan, Jimmy 71, 80, 82
Morgan, Dr. L.V. "Happy" 69, 79, 80
Morris, Edward 121–122
The Morrison Monument 109, 119, 198
Moskowitz, Sam 33, 36, 52, 144
Movie Magazine 47, 205, 210
Munsey Publishing Company 30, 46–47, 49–50, 59, 66, 203, 207
The Murder of the USA 2, 92, 104, 149, 195
Murgatroyd 147
Murry, Elizabeth Cannon 16, 17
Murry, Oliver Perry 16, 17

NASA 104–105, 148
Nathan, George Jean 3, 24–26, 28, 42
New York City 20–21, 37, 38, 41, 76, 125, 127, 135
Newark, New Jersey 20–22, 29, 36–37, 58, 60
"Night Drive" 120–121, 209
Norfolk, Virginia 6, 9, 16, 19–21, 36–37, 60, 159
Norfolk and Southern Railroad 19–20
The Norfolk Virginian Pilot 124

Office of Pubic Information, 19th Division 29
Office of War Information (OWI) 29, 62, 86–87, 90–91

The Parisienne 26, **27**, 28, 31, 207
Pierce Arrow 57, **58**
Pigs Is Pigs 66
The Pleiades Club, *Yearbook 1918–1919* 31, 207
Pohl, Frederic "Fred" v, 64, 117–119, 163
Portsmouth, Virginia 16, 36, 42, 58, 60, 124
"The Power Planet" 66, 103–104, 119, 164, 197
Project Orbiter 130

Project Vanguard 130
"Proxima Centuri" 2, 65–66, 109, 119, 136, 160, 198, 211, 212
Prudential Insurance Company 20–21, 28–29
"The Purple Hieroglyph" 41, 206, 213
Pyramid Books 133, 146, 154, 196

"Quarantine World" 61, 153, 212

"The Red Dust" 35, 50, 150, 197
Reed, Robert, 86
"Reverie" 107, 121, 213
Richmond, Virginia 14, 36, 67, 69, 83, 153
Rico, Joe 52, 65, 99, 175, 212
Rudloff, Lt. John 90–91
"The Runaway Skyscraper" 1, 3, 6, 33, **34**, 50, 109, 118, 150, 158, 197, 212
The Rural Messenger 14

St. Louis, Missouri 14, 157
St. Therese's Catholic Church 69, 127
"Sam, This Is You" 118, 126, 200, 211–212, 214
The Saturday Evening Post 30, 80, 82, 86, 90, 108, 122, 142, 146, 197, 199, 209
Saucy Stories 26, 28, 30, 207, 210
Schmunk, Robert B. 65
Shasta Publishers 64, 78, 104,119, 195, 211
Sidewise Award for Alternate History 2, 65, 162
Sidewise in Time 2, 3, 64–65, 95, 109, 119, 121, 126, 150, 162–163, 198, 211–212
Sidewise in Time (book) 65, 119, 211
Silly Putty 108
Silver, Steven H. v, 65, 132
Silverberg, Robert v, 83, 95, 103, 126
The Smart Set 3, 5, 12, 22, **23**, 24–26, 28, 30–31, 35, 50, 59, 207, 209
Snappy Stories 26, 28, 30, 41, 59, 61, 206, 210–211
Space Tug 78, 104, 120, 195
Stallings, Gail 113–114, 124–125, 127, **128**, 129, 133–**135**, 150, 153, 155, 157–158, 161, 165, 169, 171
Stallings, Pam 113–114, 124–125, 127, **128**, 129, 133–**135**, 150, 153, 155, 157–158, 161, 165, 169, 171
Stallings, Peyton "Pete" 113, 127
Stanton, Austin 129–131
Startling Stories 105, 107, 117, 137, 195, 197–199, 200, 213
Stierhem, Eleanor 5, **84**, 85, 94
"The Strange Case of John Kingman" 144, 199, 212–213
Street & Smith 30, 35, 46, 49, 62, **63**, 114, 117, 204

Stumpf, Dan 147–148
Sturgeon, Ted 108, 145, 159, 163, 166–167
Suffolk, Virginia 13–15, 36
Swanwick, Michael v, 94, 158
Swedin, Eric 99–100
Swift, Will 88
"Symbiosis" 4, 109, 197, 212
Syracuse University 154–155

"Tanks" 61–62, 197
Tarrant, Kay 59
The Tazewell 7, 19–20
Telling Tales 46, 49, 59, 211
Terrill, Rogers 108, 118, 126, 147
Thayer, John Adams 24–25
Thrill Book 35, 49, 197, 202
Thrilling Wonder Stories 105–107, 117, 121, 137, 195, 197–199, 200, 212–213
Tidewater Virginia 36–37, 42, 45
"To Build a Robot Brain" 101–102, 187–194, 213
Today's Woman 5, **84**–85, 94, 120, 209, 213
Tremaine, F. Orlin 62, 64, 67, 81, 115

"The Unkissed Wife" **47**, **48**, 209

Von Braun, Wernher 130

The Wabbler 91, 104, 198
The Wailing Asteroid 132–133, 196, 213
Warner, Eltinge 25
Washington Irving High School 38–39
Webster, Bud 159–160
Weinstein, Diane v
Weinstein, Lee v
Wells, H.G. 1, 32, 50, 136, 158
"What's in a Pro?" 171–172, 213
White, Matthew, Jr. 33
Who's Who in America 122
Wilkinson, Max 86
Williamson, Jack 1, 62, 150
Wolfe, Gary K. 160
The Woman's Home Companion 79, 208–209
Wright, Orville 7
Wright, Wilbur 7
Wright, Willard Huntington 24–25
Wright & Brown 79, 196–197, 211
Wylie, Dirk 118

Yost, Charles E. 53

www.ingramcontent.com/pod-product-compliance
Ingram Content Group UK Ltd.
Pitfield, Milton Keynes, MK11 3LW, UK
UKHW041954140426
5217IPUK00015B/792